T0360999

THE PICKERING MASTERS

THE WORKS OF
IRVING FISHER

Volume 10. *Booms and Depressions*
and Related Writings

THE WORKS OF
IRVING FISHER

EDITED BY
WILLIAM J. BARBER

ASSISTED BY ROBERT W. DIMAND AND KEVIN FOSTER

CONSULTING EDITOR: JAMES TOBIN

VOLUME
10

BOOMS AND DEPRESSIONS
AND RELATED WRITINGS

Routledge
Taylor & Francis Group

LONDON AND NEW YORK

First published 1996 by Pickering & Chatto (Publishers) Limited

Published 2016 by Routledge
2 Park Square, Milton Park, Abingdon, Oxon OX14 4RN
711 Third Avenue, New York, NY 10017, USA

Routledge is an imprint of the Taylor & Francis Group, an informa business

Copyright © Taylor & Francis 1996
Introduction © William J. Barber, 1997

BRITISH LIBRARY CATALOGUING IN PUBLICATION DATA
The works of Irving Fisher. – (The Pickering masters)
1. Fisher, Irving, 1867–1947 – Criticism and interpretation
2. Economics
I. Barber, William J. (William Joseph), 1925– II. Tobin, James, 1918–
330.1′57′092

ISBN 13: 978-1-138-76414-9 (hbk) (vol-10)

LIBRARY OF CONGRESS CATALOGING-IN-PUBLICATION DATA
Fisher, Irving, 1867–1947.
  Booms and depressions.
    p. cm. –– (The works of Irving Fisher ; v. 10)
  Includes index.
  ISBN 1–85196–235–2
  1. Business cycles. 2. Currency question. 3. Financial crises.
4. Banks and banking––United States. I. Title. II. Series:
Fisher, Irving, 1867–1947. Selections. 1996 ; v. 10.
HB119.F5A25 1996 vol. 10
[HB3711]
330 s––dc20
[338.5′42]   96–12210
                                                               CIP

CONTENTS

★ Denotes extract

ACKNOWLEDGEMENTS

We would like to thank the following for granting their kind permission to reproduce texts in this volume:

American Statistical Association: "The Stock Market Panic in 1929", *Journal of the American Statistical Association*, vol 25, March 1930, 93–6

Macmillan: *The Stock Market Crash – And After*, New York, 1932*

Professor George Fisher: *Booms and Depressions*

The Econometric Society: "The Debt-Deflation Theory of Great Depression", *Econometrica*, October 1933, 337–57

* Denotes extract

Editorial Introduction
with Selected Documents

For Fisher, the years 1929–1933 were extraordinarily trying. He was totally unprepared for the onset of the Great Depression. The lesson of the theories he had worked out in the 1920s seemed to be that significant fluctuations in economic activity were preceded by changes in the price level. But that model could not explain what had happened in the American economy following the stock market crash in the autumn of 1929. For the preceding half decade or so, the general price level had been remarkably stable – a condition that appeared to have augured well for continued economic stability. Fisher – along with a substantial number of his professional colleagues – confronted a formidable intellectual challenge in meshing his theorizing with observable realities.

The events of these years presented Fisher with more than analytic difficulties. There was a decided urgency about his financial circumstances. In his decisions with respect to his personal portfolio in the late 1920s, he certainly could not have been faulted for lacking the courage of his convictions. He genuinely believed that "new era" prosperity in the United States was solidly based and that it was prudent to accumulate common stocks on margin. Before the collapse on Wall Street, his holdings were valued at approximately $10 million. Four years later, his net worth was negative. He and his family were sustained by loans from his wife's sister.

Comprehensive reproduction of Fisher's commentary on economic matters during the early years of the Great Depression – much of it highly repetitive – would fill a shelf. The aim of this volume is to provide the reader with a representative sample of his thinking as he attempted to diagnose the condition of the economy in its unanticipated state and to prescribe remedies for its ailments. The focus here is on his presentations to professional gatherings, on books and articles he produced during this period, and on his testimony before Congressional committees. Supplementary material is to be found in the first three chapters of Volume XIV – *Correspondence and Other Commentary on Economic Policy, 1930–1947*. The documents assembled there draw on Fisher's letters to public officials and to fellow economists, as well as on the running commentary on current events he offered in his weekly newspaper column.

In October 1929, Fisher articulated forcefully his views about the American economy and its prospects. There was already evidence of turbulence on Wall Street at the time the speech reproduced below was delivered. This document – not hitherto published – might well be regarded as the high-water mark of "new era" optimism.

Address of Professor Irving Fisher

Delivered at a Meeting of the District of Columbia Bankers Association

in the Small Ball Room of the Willard Hotel, Washington, D.C.,

Wednesday Evening, October 23, 1929

- - - - - -

Mr. President, and gentlemen, it is always a pleasure to speak to bankers, and it is a special pleasure to speak to the bankers of our Capital, and an added pleasure to be present to get a glimpse of your traditions and your loyalty to your organization and to each other as evidenced by the tributes which have been given in the appreciation of them.

I am to speak on a subject of great interest to all economists, all businessmen, and particularly bankers. What is the truth regarding the stock market, regarding the level of prices on the stock market?

According to my own weekly index number of stock market prices, weighted according to the issues outstanding of each stock, the New York Stock Market is now, or has recently been, fully twice as high as in 1926, the date from which I reckon in my index numbers. Back of that, I have to depend on other index numbers.

The Dow-Jones index showed that in 1926 prices were 88 percent higher than before the war, 1913; so that the stock market is nearly four times as high today as it was before the war.

And this is not all. I have another index number basis, not on shares outstanding, but on shares traded in. The first which I have just mentioned as being twice as high as in 1926 I call, to give it a name, The Investors' Index, representing what the average investor would have if he had taken a cross section of the New York Stock Market and held it. But the Traders' Index is based on the idea of constantly reinvesting, selling, and buying, if, let us say, $100,000 had been put in the stock market in 1926, at the beginning of 1926, and at the end of the week those

3

issues had been sold and rebought on the basis of the most popular stocks during that week, and so on, week by week to the present time, always reinvesting according to the popularity of the stocks as shown by the beginning and the end of each week, the $100,000 today would be over $1,000,000, or ten times as high as in 1926.

Today the utilities yield 3 percent on the average, on the market prices, less than bonds. Allied Chemical and Dye, to take an example of those that yield even less, is giving in dividends only 1.8 percent of the market price. Many stocks are yielding to the investors less than the bonds of the same company.

Then we notice that brokers' loans have expanded, within this last year, by two billion dollars, reaching nearly seven billions in all. And yet the market seems destined, with some pronounced set-backs, to keep up, if not to go up further.

The banks, under the leadership of the Federal Reserve Board, have tried to put a stop to this rise, or, at any rate, to put a stop to the constant increase of credit put at the disposal of the stock market, especially by limiting loans at the ends of quarters, when there is a special desire for call loans and because so many corporations which have had loans on call recall them in order to use the money for dividends.

There was at one time almost a panic because of these conditions; this panic, or panicky situation, was relieved somewhat by Charles E. Mitchell, President of the National City Bank of New York, who encountered a great deal of criticism, especially from Senator Carter Glass; yet thereafter the stock market proceeded to go considerably higher than it was. The President of the American Bankers Association, Mr. Hazlewood, at its recent meeting which has been referred to here, made this the subject of his remarks, and it was the basis of a resolution passed by the Association asking that the whole subject of credit, the stock market, and brokers' loans in particular, should be studied so that we would know a good deal more about it than we do today. It is a puzzling situation, and I sincerely hope that this investigation will be made speedily and thoroughly.

What is the explanation of this mushroom growth in stock prices and brokers' loans? Is it like the Florida boom, as Mr. Babson has said, bound to collapse sooner or later? Is the stock market just going up because it is going up? Is it simply that those who have been fortunate enough to make money by buying and then selling in a bull market, are encouraged so that they buy more and drive up stocks still more? If so, it is a house of cards.

One of the financial writers in New York recently said that the prices on the stock market had gone up beyond all bounds and no longer had any relation to earnings or yields. He said, however, that when you can find a stock that you can buy at between ten and fifteen times its earnings, the stock is worth it. I would like to refer to that a little later.

The stock market, certainly at first glance, seems too high and to warrant a major bear movement, and there are many who think such a bear movement is beginning and that it got underway today. But there is another side. Many who have heard, as the whole public has in essence, what I have just said, take it for granted that is the whole story, that settles it. I fear that some bankers are prone to look at these facts and to say that all there is to it is that it is simply a Florida boom over again, that everything is out of bounds, and that there must be a collapse, that this bubble should be pricked.

But bankers do not want to be like the Irish Justice of the Peace, who, after hearing one side, got up and said, "I am going to decide this case right now." When the attorney for the other side said, "Your Honor, I would like to have you hear my side," he replied, "I don't want to hear your side; it has a tindency to confuse the court." (Laughter.)

So I think that when you hear the other side, you will find that it is really a puzzling proposition, that it is not so simple as it looks.

Of course, at the outset we must recognize that we cannot solve this problem in terms of money merely by looking at surface money statistics, because money is always the mere surface of things; there is always some kind of reason back of the money. Why the stock market is so high is our problem.

Well, there are four possible reasons, and only four. It is due possibly to a changed expectations of future earnings. In so far as the public have great expectations in the future earning power of the companies the stocks of which they buy, they will bid those stocks up.

In the second place, the rise may be due in part to the plowing back of earnings, instead of declaring them as dividends, because this reinvestment builds up the power for future earnings and dividends.

In the third place, there may be a change in the public estimate of the risk involved in buying common stocks, and, in the fourth place, which overlaps the last — and is partly identical with it, but not wholly — there may be a change in the basis on which the future dividends or earnings are discounted. Every stock is sold, as every bond is sold, upon some kind of basis representing a ratio of the price to the earnings, or to the yield or earnings as expected.

Let us take these for possible reasons up in order, and see to what extent we can explain this high stock market.

Undoubtedly the first reason does apply. There has been a changed expectation on the part of the investor as to future earnings, for many reasons. The first reason for expecting future earnings is that we are now applying science and invention to industry as we never applied it before. We are living in a new era, and it is of the utmost importance for every businessman and every banker to understand this new era and its implications.

Invention is a profession; it is recognized and appreciated and eagerly sought after. The contrast with the past, even with a few years ago, is very great, and the contrast is enormous with the old industrial revolution. We talk about power looms and steam engines and locomotives and the various elements in the English industrial revolution, which had such a profound effect on business and banking, but let us see who those inventors were.

James Watt was not a professional inventor—the inventor of the steam engine. He was a maker of mathematical instruments. Richard Arkwright, who invented the spinning machine, was a barber. Edmund Cartwright, who invented the power loom, was a clergyman. Robert Fulton, who invented the steamboat, was a portrait painter.

Even when I was a young man in college, inventing and scientific work in general were almost looked at askance by the businessman. I can remember a self-made businessman in Chicago saying he would have nothing to do with any college-bred man in his establishment. On the other hand, the university man, the academic type, was equally contemptuous, if I may use that word, of the man who was merely making money, and one university professor said, when asked why he did not use his brains in that way, that he was too busy to make money.

One of my teachers at Yale was J. Willard Gibbs, the greatest scientist America ever produced, the Isaac Newton of America or the Einstein of America; but in his day his kind of work was not appreciated. Now it is becoming worldwidely appreciated as basic, and one man said that, unlike any other scientist, none of his work has ever been undone. Probably in metallurgy alone, in the metallurgical industry, billions of dollars have been made, thanks to J. Willard Gibbs. He was the last man ever to think of making money, and he was not interested in making studies from that point of view at all.

But today there is a "hook-up" between the university and business. Business today is robbing the university very often of its brains. Our best professor of chemistry at Yale, who perhaps was as much a successor of J. Willard Gibbs as any one there, has been taken by the steel industry because, in justice to his family, he could not resist the salary offered him — several times what one can get as a university professor.

It is interesting to note that there was an exodus of professors into industry after the war, and because of war inflation. In 1920, or thereabouts, there was sort of exodus and it was applicable to some extent to the scientific bureaus here in Washington, the reason being that as prices rose through war inflation; that is, as the purchasing power of the dollar fell, those whose salaries were fixed in terms of dollars found that their salaries would not go as far as they used to and that they did not have in them the purchasing power to live according to their former standard. These naturally went into industry if they had a chance.

I believe that fact, which was originally incident to a war evil, war inflation, is providing a great blessing, and is responsible to a large extent for the great transformation in industry through the application of scientific study by university men and other scientific men.

I am told that in the laboratories of the American Telephone & Telegraph Company today there are 4,000 scientific men, and the laboratory of no university could equal that. One of our scientists at Yale, formerly the President of Dartmouth College, was attracted by the General

Electric Company and took charge of some scientific work in their laboratory at Cleveland because he found that laboratory was better equipped than any he could get in any university.

We are just celebrating the 50th anniversary of Edison's work in bringing forth the incandescent lamp. Edison is the symbol of what I am telling you. His life really links the past, when science was not appreciated, to the present, when it is almost idolized. He was almost the first professional inventor. Today the most remarkable thing about this appreciation of Edison seems to me to be appreciation of the fact that the public realizes what his work has meant to industry and what the work of the others means. He is the symbol today of the application of invention to industry.

The result of this change, most of which has occurred since the war, almost during this period from 1926 to date, during which prices have doubled on the stock market, is a congestion, re-congestion in the Patent Office, which under Mr. Hoover, when he was Secretary of Commerce, had almost caught up with its work. But now there is such a flood of inventions that the Patent Office is behind once more.

We talk about mass production. The most important mass production today is the mass production of inventions in the American Telephone & Telegraph Company laboratory, and in the General Electric Company's laboratory, in the laboratory of the Allied Chemical and Dye Corporation, and in many other laboratories.

The report on "Recent Economic Changes," prepared originally under the chairmanship of Herbert Hoover before he was President and while he was Secretary of Commerce, says there is nothing more revolutionary today in individual inventions, but that the tempo, the rate of speed of improvements through invention today is far beyond anything formerly known in the history of the world.

I picked up today's paper, and looked through it with reference to this very matter, to see how the daily news shows what I am talking about. I found an article on synthetic helium. A German thinks he has a method of freeing Germany from dependence on the United States in buying our helium, through a process by which it is made synthetically.

In that same article it stated that the capital had been raised for an inter-oceanic line of Zeppelins. You will notice that invention requires capital, and so far as that capital is raised in New York, it will lead to an increase in brokers' loans.

In the same paper I saw that the experiments in regard to the seadrome had been successful, and that the decision had been made to build a real seadrome instead of a mere model, and weighing some 40,000 tons, and to tow it out 350 miles from shore and anchor it, and that it would cost $1,500,000. That money must be raised, and that may add to brokers' loans.

I saw in the same paper that there is soon to be an air line between New York and Los Angeles, spanning the continent in 36 hours — an all-air line.

In this same paper was a report that in Poland a rivetless bridge had been constructed by a new process of welding. There is also an article on the distillation of coal to make fuel oil.

I venture to say that almost every day's paper will give you half a dozen items of this sort, showing what the new inventions are and the development and exploitation of them through the use of capital.

Leonard Ayres has called attention to the fact that in the automobile business, obsolescence is the life of trade, which merely means that old inventions are being superseded by new. There is scarcely any new automobile now produced with two-wheel brakes, because the invention of four-wheel brakes has superseded them. One concern has come out with a front wheel drive, and if that proves successful we shall again have the cart behind the horse instead of ahead of it, as in all other automobiles.

If you will notice the names of many stocks on the stock exchange, you will see that they symbolize new inventions — radio, Wright Airplane, the motion picture corporations, and, of course, the motor companies.

All the resources of modern scientific chemistry, metallurgy, electricity, are being utilized — for what? To make big incomes for the people of the United States in the future, to add to the dividends of corporations which are handling these new inventions, and necessarily, therefore, to raise the prices of stocks which represent shares in these new inventions. Particularly are we going to see a new power development, and that is the chief reason the public utilities which are representing super-power, have risen far more than the railway group or the general industrial group. Insull says that as a consequence of the added power we all have, the forty-five million and a half workers in the United States are the equivalent of six hundred million to nine hundred million workers. The public utilities are selling at a price–earnings ratio of over 20 to 1; that is, the price of their stocks is twenty times their earnings. We hear about an institute for cellulose to symbolize inventions in regard to paper, artificial cotton, and wood pulp. Professor Newman says that seventy billion out of the ninety billion of income of the people of the United States is properly ascribable to scientific research.

Now, with the scientific research that we have today, we are justified in great expectations of future dividends, future income for the people of the United States, and as this tempo increases, as it is sure to do, we shall see a still greater increase. Noted that with the newer, the more recent inventions you find a higher price ratio to earnings. In the airplane industry very little attention is paid to the earnings today, because the price of the stock is purely a speculation on the far bigger returns that are expected in the future. Any new invention, as it is exploited, at first does not give any profit, does not reach a profit-making stage, and when it does, it takes a long time before the price–earnings ratio can go up to anywhere comparable with old established, slow-going concerns. So you naturally find this price–earnings ratio tremendously high for new inventions, or for those industries like the utilities which are exploiting new inventions.

I have given one of the main reasons why we may properly expect more in the future than we are experiencing in the present in reference to dividends and earnings.

The second reason, like unto this first, is scientific management, the application of science, not to the basic processes in the factory, but to the human machines which manage the factory. Frederick Taylor is coming into his own today. He, like pioneers and former inventors, was not appreciated during his lifetime. He died of a broken heart because particularly the laboring men, the men he was trying especially to help, regarded scientific management and stop watches as a means of further exploitation. But today his methods and ideals are coming into effect under other names.

10

Mr. Hoover has his Committee on the Elimination of Waste. We now recognize the importance of scientific management under mass production; big business is coming into its own, and we talk about "Fordizing" business.

Only a short time ago there was a great prejudice against big business of any kind, particularly when it was obtained by combinations, but suddenly that pent-up pressure towards larger business units, in spite of public prejudice and the opposition of politicians, has broken loose. During the Roosevelt and Wilson regimes, there was an organized effort at trust-busting; it was the popular sport of politicians. But today, under Coolidge and Hoover, they will go the limit to stretch the Sherman Act and the Clayton Act in order to help efficiency because they believe that the interests of the people of the United States require big business. So while we do not use the word "trust" today, we do have mergers, and they have not fallen heir to the unpopularity of the trust but are recognized as means of economy and as helping the whole people.

In the third place, scientific management at last is being accepted, somewhat passively, but perhaps very soon it will be accepted aggressively, by labor. There is a new labor policy that has come forth in the last two or three years under the leadership of William Green, by which labor no longer boasts of trying to limit output in order to make jobs for working men, but boasts instead of trying to save waste, realizing that the ultimate source of wages is productivity.

In the fourth place, we may expect future dividends because of prohibition. Whatever else we may say about or against prohibition, we certainly cannot say that it is economically injurious. I estimated, or perhaps I should say I guessed, because the estimate has been taken a little more seriously than I intended it, but so far as I could discover it seemed to me, and it seems to me still, that at least six billion dollars of product is annually enjoyed in the United States because of prohibition. Professor Feldman of Dartmouth, although he has made some criticisms and just criticisms of my method of estimating, has not attempted to reduce the figure, but his book on the economics of prohibition has shown in his own way that prohibition has been very advantageous.

Prohibition Commissioner Doran recently issued a statement that he did not know of any economist who would gainsay that prohibition had been of vast help to the United States. I can verify that, because I was asked to get up a round table on this question at the St. Louis meeting two years ago of the economists' association, and to have both sides represented, and I could not find a single economist in the United States who was willing to take the offside in this round table. I found many economists who were opposed to prohibition on the ground of personal liberty or other grounds, but not a single economist who was opposed to it on economic grounds. Of course, you know that Mr. Hoover has said, before he was nominated for the Presidency, and afterwards, that it was economically valuable, and a British Commission sent over here to examine us and report on our prosperity, included among the many causes, prohibition.

In the fifth place, we have had an immense impulse towards prosperity through a stable price level, a more stable price level, that is to say, a more stable purchasing power of money than we ever had in a half dozen years in our lifetime, or in recorded history. I am talking about the level of prices of commodities, of course, and not of the stock market; but commodity prices have varied very little since 1923. We have had six years of stable money, that is, approximately stable money, during which a dollar would buy approximately the same at the beginning and the end and the middle of this period. You cannot match this so far as I know, and I have been a student of index numbers for many years, in any other time or place; and I think it ought not to require much argument to convince you that a stable price level is of very great value to business, because the dollar is the businessman's yardstick. If the physical yardstick by which we measure cloth were to vary, evidently contracts in terms of cloth would be confused, and every man who dealt in cloth or carpets or wire, or anything else measured in yards, would find it hard sledding. Sometimes he would gain and sometimes he would lose, depending on which way the yardstick fluctuated, and on which side of the market, whether buyer or seller, he happened to be.

The same is true of money, only a hundred times as true, because while yards are only used for measuring a few things, dollars are used for measuring everything. On the other side of the counter, for the yards of cloth that are sold and put across the counter there are so many dollars that are shoved across the counter in the opposite direction, and the same applies to every other unit. Dollars are used wherever yards are used, or kilowatts, or any other unit, and yet the dollar is the only unit of commerce that has been essentially unstable.

12

Through our Bureau of Standards, we have standardized or stabilized every other unit, but the most important unit of all we have not stabilized, and it is particularly important for time contracts with which bankers deal.

If I should agree to deliver one thousand yards of cloth to you ten years from now, and when I attempted to deliver that cloth I found such a yard was twice as long, I would have to deliver twice as much cloth as I had expected. The same is true if I have to deliver to you $1,000, and at the end of ten years I have to deliver the same $1,000 nominally, but if each dollar is twice as big in is purchasing power I have got to deliver twice as much purchasing power.

If I am a farmer producing wheat, the result is at the end of ten years that a dollar will buy two units of wheat where it bought one at the start, I virtually have got to raise two bushels of wheat for every one that I expected to have to raise to pay my debt.

It was just this that ruined the farmers in 1920, the deflation of 1920. I believe myself that 90 percent of the trouble of the farmer today, requiring still at this late date the aid of political or farm relief, was due to that deflation by which through the fall of the price of wheat, as the farmer put it — or through the rise of the purchasing power of the dollar, as I should prefer to put it — he found his debts impossible to pay and his loans at the bank were frozen. Many of the farmers were bankrupted and had to give up their farms.

The most important unit, the dollar, needs to be kept stable, and it has been for once, during the last half dozen years.

Now, most people do not realize the havoc that is wrought by unstable money because of what I call the money illusion; that is to say, it is taken for granted that a dollar is a dollar, and that is all there is to it. There is no attempt ever made to measure a dollar, the dollar being the unit itself, but if you really measure the dollar just as we measure a yard in the Bureau of Standards, by something else, namely, its purchasing power of our commodities, we shall find that a dollar is not always a dollar, and unstable money has done tremendous harm.

Professor W. I. King estimated that the convulsion of prices, that is, the convulsion in the purchasing power of the dollar during the war, and shortly afterwards except half a dozen years, really cost this country forty billion dollars worth of economic energy.

Now, if there had been even a forty-million dollar bank robbery, all you men would have been excited about it, but here was a silent pocket-picking to the tune of forty billion which was not realized, but which did play havoc just the same, not only with the farmer, but with all sorts of classes, with everybody, in one way or another.

Now, if it is hard to see and realize how the dollar, changing in its value, first down between 1913 and 1920, when it was only worth forty cents compared with the pre-war purchasing power, and then up again to 1922, when it was worth 72 cents in pre-war purchasing power with those sudden and great convulsions — if it is hard to realize the nature of the harm then being done, it is still harder to realize the nature of the good being done by the absence of this inflation or deflation.

It is much harder to realize that we have today an effective force at work in stabilizing money during the last six years. An unstablized currency is the most subtle cause of complaint that I have mentioned, and yet, next to invention, I should put stabilization of the dollar second on the list, and the most important. Certainly I put it above the average of the various causes I am mentioning.

Then another reason why the stock market should have risen comparable with pre-war times was the unstable money during the war which resulted in a new plateau of commodity prices. That raised prices in general 100 percent, and in the end by 40 to 50 percent, so that our commodity price level today is between 40 and 50 percent higher than it was before the war, a dollar buying two-thirds of what it did before the war.

That same effect is felt on stocks, because if the dollar changes so that it is lowered in purchasing power, everything the dollar is spent for, on the average — not everything, but the average of things — is raised, and that average would apply not only to ordinary, small commodities, but to large units like railways and ships and the other things that we do not own as we own loaves of bread, but own in share through the stock exchange. Naturally if the railroads go up in value, steamships go up in value, and the shares on the stock exchange representing parts of ownership in these things must go up in value likewise.

So far as I know, the first man to call attention to this was Mr. James H. Rand, Jr., Chairman of the Board of the Remington Rand Company, and about at the same time Secretary Mellon called attention to it also. When, in 1925, people were talking about the stock market, as they did then, as bound to come down to pre-war levels, because it was so much higher than pre-war levels, these two men said that because of the change in the purchasing power of the dollar, nothing of the sort should be expected.

The actual rise in stock prices, however, was a great deal more than the 40 or 50 percent rise in commodity prices during this period; it was 88 percent, as I said, according to the Dow-Jones averages. That, however, is also largely explained by the fact that common stocks will rise all the more if there are senior securities. If your railway has doubled in value, the share owned by the bondholders and the preferred stockholders will not double, will not increase at all — essentially it is fixed more or less by the terms of the contract for the bondholder or the preferred stockholder, and all the rise in the value of the railway will go to the common stockholder. If the common stockholder had originally a half interest in the railroad, and the railroad rose in price by 40 percent, the shares of common stock ought to raise in price by some 80 percent, and that is virtually what happened during that period.

In the next place, there has been a substantial plowing back of earnings, and more so as times goes on. Many of the stocks which sell the highest on the stock exchange and which have had the most spectacular rise are not paying any dividends, and some like the Allied Chemical & Dye which I mentioned, only paying 1.8 percent, are nevertheless earning, not the $6 a share they are declaring, but some $15 a share. I suspect that it is really a great deal more than the books show, knowing, as I do, the policy they pursue.

In the next place, we come to the estimate of risk. You remember I said there were four possible reasons why stocks should go up — one, increased earnings or increased expectation of earnings; and the second is the plowing back of earnings. I have given these two reasons, and elaborated the first under half dozen different heads. Now we come to the change in the estimate of risk. There has been a material change in the estimate of the public as to the risk of investing in common stocks. Whether this change is justified or not, the change has occurred. Only a few years ago a bond was regarded as far safer than a stock; the stock, in other words, as far unsafer than a bond.

I think I was the first to suggest that when prices are rising, the bond is not safe, and the bondholder is apt to lose with the change in the purchasing power of the dollar. I pleaded with the Treasurer of Yale University at that time to invest less in bonds and more in common stocks. Other economists said the same thing when they saw that there was a depreciation of the dollar going on, even before the war, because it would depreciate still faster. We had, however, apparently little, if any, effect upon the public mind.

Then came the war, which gave us a tremendous object lesson on the lack of safety of bonds. This lesson was not finally learned in the United States, but it was partially learned. It was, however, learned abroad, where the inflation was far more than in the United States, particularly in Germany. Professor Harnack there had accumulated a small fortune through the books he had written, and had invested that fortune in what he regarded the safest way, namely, in bonds. He expected in his declining years to live on the interest on the money which he had accumulated in this way.

At the end of the German inflation, Professor Harnack's whole fortune — not the income from it, but the whole fortune — would not buy a postage stamp. He had been defrauded of 99 percent and more of his property through the change in the yardstick in which it was measured, the mark.

In this country, nothing as great as 99 percent — we may be thankful — was ever experienced, but between 1913 and 1920, or between 1896 and 1926, to take the very worst case I can, the bondholder was defrauded, if I may use that term in an impersonal way, of 75 percent of his property, because at the end of that period the dollar would buy only a quarter as much as at the beginning. The result was — while most of this occurred during the war — that many institutions like Yale University, which were depending on the income from bonds, could no longer pay the higher costs of employing professors or paying for materials and the expense of running the college, and you found at that time, after the war, as soon as the war excitement was over, that there were "drives" in many colleges to get money, to make up the difference. Yale University went out to raise $20,000,000 and raised $21,000,000. A large part of this was due, as President Angell said when he made the appeal, to the fall in the purchasing power of the dollar.

Now, the big investors of this country, the more intelligent ones, began to realize that a bond was not as safe as they thought it was; they had less faith in bonds, and particularly after the book by Edgar Smith called <u>Common Stocks as Long Term Investments</u>, which I think was written in 1926 or thereabouts. His work was verified by Kenneth Van Strum, in another book called, <u>Investing in the Purchasing Power of the Dollar</u>, and by myself, all showing that it was perfectly true that throughout the history of the stock exchange the stockholder generally had come out better than the bondholder when there were falling prices. In other words, when there was a rise in purchasing power of the dollar, the bondholder did come out sometimes a little better than the stockholder, but taking it all in all, that was not true; the bondholder came out a great deal worse.

The result of the publication, particularly of Smith's book, and of these other studies to some extent, led to a revolution in investments. I remember telling a bond seller, a friend of mine who had been the head of an investment bond house, that he had been selling gold bricks all his life, and what I meant was that to invest in bonds was really to take a flyer in gold. Scarcely any bondholder would think of investing in a gold mine, and yet that is exactly what he was doing when he was investing in a bond, because he was betting on the value of the gold, and the gold dollar lost during the war at one time half of its purchasing power.

Now, as intelligent investors begin to see the light, they begin to lock the door after the horse was stolen. As a matter of fact, today is probably as good a time to buy bonds as we have had in a long time, because today we have a fairly stable dollar. We have had it so long, and the prospects for it for the future are good. Possibly, if anything, there will be a fall in price of bonds rather than a rise, but this is human psychology, to lock the door after the horse is stolen, and so many of the old conservative holders of gold bonds have sold out and invested in stocks. There has been almost a stampede towards stocks, and away from bonds.

Immediately as people bought stocks, because of their lack of faith in bonds — and the statistics of Edgar Smith showed in the end that their profits would appreciably be greater from stocks — they immediately wanted to know how they could make their investment safe, or moderately safe. We economists told them that there was no such thing as a safe investment until you have a safe dollar, that then a bond will be really safe, but that if they invested in stocks they could get a certain degree of safety by diversification.

The result was the springing up — and it has been common in the last few years — of a new profession, namely, the profession of investment counsel, the object of which was to supply diversification to the investor who could not give the expert attention that was required. So these investment counsel offer to review any investor's holdings and then to advise him how to reinvest, and particularly what stocks to buy.

Then, closely on the heels of investment counsel followed investment trusts, because investment trusts went investment counsel one better. The latter not only diversified, but they did more than advise the investor what to invest — they did the investing for him. All you need to do in an investment trust is to buy a trust certificate and the investment trust will do all of the buying of the individual stocks. The trust certificate ipso facto allows you to have a part share in all the holdings, bonds or stocks, but particularly stocks, that the investment trust handles; and then, besides that, unlike the investment counsel, you can have a rapid turnover. If your investment trust is really wisely run, those who invest will presumably act more wisely than the individual investor. So you get management, and Edgar Smith set up the first investment trust in this country, the Investment Managers Company.

Now we have 400 investment trusts, and they have sprung up like mushrooms. They have had, almost in the last two or three years, a great following. They are going to have perhaps just as great a following in the immediate future, and they themselves have had a big influence on investing in their stocks. They have invested for the certificate holder, but they have invested just the same, and to the tune of billions of dollars — three billion dollars have been so invested, one billion during the last year.

These are mushroom growths. They have not yet been brought under the supervision of the government as banking has, but as yet no scandals have come. It is hoped, at least, that publicity will be required, as Mr. Cheney, Chairman of the Legislative Committee of the Assembly in New York is demanding, through a state law, and recently the United States Government has started on the road towards making an investigation. It may be that as the stock market ceases to be a bull market, particularly if it turns into a bear market, investment trusts which are unwisely managed will prove to be injurious to the certificate holder, if not fraudulent. But as yet we have had no scandals, and I think such investment trusts as I have known personally have been wisely managed.

Now, the investment trusts can afford to make studies of stocks which the individual investor could not study. I am a director of Remington-Rand Corporation, and so far as I know the most expert study of this company has been made not by any director or officer, but by an investment trust with headquarters in Detroit, who wanted to study this company as they studied other companies to see if it was suitable for their buying a considerable block of stock. This investment trust has spent some $200,000 in making such investigations, something that no individual stockholder could think of doing. One reason why, it seems to me, the stock market cannot be so "unduly" high as many people think, is that the predetermination of buying these stocks has been an investigation of the potential earnings in the future. You will notice that largely, I think, as a consequence of this expert study, our stock market is highly selective today. We make these averages, these index numbers, but a true perspective of the stock market has to be more than a mere average, but a study of individual stocks, and a study of the different classes of stocks.

Mr. Babson pointed out that half of the stocks during the last year have fallen in spite of the fact that the average as shown by the index numbers had risen. The leaders are becoming fewer and fewer, and those stocks that are leading have a greater and greater scarcity value.

Now, diversification has been brought about not only through investment counsel and investment trusts, but through the mergers I have mentioned as increasing earnings. Mergers have not only increased earnings; they have also made for diversification. Remington-Rand, for instance, absorbed some hundred other companies, so that a stockholder in Remington-Rand is actually the holder of stocks in a hundred different companies. The Electric Bond and Share, you know, is noted for its diversification, and it was because of this that Sidney Mitchell conceived the idea that he did. He found that certain public utilities were enormously successful, and others were rank failures and that they were risky investments; but he concluded that the average was always fairly safe, and so this Electric Bond and Share Company was put together as a means of diversifying large investments. Many of our so-called investment trusts today are holding companies in particular lines of industry rather than investment trusts which take all lines.

Now, finally, we come to this matter of basis. Not only are the dividends to be expected in the future, and the earnings to be expected in the future, greater than we formerly dreamed of, because of invention and the various other reasons I have given, but we are, because of greater confidence through diversification and otherwise, and for other reasons, willing to discount those future earnings at a smaller rate. In other words, the price will be a larger ratio to the earnings than formerly, within the limits of justification.

Unfortunately, I know of no really dependable statistics as to what the price–earnings ratio used to be, but there was a tradition that it used to be about ten to one, and I assume that within perhaps 10 to 15 percent that was the truth, because there certainly was a very widespread impression, and it was based on averages privately made by other people.

Now, we have through the Standard Statistics Company careful studies in the price–earnings ratio, and last year, 1928, was 14½ to 1 instead of whatever it was before, which, as I say, I am assuming in the absence of perfectly dependable figures to have been 10 to 1; and this year it was 13½ to 1 until recently.

In other words, the price–earnings ratio has begun to come down. You will remember I quoted a gentleman who said if you could buy a stock between ten and fifteen times the earning power today, it was a good buy, but that stocks were unreasonably high with no return.

I venture to say that this gentleman had not looked up the facts, because the average has never been up to fifteen, and is now nearer ten than fifteen, and after these last two breaks in the market, it is probably about eleven to one.

How can we explain this fall during this last year in the price–earnings ratio, when the stock market has seemed to be sky-rocketing? We take account of the cost, of the increased earnings, and you cannot believe just because stocks have gone up that they are really high. You have got to take account of earnings, and you have got a ratio of price to earnings, but you may have this ratio lowered through a rise in earnings, and yet at the same time the price of the stock may not have fallen, but may have risen. Price–earnings ratio may come down either because prices come down or earnings have gone up, and the reason is that earnings have gone up during this last year.

I would like to read to you the latest figures from the bulletin of the Standard Statistics Company. We find that industrials, in 1928, for October, were 14.9. The price was 14.9, practically 15 times the earnings. The highest I have known in 1929, for October, was 13.5. I telephoned the company to get their revised figures, which have not been published, and they have given them to me and authorized me to make them public here tonight.

Before today's break on the market, industrials were selling on the average of 12.4. I have the number of companies averaged, but I do not have it right before me, and I won't take time to look it up, but I think it was something like 300.

Public utilities were selling in 1928, in October, at the rate of 27.3, and a year later, in October, 1929, before this last break — the last two breaks — 24.5, and after the first break, but not after today's break, of course, because this figure was obtained this morning, the figure was 21.9.

The railway shares were selling in 1928 on a price–earnings ratio of 7.4. In October, 1929, they were selling on a price–earnings ratio of 12.7. This morning I got the figure as of October 18, of 11.9. Since then all these figures have gone down because of a fall in the prices through the breaks in the market.

So, with the exception of utilities, we are within the limit when this financial writer said it would be a good buy to buy stocks, and the utilities are typical of the particularly great expectations through improved super-power that I have referred to. I have these figures for October for some 400 companies, and I have gone through this long bulletin with reference to the individual companies and I find that the price–earnings ratio has fallen in the great majority of cases. Only in one case out of five or six, that is in 73 cases out of 399, did I find the price–earnings ratio increased.

So, if there had been any tremendous wild-cat market, it was last year rather than this year according to these figures. Out of those 73 cases out of 399 in which the price–earnings ratio had increased rather than decreased during this last year, I only found six cases that looked at all suspicious of any abnormal increase. The others were either slight or due to getting into line with the rest of the market, or to obvious causes — at any rate, not surprising. But there are only six which I would like to have explained if I was trying to go into this intensively.

So we see that increased earnings are beginning to show, that the great expectations of 1928 are being justified to some extent in 1929. Presumably they will be still more justified in 1930.

It is said that the dividends coming October 1st and January 1st will be record breakers. I stated that the prosperous concerns found that profits between 1929 and 1928 had increased 20½ percent, that the dividends declared had been increased 12½ percent, and the part plowed back had increased 33⅓ percent in that one year.

Now, in order to complete the job, I want to give three more reasons why the stock market is high. One is our system of taxation — I would like to say our silly system of taxation by which we consider capital gain as income. I met on the street in New Haven the other day a gentleman who said to me, "I wish I could sell some of my Allied Chemical and Dye stock; I would like to diversify it, but not too much of it — mighty good stock, but I would like to sell some."

I asked, "Why don't you?" He said, "I got that stock at 35; it is now selling (at that time) at 330."

"Now," he said, "I will be taxed on $330 a share practically if I sell this stock, and I do not think I will sell it."

Many people feel the same way, and they feel so particularly with respect to stocks. So, in a sense, stocks are high because they are high, and stocks that have gone up most with justification will be most closely held because of this artificial cost taxation.

22

Mr. Mitchell, Chairman of the Board of the National City Bank, has claimed that he believed this cost was a very potent cause for the high stock market. I do not know how potent it is, but it certainly should be included in the list of causes.

Another cause is the foreign buying. Englishmen particularly have been buying stocks in our stock market.

Finally, I come to the reason which you are wondering why I have not mentioned it at the start, and that is speculation. Of course, all buying of stocks in a sense is speculation; that is, it is discounting an expected and hoped for future, and I would like to say that speculation to my mind is primarily and normally a good thing, and that we could not get along without it. It is only when the speculation is to be found fault with, either because of its unwisdom or recklessness or because it is a rigging of the market based upon deceit or manipulation that we can complain of speculation.

There is a popular tradition that speculation is all wrong. There is a great prejudice against it as there used to be against trusts, but I believe that we ought not indiscriminately to condemn all speculation. But there is a certain lunatic fringe in the stock market, and there always will be whenever there is any successful bear movement going on. The general public will come in after the opportunity to make real profits has passed on and will try to repeat what has already happened to the successful speculations, and they will put the stocks up above what they should be and, when they are frightened, when the president of the bankers' association says something or somebody else sounds a note of caution, this lunatic fringe will immediately want to sell out. They buy at the market and sell at the bottom of the market, and they will go into debt too much, will go on bigger margins than they should and will be wiped out and sold out by their brokers.

In the distress selling that was occurring three days ago, the next to last break, because I understand there was quite a break today at the last hour, it was noted by a very good observer that almost all the selling was in 100 share lots, that the distress selling was almost all in 100 share lots. People who had gotten in it, who had no business in the market, who were not professionals, had no expert knowledge, were merely coming in on wild tips or on the general notion that there was money to be made there because money had been made there.

Now, the problem is, how important is this lunatic fringe? How important is this cause compared with the other causes that have been mentioned, for I have mentioned altogether 15 causes why the stock market has risen, all of which I believe to be true — first and foremost, invention. All of the causes I have referred to are special causes since the war, and mostly since 1923, some of them since 1926. Therefore, they are especially fitted to explain the rapid rise that has occurred during the last three or four years — first, invention; second, scientific management; third, mergers; fourth, the new labor policy; fifth, prohibition; sixth, a stable purchasing power of the dollar; seventh, to go back, for this stands out from the rest, but you will remember that I said that the unstable dollar between 1913 and 1922 had its effect; eighth, since common stocks are equities, their value is magnified to the extent that the senior securities cannot respond to increased values; ninth, the policy of plowing back; tenth, the flight of the bondholder from bonds; eleventh, the rise of investment trusts and investment counsel; twelfth, the lowering of the basis on which stocks are bought, which, of course, overlapped with the previous; thirteenth, our confused taxation of capital, and we think we are taxing income; fourteenth, foreign buying; and fifteenth, speculation.

Until the last week, I thought that this last cause, speculation, was about the least important of the fifteen, but in view of what happened today in the stock market, I see that I was partially wrong. I still think, however, that the other fourteen causes are far more important than this one cause by itself. Not only are brokers' loans high, but there has been a great demand for money.

Right now we talk about its being low, but that is due to special conditions during the last few days. Why is this? It is because when there are new inventions, new securities, great expectations in the future, people are so eager to get the advantage of these futures, that they will not only invest what they own, but they will borrow in order to invest further.

To a certain extent it is normal that during an era such as we are now passing through, where the income of the people of the United States is bound to increase faster perhaps than ever before in its history, and it has during the last few years increased amazingly, that we should try to cash in on future income in advance of its occurring, exactly on the principle that when a young man knows he has been given unexpectedly a large bequest, and that it will be in his hands inside of a year, he will borrow against it in advance. In other words, there ought to be a big demand for loans at a high rate of interest during a period of great increase in income.

There are two principal reasons for the rate of interest, as I see it. I am just having a book coming out on the theory of interest. There is the principle of human impatience, by which we want a thing before we can get it, and borrow in order to get it, and there is the principle of return on investment, when as in the case of new inventions the return on investment is bound to be abnormally high — people will pay abnormally high rates in their borrowings in order to take advantage of those investment opportunities. Human impatience and investment opportunity are the two principles, and they are both operative today.

You all remember the tradition — it is almost a by-word today — of the opportunities of early investors in Bell Telephone stock, and it was so exceptional in those days for an invention to make a man rich so quickly with a small capital that when a person recently used to speak of the Bell Telephone, that he had a modern Bell telephone, you thought he was a swindler, but today there are many genuine Bell telephones on the market, so to speak, and they are discovered by the search of the eagle eye of the investment trusts and by other large and wise investors. It will naturally tend to increase loans and to increase the rate of interest.

Moreover, these brokers' loans are swollen largely, as Mr. Mitchell pointed out the other day, by the change in the modern method of financing by which short-term debts take the place, to a certain extent, of former long-term obligations, and by which securities are pledged instead of using the method of commercial loans.

So we have a rough picture of a situation where we are in a state of rapid transition, with great prosperity at present and greater prosperity in view in the future, and these cause, I think, rather than speculation, or these plus speculation, explain the high stock markets, and when it is finally rid of the lunatic fringe, the stock market will still never go back to 50 percent of its present level, what it was in 1926 — at least I can scarcely conceive of it, and I am surprised that it should have gone back as much as Mr. Babson said and as it actually has touched those figures. I think it will rebound again. Still less do I think that it is going to go back to anything like pre-war times, when it happened to be a third or quarter of what it is today.

Of course, I am not here to prophesy; I am not a prophet nor the son of a prophet; I am not infallible, and I hope you will check up to see if I am in error in my exposition of causes. I try to confine myself to explaining causes, and, of course, you and I are all interested in explaining the past in order that we might be more wisely guided in reference to the future.

In closing, I want to say frankly that it is my own belief that unless there is a real panic tomorrow—and I do not know what did happen today—unless there should be a very radical change in the psychology or unless this lunatic fringe is much larger than I have ever dreamed it was, we shall not see very much further, if any, recession in the stock market, but rather a ragged stock market in the next few weeks, and then, after the first of the year, a resumption of the bull market, not as rapidly as it has been in the past, but still a bull rather than a bear movement.

Fisher's initial attempt to account for the "panic" of late 1929 took the form of a talk given at the meeting of the American Statistical Association on December 28, 1929.

– Fisher, "The Stock Market Panic in 1929," *Journal of the American Statistical Association*, Vol. 25 (March 1930).

THE STOCK MARKET PANIC IN 1929

By Irving Fisher

To my mind the problem of the stock market panic is, and will be to some extent for many years, an enigma, but I think now is the time to gather data and to make preliminary estimates of what really happened and why, because as we wait, those involved are forgetting; and if we wait too long the people whose memories are most important will have died. Some one has said that the "perspective" of the historian, about which the historian boasts so, is simply due to the fact that all those people who had the data, from which they could contradict him, are no longer living.

I shall probably modify my opinion from time to time in the future as I have in the past. But I wish now to gather together what evidence there may be on the most important economic event in the lifetime of all of us here.

Perhaps some of you who are more or less familiar with my work in statistics may not realize it, but this is the first time I have ever tried to analyze an historical event and to trace all the causes at work. I have never studied or written a paper on business cycles as such. I have merely tried to trace individual threads, such as the rate of interest or the change in the purchasing power of money. Yet, much to my amazement, I have been credited with having a theory of the whole phenomena.

I conceived it to be a proper function of the analyst to trace faithfully what would occur if one individual force was at work unhindered by others, and on that basis I have tried to show how changes in the purchasing power of money, for instance, have explained a great deal in the business cycles, but I have never tried to explain "the business cycle."

Now it is my desire to try to get all the elements together in my forthcoming book on the stock market crash. It is an exceedingly complicated problem. For this reason it would be impossible to present all aspects at one short meeting like this.

I wish this preliminary explanation to be made and emphasized in order that you may not think that by picking out a few outstanding factors I am pretending to represent a complete view of the subject. To do so must, of course, over-simplify the problem. No problem as complex as that before us now can be expressed in two or three outstanding influences.

27

Nevertheless, if I were to try to pick out those influences which seem to me most important, they would be somewhat as follows:

The stock market crash had its roots primarily in the bull movement. If we want to explain the crash, we must explain the bull movement that preceded it.

As I see it, this bull movement was justified to a very large degree. Last night I was talking with a fellow student of this problem, whose judgment seems to me as good as anybody's, and who stated that, in his opinion, two-thirds of that spectacular 100 per cent rise in the stock market between 1926 and September, 1929, was justified by prospective earnings while the other third was due to unjustified speculation. I would concur in this conclusion as representing the composite of my own judgment, estimate or guess, whichever you choose to call it; although I would raise the figures a little and say that between two-thirds and three-fourths of the rise in the stock market between 1926 and September, 1929, was justified. The unjustified character of the remainder is best registered by the swelling of brokers' loans. This unjustified part was the outgrowth of the other part. It was just because there were great chances to make money such as have seldom if ever, in the aggregate, occurred before in the history of the world that so many people were eager to profit by them and went into debt for this purpose. They thereby erected a great credit structure beyond anything that had previously been erected.

On the face of it, it looks absurd to justify even two-thirds of the 100 per cent rise in the stock market. After this tremendous crash, it has become the fashion to decry the phrase "The New Era," which so many were using a few months ago. That phrase may perhaps be exaggerated in its implications, but I do believe that the Hoover Committee on Recent Economic Changes was right when it said that the "tempo" of invention and improvement in the arts was greater since the War than ever before, and I point out that even a slightly increased tempo is magnified in the equities of common stocks.

I think that what Mr. Snyder has pointed out is of very great interest—that the general rate of growth of production has been fairly constant for a long time. But we must not slur over the variations from the general trend.

I call attention to the particular line signifying the product per man. The product per man, according to Mr. Snyder's line, went up sharply in the last few years.

This has been due largely to inventions, and inventions have been due largely to the fact that invention for the first time in history has been making use of science where only a few large corporations had been doing it before the War, and, after the example of Germany, almost all important corporations now have their development and research laboratories. One has four thousand scientists at work all the time to improve its products. We have mass production of invention, and it is shown in the lagging of the Patent Office. The war inflation led a great many college professors who were living on their salaries to discover that they could no longer do so because the purchasing power of the dollar had fallen. It was necessary for them to increase their incomes, and they accepted whatever opportunities came to them to go into industry, and industry found it was the most profitable investment ever made.

Besides this historical accident of inflated cost of living there was another. The same inflation had brought up wages. This was aided by a stoppage of immigration. When deflation came, organized labor was strong enough to resist recession of wages. Industry had to put up with high wages, and decided that it should save labor by labor-saving inventions.

So there was a great impulse toward labor-saving invention. Besides, those owners introduced industrial management as never before. The War pyramided trusts, and we have been condoning them ever since. We have been praising mass production and scientific management where before we criticised them. Labor has been coöperating as never before, especially under the leadership of William Green. These causes and the flight from bonds to stocks, especially after the publication of Edgar Smith's book on stocks and long term investments, and the coming of investment trusts that exploited that idea, have led to greater confidence in common stocks.

These are some of the reasons why there was a bull market, and a justified bull market. How did it happen that there was an unjustified expansion of loans? It would happen necessarily, I suppose, to some degree anyway because whenever there is a good thing to be exploited people become over-enthusiastic and swing to extremes. But aside from this, there were special reasons why there should be a going into debt. One reason was that during the War many people, who had never before known what investment was, were induced to buy Liberty Bonds and to do so on borrowed money, and when the Liberty Bonds were paid off, as they have been to a large extent, those funds were then seeking investment by the same process—borrowed money. The psychology had been set for investing in whatever seemed most profitable on borrowed money.

Then again, and this I think is of very considerable importance, the rate of interest ought to have been raised in sympathy with the big investment opportunities. I have a book that is in the course of preparation on *The Theory of Interest* in which I have emphasized the importance of invention, and when new invention gives an opportunity to make more than the current rate of interest there is always a tendency to borrow at low rates to make a higher rate from the investment.

Now the rate of interest was artificially low, partly, because we had so much gold after the War and gold had a fictitious influence upon the rate, and then, a little later when Europe began to get back on the gold standard, we tried to help Europe by not re-attracting that gold to this country by raising the rate of interest. And finally, when the bull market came into being the Federal Reserve system not only still wished to prevent the exodus of gold back from Europe to the United States but also wanted to maintain the low rate of interest for what it considered legitimate business as distinct from speculation. It was confronted with the problem of how to discourage the speculation in Wall Street and at the same time not to discourage business by a too high rate of interest. It tried to make a discrimination, but it was like putting a log across half the stream. The water merely went around it. In so far as the banks coöperated with the Federal Reserve system, in not loaning in Wall Street, to that extent the "bootleg" lenders, came into the market and supplied the deficit.

I think, as we look back—and hindsight, of course, is always better than foresight—we may now say that it would have been wiser had the Federal Reserve system, in order to nip this speculation in the bud, raised the rate of re-discount indiscriminately over a year ago. It certainly would not have deterred business as much as the stock market crash, which was the fruit of the other policy.

In other words, the same mistake, in a different form, was committed as was committed in 1919 when in order to encourage business after the War there was an easy money policy. It then led to commodity inflation while this time it led to stock market inflation.

So, without trying to introduce any complications into this over-simple statement of the situation, I shall conclude that there was underlying this bull movement a justification in fundamental conditions, and on top of that justified bull movement there was an unjustified going into debt, encouraged by the fact that investors found themselves confronted on the one hand by wonderful opportunities to make money and, on the other, a low rate for loans. They could borrow at much less than they expected to make.

In short, both the bull movement and the crash are largely explained by the *unsound financing of sound prospects*.

Fisher hastily put together a book – published in February 1930 – entitled *The Stock Market Crash – and After*. More than trace elements of "new era optimism" then survived, as was evident in its concluding paragraphs.

– Fisher, *The Stock Market Crash – and After*, New York: Macmillan, 1932, 268–69.
". . . Because of these solid achievements of the past seven years, their present continuance, and the assurance that they will be prolonged into the immediate future, I feel that the threat to business due to the dislocation of purchasing power by reason of transfers of stock holdings will be temporary. Fulfillment of the pledges by the nation's business leaders that industrial programs will be adhered to, that wages will not be reduced, and that the 'tempo' of production on which all our prosperity has been built will be maintained, should suffice to bridge across the business recession that slightly antedated and accompanied the crash. The effects of the crash were largely psychological. President Hoover's instant realization that the panic of 1929 was peculiarly dominated by the psychological factor, enabled him to give useful reassurance to the nation in the business conferences held in Washington. Of course, he did well to emphasize the purely temporary help to be derived from an extended program of public works. He was not tripped by the 'make-work' fallacy, and he regarded the expedient merely as a balance-wheel in an emergency. When increased business again suffices to take up the slack in unemployment, public works should be restricted accordingly. In the circumstances Mr. Hoover's remedy, which consisted chiefly of reassurance, was more efficacious than any of the other remedies to counteract a repetition of the panics that are discussed in this book. As a means of further present reassurance I trust that the book itself will be of some use, besides affording substantial reasons for practical optimism for the future.
The only "fly in the ointment" is the danger in a few years of gold shortage and long gradual deflation like the deflations after the Civil War and after the Napoleonic Wars. And even this danger may be averted if wise banking policies and gold control are adopted in time. For the immediate future, at least, the outlook is bright."

When *Booms and Depressions* appeared in 1932, Fisher spoke in a quite different tone about the causes and cures of depressions. In the preface to this work, he observed that it was an outgrowth of an address he had given to the American Association for the Advancement of Science on January 1, 1932. The full text of that speech was never published. Its essential message can be gleaned, however, from extracts quoted in the *New York Times*.

– Fisher, "First Principles of Booms and Depressions," Address to the American Association for the Advancement of Science, January 1, 1932 (extracts as reported in the *New York Times*, January 2, 1932).

"If the total amount of society's collective debt is unusual, an unusual amount of distress selling naturally follows. And when the volume of such selling gets too unusual, it spells general and serious deflation.

For, in the first place, when there are more sellers than buyers, the selling itself deflates prices.

In the second place when such wholesale liquidation occurs, the bank deposits of the borrowers are automatically wiped out, thus wiping out the credit currency that was built on them.

In the third place, after all this has gone far enough, and perhaps broken a few banks, people get scared and begin to hoard, thus wiping out still more currency. And with the currency thus shrunk, prices shrink still more.

Now shrunk prices are the same thing as bloated dollars. That is, not only do you have to pay the same number of dollars on your debt, but you have to pay in dollars which are worth more than they were when you contracted the debt. This means that all debts have become bloated through the bloated dollar, and so the securities for all these other debts have become insufficient.

Thus, the contagion spreads to the debts of the most staid and conservative. Either you go to the wall, or the shrunk prices on one side of your books, and the bloated interest on the other side squeeze your profits dangerously. When discreet citizens are thus sucked in with the indiscreet, we have a depression.

Now please note the paradox. A little individual liquidation reduces debts; but when liquidation becomes epidemic – why, then, the more society pays on its debts the bigger it makes those debts, because the bigger it makes each dollar through deflation."

Fisher took this message into the chambers of Congress in the Spring of 1932.

– Fisher, Hearings before the Committee on Ways and Means, House of Representatives, 72:1, April 29, 1932, 684–712 (extracts).

". . . A year ago I had never made any intensive study of depressions. My work in economics has been in writing special monographs on special small subjects and this is one that had always seemed to me a pretty big subject and I was putting it off. But a year ago I began to study it, because I was asked to make an address upon it before the American Association for the Advancement of Science. Since that time I have given this all the attention that I could, in view of a good many other engagements.

As I say, I am writing a book upon it, and now I feel, as I did not a year ago, that I do understand the real diagnosis of this depression. . . .

It is impossible to ever give a complete explanation, and we shall be debating for 100 years the history of this depression and trying to unravel all the tangled skeins, threads, and causes involved.

I do not mean to say, therefore, that I am cocksure I can tell you 100 per cent the explanation of this depression, but I do feel very confident that I can tell you what has caused 90 per cent of it.

We are suffering from two economic diseases, the debt disease and the dollar disease. The debt disease has led to the dollar disease.

By the debt disease I mean that in 1929 we had accumulated a tremendous overindebtedness. It showed itself first in the collapse in the stock market, because the American public had been speculating to such a tremendous degree, and speculating in the stock market is simply going into debt. The fact that it is done on margin through the broker merely puts the debt out of sight. The broker borrows, but the customer is the one who is really borrowed for. So that he goes into debt through the broker, and it is that debt that was his undoing. Not only was he in debt, but the farmer was tremendously in debt ever since the war days. He has never gotten out of debt. Then there were the tremendous intergovernmental debts, the reparations debts, and the tremendous internal Government debts.

Then there were the international debts that we extended to Europe in the way of credit to help Europe to recover. Then there were the consumer debts to finance installment buying.

Then there were the great debts at the banks, and I fear that catalogue is not complete, but the total runs up, in 1929, to over $200,000,000,000, whereas the assessed valuation – that is, the estimated value of the physical capital of the United States – was only $360,000,000,000, and it is probably not more than half of that to-day. But the debts to-day are in effect greater than then – nominally less, but really greater because of the enlargement of the dollar. That is the dollar disease. The debt disease has led to the dollar disease through distress selling and the contraction of the currency.

When people are in debt and find that they are too much in debt, or their creditors find that they are too much in debt, and either the debtor, because he realizes that he is too much in debt and tries to pay it off, or the creditor, because he realizes that the debt may not be good and is demanding payment, makes an effort to pay off, to liquidate. In either case the effect is deflationary.

The first effect is to force sales. The margin dealers in 1929 at the time of the stock-market crash were doing just that. Borrowers were called by their brokers and told that their margin was not sufficient and that they must put up more securities or else sell, or be sold out.

Now, the effect of that selling was to reduce the prices. The effect of any selling is to reduce the prices; and when the prices are reduced, the margin is reduced still more, and then the broker comes back again and demands more margin or more selling. And so you have this distress selling. Distress selling is different from normal selling. Normally a person sells because the price is high enough to suit him, give him a profit; but in distress selling he sells not because the price is high but because it is low, and that forces him to sell in order to save his solvency. When the stock-market crash started this avalanche of selling, it proceeded from the stock market to the real-estate field and to the commodity field, and lower prices generally. And it was not simply the physical process of distressed selling that lowered prices. It was more vitally the contraction of the currency which that involved; because when a person pays his debt, if he pays it to a commercial bank, he reduces the circulating medium by the amount of his payment....

Now, when you have this decrease of prices, you find that all the phenomena that we recognize in a crises such as this grows out of that together with the debt. That is, the debt disease and the dollar disease cause all our miseries – 90 per cent of them, at least.

In the first place, take a business man's balance sheet. His assets shrink in value with the general shrinkage in prices. His liabilities do not shrink, because they are fixed by contract. Therefore, the difference, the net worth, shrinks even faster; and in the cases of business men who are on the ragged edge anyway, that shrinkage brings it below zero, and they are bankrupt. You get the phenomenon of bankruptcy immediately out of this fall in prices.

The same thing which I have applied to the capital account or balance sheet applies to the income account. The balance sheet relates to a point of time, and the income account to a period of time. The receipts reduce because the average business finds that it can not charge the same prices, and as the shrinkage of prices goes on the receipts reduce in dollars, but the expenses do not reduce, or do not reduce so fast, because some of them are fixed by contract. Interest on debts, rent, salaries, and even to some extent wages, are relatively fixed. The result is that the receipts shrink a great deal faster than the expenses, and the difference between them, or profits, shrink very fast, and for those businesses that are on the ragged edge the profits are turned into losses.

So that is the next phenomenon that we recognize in a crisis; that business is unprofitable, and when business becomes unprofitable you have the next phenomenon, unemployment. Because in a capitalistic society – in other words, a profit society, in which the profit-taker has the say as to whether a business will run or not, or how far or how fast it will run – as soon as profits turn into losses he begins to shut down, either wholly or in part, which means discharged workmen and unemployment, and also a reduction in volume of trade. So you have all these phenomena coming directly out of the two things: the debt disease – overindebtedness – and the dollar disease, namely, falling prices.

I will not go into the analysis any further, but, as I diagnose the situation, those are the two diseases from which we suffer.

Now, even granted that the debt disease was not preventable the dollar disease is wholly preventable. It was not necessary, because the patient had grippe, that he should have pneumonia. You could have the debt disease without having the dollar disease. There could have been something to prevent the fall of prices, namely, the very thing that now is being applied, and which could have been applied long ago – the open-market operations and various other devices.

People say that this depression is natural; that it is natural that there should be a fall of prices; that it is supply and demand. That shows a total lack of understanding of the situation. Moreover, it is foolish to say that because a thing is natural, therefore we should endure it. It is natural for a boat to capsize if the passengers all rush to one side. In the fjords of Norway, where the sightseers sometimes are suddenly attracted to one side of the boat and all rush over there, they will have some sailors push a heavy weight in the opposite direction to rebalance the boat. And that is, as I see it, what ought to be done through the Federal reserve of the Government, or some agency – open-market operations, rediscount rates, or what not – there should be something to prevent the boat from capsizing, or even from tipping. And it can always be done, because the price level is the one thing that is easy to control. . . ."

In his Congressional testimony, Fisher insisted that economic recovery would be assured if measures were taken to restore the general price level to its pre-crash average. (In much of the discussion at the time, the 1926 price level was regarded as the target to be sought.) He strongly supported yet another version of a Goldsborough Bill in 1932. Unlike the bills Congressmen Goldsborough had introduced in 1922 and 1924, this one made no mention of varying the gold price along the lines of Fisher's compensated dollar plan. Emphasis was placed instead on requiring the Federal Reserve to use all of its weapons to "reflate" – i.e., to raise the general price level to, say, its 1926 height – and thereafter to stabilize. Fisher was sympathetic as well to another technique which allegedly would work automatically to serve these purposes. Under its proposed terms, the reserves which member banks were obliged to deposit with the Federal Reserve would vary directly with changes in the velocity of monetary circulation. Thus, if velocity fell, required reserve ratios would be reduced in the same proportion. This scheme was a non-starter. The

Goldsborough Bill of 1932, however, cleared the House of Representatives by an overwhelming margin, though it died in the Senate.

In the debates on monetary policy in 1932, the contrasts between Fisher and Kemmerer – both of whom took their bearings from the quantity theory of money – were revealed in sharp relief. As Kemmerer read the situation, little could be accomplished by increasing the money supply or by pressing the central bank to expand the lending capacity of banks still further. Attention should instead be directed toward creating conditions conducive to stimulating the velocity of monetary circulation. The basic requirement here, in Kemmerer's view, was the restoration of confidence. From his perspective, heterodox interventions of the type Fisher called for would simply erode confidence still further. Fisher had no quarrel with the proposition that confidence was lacking in the environment of 1932. But that aspect of the problem, he maintained, should be addressed by a program of Federal guarantees of bank deposits. As he set out that case to a Congressional Committee:

"If you really could convince people that member banks were safe, hoarding would stop overnight and ... if hoarded money were put back into banks, it would soon go on its way, to be multiplied by 10. There are plenty of people who are willing to borrow at banks."[a]

Fisher's new-found interest in the topic of business cycles did bring him at least a step closer to Wesley C. Mitchell than he had been a decade earlier. Fisher continued to maintain that there was nothing preordained about alleged cyclical phenomena. Nonetheless, he chose to dedicate *Booms and Depressions* to Mitchell, hailing him as "the world's acknowledged leader in the study of the subject of this book."

The distance between Fisher and Mitchell's Columbia colleague, Edwin R.A. Seligman, widened over this issue. Seligman had been among those invited to read the manuscript of *Booms and Depressions*. In his comment, he chose to be "entirely frank." He feared that Fisher was "incurring the danger of being classed with the horde of panacea-mongers." For his part, Seligman did not share Fisher's faith in monetary stimuli and maintained that Fisher had "greatly underestimate[d] the importance of a great constructive program of productive government outlay even, if necessary, through an immense loan." Nor did Seligman discern "any advance of theory at all" in Fisher's manuscript. The work, as Seligman read it, was "meant primarily for the general public." And he added:

---

[a] Fisher, Hearings before the Committee on Banking and Currency, House of Representatives, 72:1, March 30, 1932, 144.

"Now so far as the general public is concerned, you are known chiefly for three doctrines.

1) That common stocks are a better and safer investment than bonds and that the level of stock values in 1929 was not an exaggerated one.

2) That stabilization of money can best be secured by changing the content of the gold dollar without any regard for what is done in other countries and for its effect on international exchange.

3) That prohibition has spelled economic progress because of alleged steadiness of the workman – without any regard for the vast economic and fiscal sacrifices involved

a) In the abandonment by the country of about a billion and one-half of revenue

b) By the immense increase in the price of liquor, the amount of which is greater than before prohibition, and,

c) By the heaping of immense profits to bootleggers.

None of the above doctrines is shared by the overwhelming majority of your economic colleagues, yet I find repeated allusions to those broad and in my opinion unfounded generalizations in your book."[a]

Fisher was undeterred by criticisms such as these. In a letter to Ragnar Frisch in Norway (to whom he also sent a mimeographed draft of *Booms and Depressions*), he described his own assessment of this project as follows:

"The book is intended to be a real contribution to cycle theory and yet to be understandable by the man in the street – a difficult combination!"[b]

---

[a] Edwin R.A. Seligman to Fisher, April 27, 1932, Seligman Papers, Columbia University Archives.
[b] Fisher to Ragnar Frisch, April 21, 1932, Frisch Papers, University of Oslo Archives.

BOOMS AND DEPRESSIONS

Booms and Depressions

Some First Principles

By

IRVING FISHER, LL.D.

Professor of Economics, Yale University

NEW YORK · ADELPHI COMPANY · PUBLISHERS

To

WESLEY CLAIR MITCHELL

THE WORLD'S ACKNOWLEDGED LEADER
IN THE STUDY OF THE SUBJECT OF THIS BOOK

"Money, as a physical medium of exchange, made a diversified civilization possible. . . . And yet it is money, in its mechanical more than in its spiritual effects, which may well, having brought us to the present level, actually destroy society."

SIR JOSIAH STAMP

(From Foreword to the English edition of *The Money Illusion* by Irving Fisher)

PREFACE

This book grew out of an invitation to speak on the Depression of 1929–32 before the American Association for the Advancement of Science and is an elaboration of my address at the meeting of the Association, held at New Orleans, Jan. 1, 1932.

The vast field of "business cycles" is one on which I had scarcely ever entered before, and I had never attempted to analyze it as a whole.

The scope of the present work is restricted, for the most part, to the rôle of nine main factors, not because they cover the whole subject, but because they include what seem to me to be the outstanding influences in the present, as well as in most, if not all, other major depressions.

By this restriction it has been possible to make the book much shorter and, I hope, much more intelligible to the lay reader than if it set out to be an exhaustive treatise on an inexhaustible subject.

At any rate, the nine factors are so inherently and obviously related to each other that we are not compelled to resort entirely to empirical correlation. Empirical studies are important and essential in this field; but, by excluding those which apparently have no rational basis, it is possible to mark out a clear cut set of "first principles."

The results of the analysis here presented seem largely new. But, being so unfamiliar with the immense literature, I decided to submit the first draft of this book in mimeographed form to a number of authorities, several of whom had given much of their lives to the study of the so-called business cycle. With few exceptions these have found in the theory much that they regard as both new and true.

Yet, as I could not, without years of searching, be sure how far any or all of what to me seems new may have been anticipated by previous writers, I leave to others to determine how far this book is the original contribution which it is intended to be.

As will be seen, the main conclusion of this book is that depressions are, for the most part, preventable and that their prevention requires a definite policy in which the Federal Reserve System must play an important rôle. This problem is of even greater importance than the problems of our old national banking system which led, after two generations of delay, first to the Aldrich Report and then to the establishment of the Federal Reserve System.

In my opinion, no time should, in this case, be lost in grappling with the practical measures necessary, including international coöperation, to free the world from such needless suffering as it has endured since 1929.

If this very practical task is not soon undertaken in earnest, nor brought to a successful conclusion before another such disaster overwhelmes the world, we may expect that a great body of informed public opinion will then hold specific individuals responsible. In short, ignorance cannot much longer serve as an excuse for neglecting this greatest of all practical economic problems.

But, having myself only recently acquired such knowledge as I possess on the subject, I have felt constrained, in this book, studiously to avoid casting blame on those who, here and abroad, might, had they done the right things, have prevented the depression.

I am indebted to several of my own students for helpful criticisms, Lester V. Chandler, J. Edward Ely, Florence

Helm, Harold D. Koontz, J. N. Lindenberg, Taulman A. Miller, Jr., and Hildreth Winton.

I also wish to thank the many economists and others who have kindly read and commented, in a general way, on the first draft, including, James W. Angell, Leonard P. Ayres, J. M. Clark, Victor S. Clark, John R. Commons, John H. Cover, Alfred Cowles, III, W. L. Crum, H. C. Cutting, Davis R. Dewey, Charles E. Duryea, Lionel D. Edie, Henry W. Farnam, Warren F. Hickernell, Jacob H. Hollander, W. I. King, R. R. Kuczynski, William C. Lee, Edmund E. Lincoln, H. L. McCracken, Ernest M. Patterson, Nicholas Raffalovich, Malcolm C. Rorty, E. R. A. Seligman, Carl Snyder, G. F. Warren, Frederick V. Waugh, E. B. Wilson, Ivan Wright, Quincy Wright, and Edgar H. Yolland.

I wish especially to thank the following who, evidently at personal sacrifice, gave considerable time and thought to studying, in a detailed and intensive way, part or all of the manuscript,—Harry G. Brown, J. D. Canning, C. O. Hardy, Harold L. Reed, N. J. Silberling, and Charles Tippetts.

Finally, I wish to thank my associate, Royal Meeker, who has assembled most of the factual material as well as scrutinized the entire manuscript and helped in rewriting it, and my brother, Herbert W. Fisher, who at every stage has helped in the exposition, from a layman's point of view, in the endeavor to make an obscure subject clear. With his help I have tried to write the book in such language that "he who runs may read."

Irving Fisher

New Haven, Conn.
July, 1932

CONTENTS

PART I THEORETICAL

PART II FACTUAL

APPENDICES

LIST OF TABLES

xix

57

LIST OF CHARTS

59

PART ONE

THEORETICAL

CHAPTER I

INTRODUCTION

WHAT IS A DEPRESSION?

A DEPRESSION is a condition in which business becomes unprofitable. It might well be called The Private Profits disease. Its worst consequences are business failures and wide-spread unemployment. But almost no one escapes a degree of impoverishment. Some of the mightiest and best managed enterprises, such as railroads, are among the worst sufferers. If they do not break, it is often only because they are saved by their reserves. Many rich stockholders, too, are compelled to live on reserves; while many persons who had lived modestly are compelled to live from hand to mouth; and many who already lived from hand to mouth become jobless and live on charity, or die, or become thieves. In a word, a depression is a form of almost universal poverty, relative or absolute. And though this poverty is transient for society as a whole, it is, for countless individuals, tragically permanent.

THE RECENT PICTURE

A great orator of New England has put it thus:

"A few months ago, the unparalleled prosperity of our country was the theme of universal gratulation. Such a development of resources, so rapid an augmentation of individual and public wealth, so great a manifestation of the spirit of enterprise,

3

so strong and seemingly rational a confidence in the prospect of unlimited success, were never known before. But how suddenly has all this prosperity been arrested! That confidence, which in modern times, and especially in our own country, is the basis of commercial intercourse, is failing in every quarter; and all the financial interests of the country seem to be convulsed and disorganized. The merchant, whose business is spread out over a wide extent of territory, and who, regarding all his transactions as conducted on safe principles, feared no embarrassment, finds his paper evidences of debt, and acceptances and promises which he has received in exchange for his goods, losing their value; and his ability to meet his engagements is at an end . . . and loss succeeds to loss, till he shuts up his manufactory and dismisses his laborers. The speculator who dreamed himself rich, finds his fancied riches disappearing like an exhalation.

*   *   *

"Already, in many a huge fabric that but a few days since resounded with the roar of enginery, all is silent as in a deserted city. Already many a great work of public improvement, upon which multitudes were toiling to bring it to the speediest completion, that commerce might rush upon its iron track with wings of fire, is broken off, and stands unfinished, like the work of some great conqueror struck down amidst his victories. Already want, like an armed man, stands at the threshold of many a dwelling, where a few days ago, daily industry brought the supply of daily comforts.

*   *   *

"What more may be before us in the progress of God's judgments—what tumults—what convulsions—what bloody revolutions—we need not now imagine. It is enough to know that this distress is hourly becoming wider and more intense; and that no political or financial foresight can as yet discover the end.

*   *   *

"Amid these present calamities, and these portentous omens of the future, it is not strange that many minds are seeking, and all voices are debating, the cause and the remedy."

A truer picture of 1932 could scarcely be found. Yet this speech was delivered 95 years earlier, on the 21st of May, 1837, by the Reverend Leonard Bacon, from the pulpit of Center Church in New Haven, Connecticut!

THE MYSTERY OF A DEPRESSION

Similar utterances have been made during other depressions, especially those of 1857, 1873, and 1893. And yet, despite all these duplications of experience and despite the enormous mass of literature on depressions which they have brought forth, a banker in 1931 could say: "This depression is beyond me."

A depression seems, indeed, to fall upon mankind out of a clear sky. It scorns to choose a moment when the earth is impoverished. For, in times of depression, is the soil less fertile? Not at all. Does it lack rain? Not at all. Are the mines exhausted? No; they can perhaps pour out even more than the old volume of ore, if anyone will buy. Are the factories, then, lamed in some way—down at heel? No; machinery and invention may be at the very peak. But perhaps the men have suddenly become unable or unwilling to work. The idea is belied by the spectacle of hordes of workmen, besieging every available employment office.

Perhaps, then, the world has become over-populated. But how could that happen in so short a time? When the calamity starts there seems to be (at least in America) enough of every good thing to go around; everybody wants it, and nearly everybody wants it enough to work for it; yet some cannot get it, and many who can get some of it must be content with less.

There are those who ascribe this individual impoverishment to the very fact of collective wealth—not over-population, but "over-production"—too much food and too much of all else.

Later in these pages there will be more about this. It is enough here to note that those who, at the beginning of a depression, cry "over-production" and expect recovery as soon as over-production ceases usually become disillusioned when later almost universal poverty appears. If, in 1932, anyone thought there was still over-production, he should follow his own argument all the way through as follows: "How do I know there is over-production of goods? Because more goods are for sale than the public will buy. And why, then, will the public not buy? Because they haven't the money. Why haven't they the money? Because they are not earning it. Why aren't they earning it? Because they are not producing: men and machines are idle!" But if *non*-production is the trouble, why call it *over*-production?

Perhaps the secret, then, is to be found in the machinery of distribution. Between the producer and the consumer there must be a chasm in need of a bridge. But no; at this very moment, the Hudson River has a brand new bridge. There are plenty of *physical* bridges, and the railroads that cross them are in good condition. As for ships and ship-canals, they are as well equipped as ever, and as eager to serve—only the shippers are few.

There is, however, another distributive mechanism whose name is money. There is no more reason why this money-mechanism should be proof against getting out of order than a railroad or a ship-canal. Moreover, profits are measured in money. If money, by any chance, should become deranged, is it not at least possible that it would *affect all profits, in one way, at one time?*

CHAPTER II

FIRST THREE OF NINE MAIN FACTORS

OVER-INDEBTEDNESS

(The First Main Factor)

DEBTS are tied in with the money mechanism. In fact, what is called the "money market" is really the debt market. Most kinds of pocket money, such as bank notes, take the form of debts to the bearer. Bank checks, which the depositor thinks of as representing his "money in the bank," really represent a debt of the bank to the depositor, and usually the depositor obtains his checking account by going into debt to the bank.

Debts are essential to both production and distribution. Even in "normal" times,—that is, in times of neither boom nor depression,—practically every adult person is in debt, if only for last week's groceries. The primitive notion which associates debt with the pawn-shop, and regards the debtor as a victim of misfortune is, of course, quite errone-ous, especially in this modern world. The really typical debtors of today are the alert business men and corpora-tions. Every business balance sheet has its "liabilities."

Yet for individuals, for corporations and for society as a whole, debts have differences of degree. In each case debts may be too much or too little. The golden mean or point of equilibrium is a matter of balancing opposed considera-tions. Each person decides for himself how far it is well to go into debt, or how long it is well to stay in debt, just as he decides how far it is well to save or to spend, or how

8

much of his income it is well to apportion to clothes and how much to food. As in other economic adjustments, so in the adjustment of debts, the individual stops "at the margin" where, in his judgment, the desirability of a further expansion of his debts is balanced by the undesirability of further sacrifices and risks. In each case, the point of equilibrium is where opposed considerations balance.

Where do they balance?

Chance is inseparable from life. Every transaction is a taking of chances, and over-indebtedness is whatever degree of indebtedness multiplies *unduly* the chances of becoming insolvent. Everyone who is not a gambler, provides himself with a margin of safety. He puts a buffer between his debts and the collector. This buffer is the difference between assets and liabilities. Corporations call it "capital and surplus." But the sufficiency of the buffer is not solely a matter of quantity. It must be varied according to the quality of the assets. It must also be varied according to the quality of the liabilities. Slow assets and quick liabilities (such as call loans) require a larger buffer than quick assets and slow liabilities. The quickest asset, and therefore the safest when pressure comes, is cash. The quickest liability, and therefore the most unsafe in times of pressure, is the call-loan. Over-indebtedness is largely a question of dates of maturity. The entire set-up of assets and liabilities, therefore, has to be considered,—and not only the ratio between the two sides of the capital account, and between current assets and current liabilities, but the ratio between the two sides of the income account; the ratio between the income and the assets, between the income and the debts, between the income and the balancing item of capital and surplus. A balance sheet is the result of anxious efforts to weigh correctly these and many other considerations.

CRITERIA OF OVER-INDEBTEDNESS

Banks, in extending credit to different sorts of borrowers, have to consider questions of liquidity and of safe margins on collateral. Credit men, accountants, lenders on real estate, brokers, governments and legislators, all have some sort of standards of over-indebtedness. The standards are somewhat rough. The line of balance is more or less a twilight zone; but an entire book could be written about the history and the current practice of stopping the debts at a point which is neither too rash nor too conservative.

Can a more definite criterion be devised for the community than the individual? In any event, such guides will have to be considered as the ratio between the nation's income and certain fixed expenses, like taxes, rent, and interest; the ratio between the income and the accumulated volume of outstanding debts; the ratio between debts and the gold on which the banks (in a gold standard country) base their loans. As low income endangers the debtors, low gold endangers the creditor banks, which then begin to press the debtors. On these last two criteria—national income and national gold reserve—some interesting remarks have been made by Mr. Warren F. Hickernell.[1] He concludes that, at a given moment, the outstanding total of bank loans and investments should not exceed one half of the country's income for one year; and that the country's gold should always be at least equal to 9 per cent of the outstanding bank loans and investments. The overstepping of either of these limits, Mr. Hickernell regards as jeopardizing the solvency of an undue proportion of the community.

This national gold buffer is exposed to one adverse

---

[1] *What Makes Stock Market Prices?* by Warren F. Hickernell, Harper & Bros., 1932.

chance seldom considered by either lender or borrower—the chance of the mal-distribution of gold internationally. Such mal-distribution may be caused by a one-sided condition of international indebtedness, both public and private, and by tariffs which prevent international payment in goods and compel payment in gold. If these or other causes should drain a country of too much of its gold, the banks of that country would begin to cancel loans, including some which looked conservative enough when made. Thus, what was not over-indebtedness may be transformed into over-indebtedness by depriving the creditor banks of sufficient gold or sufficient access to it. Thus an unexpected rise in the tariff of one country, say the United States, renders unsafe a volume of indebtedness to that country from another country, say Germany, which without that rise would be safe, simply because the creditor has made it hard for the debtor to pay.

Over-indebtedness means simply that debts are out-of-line, too big relatively to other economic factors. If the debts are out-of-line relatively to only a few unimportant factors, little harm may result. The great disturbances come when the debts are decidedly out-of-line with practically everything—including assets, income, gold and liquidities (i. e., quickness or slowness of assets and liabilities.)

THE DEBT CYCLE

What, now, are the consequences of a mistake of judgment on the part of debtor or creditor or both? First, consider the individual debtor. If he has not borrowed enough, he can, under normal conditions, easily correct the error by borrowing more. But, if he has gone too far into debt, —especially if he has misjudged as to maturity dates— freedom of adjustment may no longer be possible. He may find himself caught as in a trap. If he cannot pay his debt when it comes due, he will try to put off the evil day. Governments and corporations accomplish this by refunding their maturing and short term obligations. But this is not always possible and if insolvency threatens the debtor, the creditor often makes matters all the harder by pressing for payment.

Ultimately, of course, the over-indebtedness, whether of one individual or of a whole community, will be wiped out, with or without business failures. But sometimes the liquidation, or the psychology accompanying it, does more than restore a normal debt situation. Those debtors who have burned their fingers by over-indebtedness, and those creditors who have burned theirs by over-lending—especially if the two groups comprise most of the community—become over-cautious, and end in an undue reaction against borrowing. Then the pendulum may gradually swing back, caution may again be thrown to the winds, and over-indebtedness again prevail. The pendulum may even swing back *beyond* the point of equilibrium, where people will again go too far into debt, but presumably not so much too far as the first time. This swinging back and forth may go on indefinitely, constituting a debt cycle; but, unless some outside force intervenes, each successive swing of the pendulum will have less scope than the last.

NINE MAIN FACTORS

This, however, is not the whole story of the expansion and contraction of debts. If it were, no one would think of devoting a whole book to it. But it happens that the cycle tendency of debts is the initiating one of at least nine main cycle tendencies which carry in their vitals much of the tragedy of economic life. The nine are listed here, and each will be discussed on its downswing to Depression, before the upswing of any of them is considered; for the first task is to see how the debt-structure, once erected, may topple into the trough of depression and take us with it.

Following are the nine oscillating factors to which reference has just been made:

1. The Debt Factor
2. The Currency-Volume Factor
3. The Price-Level Factor
4. The Net-Worth Factor
5. The Profit Factor
6. The Production Factor
7. The Psychological Factor
8. The Currency-Turnover Factor
9. Rates of Interest

The depression tendencies of the first three of these factors (Debts, Currency, and Price-Level) are closely locked together, and the key that locks them is distress-selling.

DISTRESS SELLING

When over-indebtedness, whether by sheer bulk or by rashness as to maturity dates, is discovered and attempts are made to correct it, distress selling is likely to arise. That is, in order to protect the creditors, some of the possessions of the debtor may have to be sold—his stocks, his bonds, his farmlands, or whatever his available assets may be. The debtor may choose, on his own responsibility, to facilitate liquidation by selling some of his property, even though he never pledged any of it for the debt; or his bank or his broker may cash in on the debtor's collateral; or the mortgagee may foreclose the mortgage; or the debtor may go into bankruptcy, and the trustee in bankruptcy may then auction off his assets. In short, the debtor becomes the victim of distress selling either on his own initiative or on the initiative of his creditors.

Distress selling perverts the operation of the law of supply and demand. Normally, sales are made because supply-and-demand has worked out a price attractive to the seller; but when the seller is in distress, the sale is made for precisely the opposite reason; not the attraction of a high price, but the compulsion of a low price, which threatens his solvency. The danger or the fact of insolvency is the all-important consideration in distress selling.

When a whole community is involved in distress selling, the effect is to lower the general price level.

VOLUME OF CURRENCY
(The Second Main Factor)

This excessive eagerness on the selling side of a market may seem enough to explain how distress selling tends to lower the price level; but it is not the fundamental influence. In fact, the buyer largely gains the spending power which the seller loses, and spending power is what sustains prices. But the *stampede liquidation* involved in distress selling has a radical effect on the price level, by actually shrinking the volume of the currency—that is, of "deposit currency."

Deposits are the balances on the stubs of check books— the "money" which people have in banks and which they transfer by check. A typical depositor deposits neither gold nor silver nor any other money but merely his promissory note. What he thus accomplishes is to trade his debt to the bank for a debt from the bank to himself; the object being that he may get something which will circulate. His own note will not circulate, but the bank's deposit-liability to him will. Against this, he can draw checks which, in his own business circle, will be accepted almost as freely as legal-tender money. In short, he converts his own non-circulating credit into the bank's circulating credit. New "money" is thereby created, not by the mint nor the Bureau of Engraving, but merely by the pen and ink of the banker and his customer. But when the customer *pays* his note, he undoes the whole transaction; that is, he wipes out an equal amount of circulating credit. In this respect, the payment of a business debt owing to a commercial bank involves consequences different from those involved in the payment of a debt owing from one individual to another. A man-to-man debt may be paid without affecting the volume of outstanding currency; for whatever currency is paid by one, whether it be legal tender or deposit currency transferred by check, is received by the other, and is still outstanding. But when a debt to a commercial bank is paid by check *out of a deposit balance,* that amount of deposit currency simply disappears.

Thus to pay a debt at the bank tends to contract the circulating medium. But this tendency is, in normal times, neutralized by a counter-tendency. For generally, as fast as some bank debtors pay off their debts, the extinguished currency is replaced by new depositors who obtain new credits. When, however, by reason of a general state of *over*-indebtedness, there is a stampede of liquidation, then the new borrowings will by no means suffice to restore the balance, and there must follow a net shrinkage of deposits, or "credit currency."

In this process of contracting credit currency, commercial bank debts are the only kind of debts directly involved. Yet other debts may aggravate the process of contraction.

A man may owe very little to his bank, and yet owe so much in other directions that, in order to reduce the total, he will choose to pay off his bank debt. Or a debtor, without any bank debt at all but owing money abroad, may have a deposit in a bank—say, a thousand dollars—and withdraw it in gold to pay some of his foreign debts. When he does this, he deprives the bank of the lawful right to issue credit currency to an amount far in excess of the thousand dollars thus withdrawn.

This sort of contraction by means of cash drawn from banks may be on a large scale, especially if the debtor is a bank or a savings bank, which, in order to replenish its own cash—gold, silver, or paper—so as to meet a run by its depositors, may draw on other banks. Even public debts —debts of city, state or nation—may have a contracting effect on deposit currency, through the pressure of taxes upon citizens already in debt. This pressure, to be sure, is spread over so many people that its effect is light in proportion to the huge size of the public debts, but the pressure is always there, and often reveals itself, not only in the ways mentioned but in tax-sales with all the usual effects of distress selling.

Credit currency is recorded in the statistics of the Comptroller's Office, under the heading, "Individual deposits subject to check without notice." Its shrinkage is of vast importance; for, in the United States at least, credit currency is the most important kind of Twentieth Century currency. It transacts nine-tenths of the country's business, and, when it is deflated, the general price level tends to fall, because, with less funds less buying can be accomplished.[2]

[2] This is in accordance with well known principles. See, for instance, *The Purchasing Power of Money*, by Irving Fisher (Macmillan, New York, 1931).

THE PRICE LEVEL

(The Third Main Factor)

Thus, the volume of the most important circulating medium is tied to the volume of debts, especially debts at the banks, one of the most important kinds; so that a sudden disturbance of this debt-volume is passed on to the currency-volume and consequently passed on to the general price level; for, as all authorities agree, an increase in the volume of currency tends, in some degree at least, to raise the price level and a decrease, to lower it. What we now have to consider is the way in which a changed price level changes the burdensomeness of all outstanding debts—in a word, changes *real* debts, as distinguished from nominal or money debts.

"REAL" DEBTS

There are few people today who do not grasp the difference between nominal or money wages, on the one hand, and "real" wages, on the other. Let money wages remain unchanged, and we all acknowledge that, if the cost of living rises, real wages fall; or, if the cost of living falls, real wages rise. We know that money wages may rise and yet real wages fall, as in the case of Germany's post-war inflation. For real wages are the budget of goods—the composite of commodities—the "living"—which the money wages will buy. Only by translating money wages into real wages can we express the true economic state of the nation.

This same principle applies to debts. Though a debt be paid with the same number of money dollars, yet these dollars, when prices are falling, will cost the debtor more goods. To earn them, he must sell more goods. In other words, when the price level falls, each dollar, to all intents and purposes, is a bigger dollar.

For instance, suppose a farmer contracts a debt when wheat is $1.00 a bushel, and pays it when wheat is 50 cents a bushel. Obviously, to him the dollar has doubled in terms of wheat; he must use twice as much wheat to pay each dollar of his debt. That is, when the price of wheat is halved, the farmer's *real* debt is doubled. Likewise, if the general price level is halved, the real debt of the average man is doubled.

And this is but half of the debtor's predicament; for first, he gets fewer of these bigger dollars for his goods (while owing the same number of them on his debts); and second, his security is worth fewer of these bigger dollars in the market, and therefore worth less in the eyes of his creditor. The creditor is unaware of receiving more than he is properly entitled to, and the debtor is unaware of paying more than he properly owes. One gains and the other suffers—but both suffer from what is about to be discussed as the Money Illusion.

THE MONEY ILLUSION

Few people look at money for their explanations, because most people simply look *through* money, think in terms of money, take money for granted, assume that a dollar is always a dollar. Since we measure everything else in dollars, it does not readily occur to us to measure the dollar itself. Few people realize, for instance, that the depression dollar of 1932, as compared with the pre-depression dollar of 1929, became really a dollar and two thirds; and still fewer realize the tremendous significance of this fact. Yet its significance is all the greater just because it is not clearly realized.

The real meaning of a unit of money is the goods which that unit will buy. Instead of measuring goods by dollars, the economist is accustomed to measure dollars by goods—not by any one article of goods such as bread, but by the general budget of goods such as food-stuffs, clothing and cloth, furniture and houses, building materials, services, amusements and so on. When the price of bread alone changes, this is presumably due to some change in the quantity or quality of wheat, and not to any change in the dollar. But when a thousand other prices change at the same time, and all change in the same direction, or all change *on the average* in the same direction, we are, in general, justified in saying that the dollar has changed in the *opposite* direction.

Nevertheless, the Money Illusion [3] goes on telling us that the dollar stands still while other things move. This Money Illusion is analogous to the illusion of a passenger on a train who seems to see the landscape rushing past him. It is analogous to the illusion of sun-rise and sun-set, which makes the earth appear fixed with the sun swinging 'round it once a day. So when prices change, we forget the money on which we ride and ascribe the change to something outside—the goods, the merchant, the consumer, the producer, the fertility of the earth—anything at all except the money in terms of which we think.

German money, after the World War, furnished a good example. We in America, measuring everything in dollars, said the mark had fallen. But Germans, measuring everything in marks, said the dollar had risen. In 1922, I visited Germany and took particular pains to learn from many representative citizens how they accounted for the sky-rocketing of German prices. Practically all ascribed it to

[3] See *The Money Illusion* by Irving Fisher. (The Adelphi Company, New York, 1928.)

some misbehavior on the part of commodities, or to the after-effects of the war, or to the Allied blockade, or to the wastefulness of the new German government, or to almost any cause but the important one; which was, of course, that the German government was paying its debts and other expenses with new paper money manufactured for the purpose.

Yet Germans are no more prone to the money illusion than others. Over a generation ago, when England was on the gold standard and India on the silver standard, General Keating, in conversation with an Indian merchant, mentioned the then recent fall in the value of the silver rupee. The Indian merchant was non-plused. He said that he had never heard of any fall of the rupee, although he had agents all over India. After a pause, he added, "But my agents have mentioned the rise of the pound sterling. Perhaps that is what you are thinking of."

Sometimes both observers (even if one be an American) are equally deluded. Before the World War, an American woman owed money on a mortgage in Germany. After the war, she went to the German bank and offered the amount which she conceived to be due—$7,000. "But," said the banker, "The debt is in marks, not dollars—it is 28,000 marks; and today that comes to about $250."

"Oh!" she said, "I am not going to take advantage of the fall of the mark. I will pay the full $7,000." The banker, thinking in terms of marks, could not see the point. Indeed, the fair-minded American lady only half saw it, and "cheated" her creditor after all; for even American money was worth less than when the debt had been contracted. To pay the full amount in terms not of marks, or dollars, but in terms of the purchasing power which she had borrowed, the lady should have paid not $7,000 but $12,000. Yet, had the German banker known this and suggested it, the lady's indignation at such an "unfair" suggestion would doubtless have exceeded the banker's astonishment at receiving 28 times as much as he thought was due.

GOLD AND CREDIT

When it comes to gold money, we are even more apt to be deceived. The reverence for gold, as if it were something ultimately stable, is a form of ancestor worship. Money was invented by primitive man, unconsciously; and modern man has taken it for granted ever since. A certain amount of evolution has been at work upon money, but very little conscious invention. The first great step in its evolution was the unconscious trying-out of one substance after another—oxen, wampum, silver, gold. Gold finally prevailed, not for any stability of purchasing power, but for sheer physical convenience. Stability was scarcely thought of, until something else came on the scene to afford a means of comparison. That something was paper money. Gold is not so easily inflated as paper; but gold is by no means stable. It comes out of mines, subject to the will of mine-owners and to the accident of discovery; and if a dozen new gold mines should open at one stroke, the influx of gold would tend to depreciate the purchasing power of each individual gold dollar and of every paper dollar redeemable in gold. And this very thing has sometimes happened—with serious effects on the price level.

Moreover, and conversely, gold has now become dependent on paper money and checks. When modern man invented the check system, he did not dream that deposits subject to check would come to be regarded as money. But to all intents and purposes they are money, and they largely determine the purchasing power of gold. A gold dollar and a dollar-check and a paper dollar, so long as

they are mutually exchangeable, must all have equal purchasing power; but that power depends upon the influence
of all, not of gold alone; and the checks, or deposits,
furnish so much the greater volume that their total effect
on the purchasing power of gold, though few people except economists realize this important fact, is incom-
parably greater than the effect of the gold on the checks.
And, by the same token, disturbances of deposit currency
disturb the price level far more than do the very considerable disturbances of the gold supply.

The price level aberrations hitherto mentioned were all
cases of inflation. But deflation, which furnishes the principal key to a depression, is equally stealthy; and the Americans of 1932 who talked of low prices instead of swollen
dollars were just as befuddled as the Germans of 1922 who
talked of high prices instead of shrunken marks. It is time
that we knew how to detect the dollar when it indulges
in either of its stealthy monœuvers—whether shrinking or
swelling.

THE INDEX NUMBER

There is now available a statistical measure which ought
to go far toward dispelling the money illusion. This
measure is the "index number" of prices. Its function is
to measure the *average percentage change* in prices; that
is, the change in the *general price level*, or *general scale of
prices*.[4]

---

[4] There are, of course, many sorts of index numbers differing in the
method of averaging (whether arithmetic, geometric, aggregative,
weighted or simple), in the field covered (whether stock prices, or commodity and, if the latter, whether wholesale, retail, general), and in the
assortment of samples representing that field (whether 100 commodities
or 500, whether largely food and farm products or not). The best developed index number is that of the United States Bureau of Labor
Statistics for wholesale prices, using 784 commodities weighted in proportion to their importance in trade, the averaging being done by the

Such act of measuring should bring home to us the difference between the scale of prices and an individual price. The scale of prices (or the general price level) is analogous to the scale of a drawing or a statue. To say that, in a certain statue of Abraham Lincoln, the right leg is too long is to say that it is too long *relatively* to the other leg, or to the arms, or body, and is quite different from saying that the *scale* of the statue as a whole is more than life size; and there is the same distinction between saying the price of wheat is high relatively to other commodities and saying that there is a high general price level, or scale of prices. The Law of Supply and Demand regulates prices *relatively to one another;* but money is the medium in which Supply-and-Demand *registers;* and if the whole scale of prices moves, it is usually because this registering medium has moved.

Or we may think of money as a changeable lens, through which price-changes are seen. Prices may all change *en masse* at the same time that they are changing relatively to one another. The money lens magnifies all prices without interfering with the action of supply and demand on any price. What the index number has done, therefore, is to show up (to an unfortunately limited number of observers) the difference between a mass movement of prices and the individual price movements.

Changes in the price level and changes in the dollar are reciprocal. For instance, if a new price level (or scale) is double the old price level (or scale), the new dollar is half the old dollar—or has lost 50 per cent of its purchasing power. This scale-principle was never better illustrated than in German hotels during the period of the greatest

aggregative method. For discussion of these differences and especially of the formula problem, see *The Making of Index Numbers,* by Irving Fisher, Houghton, Mifflin & Co., 1927.

post-war inflation. A so-called "multiplicator" was supplied by the hotel; and, by means of it, each guest could translate [5] the printed prices on his bill of fare. He found the price of his dinner listed as, say, "6 marks," and the price of his room as "9 marks"; but, before he paid his bill, these figures had to be multiplied by the "multiplicator." This was a factor, or index, representing the price level, or scale of prices, and varied from day to day, going up as the mark went down. It had nothing to do with the real price of the dinner, either in terms of labor, or relatively to the price of the room. Whether the multiplicator was 100,000 or 1,000,000 made no difference to these relations, but only changed the dinner and room from 600,000 and 900,000 to 6,000,000 and 9,000,000. The multiplicator, or index, saved the trouble of too frequently reprinting the price lists when the price level was changing so fast.

The almost universal failure to distinguish between a price and a price *level*, or *scale* of prices, is responsible for untold confusion of mind on the subject of this book. This confusion is characteristic of most speeches and writings on economics, including the pronouncements of editors, officials, business men, and bankers, and even of some who bear the title of economists but who have not, for some reason, separated supply and demand on the one hand from the "equation of exchange" on the other.[6] The concept of a price level, its measurement by an index number, and its reciprocal, the purchasing power of the dollar, are pre-requisites for understanding what happened in 1932.

[5] See *The Money Illusion*, by Irving Fisher (The Adelphi Co., 1928), pp. 48–9.

[6] See *The Purchasing Power of Money*, by Irving Fisher, (Macmillan, 1931).

THE VICIOUS SPIRAL DOWNWARD

We are now in a position to explain the statement that a disturbance of the price level—or (as we may now express it) the alteration of "the real dollar"—*reacts* on the debt situation which first caused the alteration. When a whole community is in a state of over-indebtedness, the dollar reacts in such a way that the very act of liquidation may sometimes *enlarge the real debts instead of reducing them!* Nominally, of course, any liquidation must reduce debts, but really (by swelling the worth of every dollar in the country) it may swell the unpaid balance of every debt in the country, because the dollar which has to be paid may increase in size faster than the number of dollars in the debt decreases. And when this process starts, it may go on and on, much after the fashion of a vicious circle. First, mass payment by the weaker debtors swells the whole community's dollar, and so weakens the financial position of stronger debtors; whereupon, many of these rush to liquidate too, thus further swelling the dollar, till it weakens the position of still stronger debtors; whereupon many of *these* in turn rush to liquidate, thus further swelling the dollar and weakening still other debtors—and so on in a vicious circle; or, rather, in a vicious spiral *downward*—a tail spin—into the trough of depression.

TWO PARADOXES

After the weak, or rash, or improvident debtors (or their creditors) have started the vicious spiral, we can scarcely blame the others individually for going on with it, through further liquidations, even though every liquidation makes bad matters worse—accelerating the tail spin. For, granting that mass liquidation has once started, each individual who does not join in will come off still worse. For, even if he stays out, his ten thousand neighbors will liquidate just the same, and thereby swell his dollar— and thereby swell his *whole* debt instead of *part* of it.

The same principles apply to creditor banks. When a bank calls a loan, it helps deflate the credit currency; but other banks, equally scared, would deflate it anyhow; and if one bank stayed out, its debtors would go insolvent before they could be dunned. In a word, the banks, too, are forced into cut-throat competition for cash or "liquidity."

THE MAIN SECRET

When over-indebtedness thus goes so far that the resulting mass liquidation defeats itself, we have the paradox which, as I think, explains the so-called mystery of depressions—at least of many depressions. It is more than the fact that the dollar, when thus expanded, adds to the burden of every debtor. It is rather that this expanding dollar may (and sometimes does) not only grow, but grow *faster than the reduction of the number of dollars of debt.* When this happens, liquidation doesn't really liquidate, so that the depression goes right on—until there are sufficient bankruptcies to wipe out the activating cause— the debts.

SUMMARY

We have now mentioned, on their depression side, the cycle-tendencies of three of our eight economic factors.

1. Debts (their liquidation)
2. Volume of Currency (its contraction)
3. The Dollar (its swelling—usually considered in terms of a shrinking scale of prices).

Of these three depression tendencies, the second (cur-

rency contraction) is important only as a connective process between the other two—which two should be called

The Debt Disease (too much debt)

The Dollar Disease (a swelling dollar)

That the dollar disease—falling prices—is the main
secret of great depressions is confirmed by the observations
of Professor Wesley Clair Mitchell and Dr. Thorp to the
effect that depressions last three or four times as long
when prices are falling and are very short when, by some
good fortune, an up-tide of prices intervenes.

THE DOLLAR DISEASE IS NEEDLESS

But the mere fact that the debt disease may lead to the
dollar disease does not prove that it must do so. The dollar disease will be unavoidable only "if other things remain equal." Should other elements in the body of the
currency not remain equal—should gold coin, for instance,
become copious in the nick of time—this gold *in*flation
might counteract the credit *de*flation. Prices might even go
up instead of down; that is, the dollar might dwindle
instead of swell. And the same result might come from
paper inflation—for instance, by way of financing a war.

And it should be equally clear that deflation, or dollar
bulging, is not an "Act of God" with a special mandate to
baffle the human race. We need not wait for a happy accident to neutralize deflation. We ourselves may frustrate
it by design. Man has, or should have, control of his own
currency.

Such a control, so exercised as to neutralize the influences which tend to swell the dollar, would, of course,
not avert from any rash initial debtor the measured consequences of his own rashness; but his punishment would
be due to the nature of his separate debt and would, there-

fore, be chiefly confined to himself and perhaps a small circle of associates. The rest of the community would not suffer from any vagaries of the universal dollar. And even the rash debtor has a right to pay his debt in the same dollar in which he contracted it. It is manifestly unfair to require even a rash debtor to pay $1.50 or $2.00 for every dollar he really owes. The principle of simple justice implied in the term "real wages" is no more applicable to wage earners than it is to debtors.

In a word, if we *must* suffer from the debt disease, why also catch the dollar disease? If we catch cold, why let it lead to pneumonia?

CHAPTER III

REMAINING SIX MAIN FACTORS

NET WORTH

(The Fourth Main Factor)

BUT, assuming for the present, that neither accident nor human currency-control has forestalled the Dollar Disease, let us trace its further consequences through the series of economic factors, of which we have thus far discussed but three:

1. Debts—their liquidation
2. Currency—its contraction
3. The Dollar—its swelling (usually considered in terms of a falling price level).

The fourth factor is Net Worth.

The fall of prices reduces the money value of a business man's assets (except cash and debts due from others), while his liabilities, being debts, remain "fixed." Therefore his net worth, which is the excess of assets over liabilities, must shrink. Indeed, it will shrink *faster* than the assets do, because net worth is smaller than the assets, and yet takes the entire loss. Net worth is squeezed between the upper and the nether millstone; and often it passes below the zero mark, pushing the owner into business failure.

PROFITS

(The Fifth Main Factor)

Profits are, in the same way, squeezed between an upper and a nether millstone. Profits are the spread between the

29

receipts which fail when prices fall and the expenses which are, if not quite fixed, at any rate less responsive to the assault of deflation than prices are. These relatively unyielding expenses in the profit account include interest, taxes, rent, salaries, and to a less extent wages. The more unyielding the expenses the worse they pinch.[1] In this way, profits are reduced,[2] and often turned into losses—just as net worth is reduced and sometimes turned into failure and bankruptcy.

A depression might be defined as the contraction of net worths and profits.

So our list lengthens to:

1. Debt Liquidation
2. Currency Contraction
3. Dollar Swelling
4. Net Worth Reduction (turned sometimes to failure)
5. Profit Reduction (turned sometimes to losses)

But, once more, it should be noted that the drop, both in net worths and in profits, will be largely forestalled if the drop in the price level is forestalled.

PRODUCTION, TRADE, EMPLOYMENT

(The Sixth Main Factor)

In a capitalistic, or private profit, system, it is the profit taker who usually makes the decision as to the rate at which his enterprise is to be run. Therefore, variations in

---

[1] It follows that the pinch is especially felt by modern business because of its greater proportion of overhead and fixed expenses. If, as seems likely, business organization continues its tendency toward more fixed charges and less running expenses, its profits will be more and more sensitive to changes in the price level.

[2] This effect may be mitigated or escaped when through inventions, technological improvements and improved scientific management, expenses are greatly reduced.

profits, or in the expectation of profits, lead the business man to vary correspondingly the general policy of his enterprise.

When his profits are squeezed too thin for comfort, naturally he will cut his production and release some of his employees, so that the community's general out-put, trade and employment, will take a slump.

That is, current out-put varies with current profits.

Thus, currency contraction reduces out-put by reducing prices and so reducing profits.

There is a special category of production, namely construction—or the production of new equipment, such as buildings and machinery, intended to increase the capacity for current out-put. Construction is much more sensitive to changes in profits than is ordinary production or current out-put. Construction increases fastest with the approach of a peak load, or a strain upon existing equipment. And it is not much more sudden in starting than it is in stopping. Right amid the new-equipment fever, at almost the first sign or forecast of impending trouble, new construction may abruptly fall. It falls earlier and faster than current out-put; and it produces a greater reaction in employment. In fact, construction affects the slump in profits, employment and so on, like an amplifier.

The derangement of this group of factors (production, trade, and employment) covers the most obvious and commonly recognized symptoms of a business depression. In fact, it is often called a depression of trade.

Again our list grows:

1. Liquidation
2. Currency Contraction
3. Dollar Growth
4. Net Worth Reduction
5. Profit Reduction

6. Reduced Production (especially of equipment) along with reduced Trade, and reduced Employment.

But once more be it noted: if something will only forestall the price deflation (the Dollar Disease), thus largely forestalling the reduction of Net-worths and of Profits, then the slump in Production, Trade and Employment will also, to a large extent, be forestalled.

In passing it may be noted that currency contraction also reduces the demand for goods by reducing purchasing power; thus demand and supply shrink together. That is, currency-contraction not only acts indirectly on production and trade through the above series of six steps but also acts directly by reducing the wherewithal for buying goods. This effect (of Factor 2 on Factor 6) would be felt even if there were no fall of prices; in fact, it would be greater. Also unemployment means reduced purchasing power.

OPTIMISM AND PESSIMISM

(The Seventh Main Factor)

All of the down movements thus far mentioned—especially the down movements of Net-worth, Profits, and Employment—have psychological effects. Already we have seen that shrinking net-worth leads to distress selling. But distress selling implies distress. A conscientious business man, caught too deeply in debt and forced into bankruptcy, may become despondent, even to the point of suicide. Distress also occurs when profits merely decline, though there may still be hope for a better future.

Yet those who reckon their net-worths and their profits are a very small class compared with those whose employment is affected by a depression; and to be employed or unemployed is, to the employee class, a question almost of life or death. Therefore, a depression affects the moods of that class with especial force.

There are, of course, some persons whose incomes run opposite to the general trend. That is, certain bondholders and salaried folk have fixed and safe money incomes; and whenever prices fall, these incomes will buy more. In terms of real income, their fortunes have actually improved. But even most of these people share the general fears. In fact, they are the very type most accustomed to play safe and are, therefore, the most easily alarmed by general conditions. They begin to wonder if their incomes are safe after all. Indeed, they see some of their own class either out of employment or ruined by the ruin of the enterprises on which they had depended for their supposedly safe incomes. In a word, pessimism, in a depression, becomes practically universal.

Nor is this psychological movement only emotional. Partly it is intellectual as well; for it involves illusion and misjudgment. During depressions, the sober judgment of many people gives way to over-estimates of the degree and permanence of "hard times." And, as our estimates are largely guesses—guesses as to what other people will do or think, and as to what and how much they will buy or sell—there enters the element of mass psychology. Everybody's opinion is largely guided by the opinion of everybody else; even the people with the coolest heads will at least "fear the fears of other men" and contribute to the panic of which such fears are a part.

Our list now is:
1. Liquidation
2. Currency-Contraction
3. Dollar Growth
4. Reduced Net-Worth
5. Reduced Profits

6. Reduced Production

7. Increased Pessimism and loss of confidence.

But here again, if (by the checkmating of deflation) the failures and the unemployment be forestalled, pessimism and loss of confidence will also be forestalled.

THE VELOCITY OF CIRCULATION

(The Eighth Main Factor)

Hitherto, under the head of deflation, we have considered only the *contraction* of currency (meaning deposit currency). But now we come to the *slowing* of currency through pessimism. For, while distress liquidation is contracting deposit currency, the loss of confidence that accompanies the distress slows down *all* currency, bank deposits included; for scared people hold on to their money (of all kinds) a little longer—they spend it a little more slowly.

And here again, *all* kinds of debts (including public debts through the pressure of taxes) have their effect in slowing the turnover of currency, because all kinds of debtors (including taxpayers) are especially subject to caution and fear. Even buyers at distress-sales, who gain the buying power that the sellers lose, will be cautious and postpone their buying and hold on to their money a little longer.

It takes contraction and slow turnover together to make up the full dose of deflation. Suppose, for instance, that the currency, besides being contracted 50 per cent is slowed another 50. This means that there is only half the currency moving half as fast. Therefore, the currency as a whole will do only a quarter of its former work. Either Prices must drop three-quarters, or Trade must contract three-quarters, or else both Trade and Prices must drop in some degree. And this combination effect is what usually happens.

No one incident unites both contraction and slowing so effectively as a stock market crash. A stock market crash wipes out great masses of credit currency with unusual suddenness; and, at the same time, it so stirs the cautious side of human nature that men hang on harder than ever to their available money of every remaining sort. In combination, these two sequels of a stock market crash (contraction and slowing of currency) constitute a dose of deflation almost as good (or as bad) as a bonfire of a large part of the nation's cash. A stock market crash is evil enough in itself; but it is not confined to itself. Through its double effect on the currency in which commodity prices are registered, it sets commodity prices sinking in sympathy with the stock prices—more slowly but also more injuriously to the foundations of the economic structure. And at last, something like a panic develops in the commodity market.

HOARDING, A SLOWING OF VELOCITY

Hoarding is a slowing of currency turnover of the extremest kind. It is the supreme manifestation of popular moods in a depression. Housewives and their breadwinners then become distrustful of everything except money. Bills and coins are confided to stockings or mattresses, or are put underground, or (in a larger way) stored in safety deposit vaults. Credit deposits may be hoarded too. In such banks as are considered safe, large credit deposits will be kept, but kept idle. Checking accounts, based on *cash* deposits, will often be changed into time deposits, bearing more interest than checking accounts. Finally, if there be any reason to fear for the solvency of a bank, it will be subjected to a "run"; and the money, after it is withdrawn, will be hoarded at home.

It should be clear that hoarding, once introduced, becomes a tremendous factor in the vicious spiral, and can continue it with or without over-indebtedness. Hoarding lowers the price level. The lowered price level hurts business (debts or no debts); hurt business increases fear, and the fear increases the hoarding.

THE TWO PARADOXES AGAIN—APPLIED TO HOARDING

We have seen, with respect to the contraction of the currency by mass liquidation, how debtors and their creditor-banks, by making, or trying to make, things better for themselves individually, make things worse for themselves collectively. The same applies to the slowing of the currency by hoarding. Every man who hoards does it for his own protection; yet, by hoarding, he aggravates the very condition that started his fear. This is especially true when his panic puts panic into the banks. They sometimes make runs, so to speak, on their customers before the customers can make runs on them.

In fact, banks find themselves engaged in a race for "liquidity." They begin to call their loans; but by calling loans, they help further to extinguish deposit currency. Moreover, the cash which each bank collects comes largely out of other banks; and these, in turn, have to replenish their cash, which they can do only by, in turn, calling loans, thus further extinguishing currency. This hoarding of money by banks has a magnified effect on deposit currency; for every dollar of reserve in a bank may support, say, ten dollars of loans. When, therefore, one bank forces another bank to surrender one of its physical reserve dollars, it forces a potential reduction of ten dollars of deposit currency. Even the bankers often fail to appreciate this ten-fold effect, because the initial effect of a physical dollar withdrawn is only one dollar of deposits withdrawn.[3]

POSSIBLE CONSEQUENCES OF CONTRACTION AND HOARDING

If all deposits were thus extinguished, as is not impossible theoretically, then the only circulating medium remaining would be physical, hand-to-hand, or pocket, money. There would then be a 90 per cent shrinkage in the circulating medium, and a slowing down of such currency as remained. The price level might readily sink to less than one-tenth of what it had been, despite a reduction in the volume of trade. Then almost all business men in debt, including farmers, would be completely ruined.

We thus again add to our list:
1. Liquidation
2. Contraction
3. Dollar Growth
4. Reduced Net-Worth
5. Reduced Profits
6. Reduced Production
7. Pessimism
8. Hoarding and a general slackening in the velocity of circulation, both of deposits and of physical money.

But here again, if deflation—or the swelling of the dollar (due to both the contraction and the retardation of the currency) be checkmated, the slowing of velocity and hoarding will be checkmated too. For instance, an increase in volume, if sufficient, may conquer a decrease in Velocity.

[3] The details of the magnifying process have been set forth by Dean Chester Phillips of Iowa University in his *Bank Credit* (Macmillan, 1920) and have recently been further worked out mathematically by Professor James Harvey Rogers of Yale University.

(The Ninth Main Factor)

Debts bear interest. Consequently, a cyclical tendency in debts will involve a cyclical tendency in interest rates. In a word, as borrowers grow discouraged and therefore scarce, interest (in the large centers at least) tends to go down. Nor can we say of this disturbance of interest rates, as we have said of other cycle-tendencies, that if the deflation were annulled, the disturbance of the interest would be entirely forestalled. For the cycle-tendency of debts carries with it *directly and necessarily* a corresponding tendency in interest rates. This, however, is relatively harmless.

"REAL" RATES VS. MONEY RATES

But here enters another paradox: the inconsistency between this nominal or money interest and *real* interest. If, last year, I borrowed 100 dollars and am to pay 105 this year, my *nominal* or money rate of interest is 5 per cent. But if, meanwhile, the dollar has swollen so that, when the due date arrives, 105 dollars have become worth 106 of last year's dollars, my *real* interest is not five per cent but six per cent.[4] In a depression, therefore, when interest is *meant* to be low, the real interest amounts, sometimes, to over 50 per cent per annum![5] The really important dis-

[4] The distinction between the money rate of interest and the real rate of interest is like the distinction between money wages and real wages, and between money debts and real debts. But it is more complicated, and so more often overlooked. We translate money wages into real wages or money debts into real debts *at one point of time*. But to translate money interest into real interest we must take account of at least *two* points of time, namely the time when the debt is contracted and the time (or times) when it is repaid. For further analysis, see Chapter XIX of *The Theory of Interest* by Irving Fisher (Macmillan, 1930).

[5] But the various nominal rates themselves move unequally. The pes-

turbance is this discrepancy between real interest and money interest; and *this* would be forestalled if the deflation were annulled.

DEFLATION THE ROOT OF ALMOST ALL THE EVILS

We see, then, that if the liquidation were prevented from bulging the purchasing power of the dollar—that is, if the dollar was safe-guarded—all the other depression consequences in our list (except as to money interest) would be forestalled, and the consistency between money interest and real interest would be preserved.

Practically the only evils would then be the disturbance in the debts themselves and in their money interest; and these would be relatively tame affairs. Of a depression as we know it, there would be little left.

CHRONOLOGY OF THE NINE FACTORS

Our nine factors have been set forth in the following order:
1. Debt Liquidation
2. Currency Contraction
3. Dollar Growth
4. Net-Worth Reduction
5. Profit Reduction
6. Lessened Production, Trade, Employment
7. Pessimism and Distrust
8. Retarded Circulation
9. Lowered Money Interest—but raised real interest.

simism of the lenders causes them, for *inferior* borrowers, to *raise* their rates, instead of lowering them—at least to raise them relatively to the rates allowed on safer loans. That is, in a Depression, any natural divergence between the two classes of loans is increased.

But, while the order of the nine major events as above set forth is a good pedagogical order, it is not a strictly chronological order. Its principal departures from chronology lie in the items of interest and pessimism, both of which, if treated chronologically, should come earlier. Pessimism was purposely delayed in the exposition until all the chief reasons for it had been catalogued. It was then inserted once for all. Perhaps, more than any of the other factors, it really comes in progressively all along the line. The first touch of liquidation has a depressing effect on moods; and this first approach of the pessimistic mood retards circulation.

Even the very start of the liquidation may be the psychological discouragement—either of the debtor or the creditor—from a realization that the debts they owe, or the debts owing to them, are too high and should be reduced. This realization may be borne home by many causes; but the chief cause may well be that earnings, current or expected, have begun to disappoint the excessive expectations which originally led to the debts. It is often said that the "turn of the cycle" may be due to a very trivial precipitating cause. Anything which causes a slight revulsion of mood may be the last straw. Then, with liquidation and distress selling, the depression spiral begins its tail spin.

So the slowing of circulation may show itself statistically in advance of the credit contraction, though the contraction was listed first for convenience of exposition and the retardation of velocity was not mentioned until the full reasons for it had come into view.

Not only may the retardation of currency begin before its contraction, but there may be at first an actual expansion of currency, if enough cautious people set about accumulating cash studiously.

Nor are these the only chronological complications. Our

Nine Factors are only a part of the whole complex picture in any actual depression, and their many effects on each other have not been exhaustively stated. If we may mix our metaphors, a depression may be said to be full of tangles and cross-currents. Moreover, dislocations may occur through a great variety of interferences.[6]

THE TROUGH OF DEPRESSION

But no downswing goes on forever. Let us trace the first factor, debts. The process of liquidation may persist until at last it overtakes the swelling of the remaining debts, and begins to reduce not only their number but their real size. Every business failure, every bankruptcy, every reorganization grimly speeds the liquidation by striking off a certain proportion of the world's debts without even paying them; so that these failures may prevent the vicious spread of liquidation from swelling the dollar to ten fold dimensions. Moreover, the reduction in the volume of trade, caused by the fall of prices, tends to check that fall. That is, the shortage of money and credit relatively to the needs of commerce becomes a less serious shortage when the needs of commerce have also shrunk. Thus, through *real* liquidation, or failures, or both, and a diminution of Trade, the bottom of the descending spiral is finally reached.

The time comes when the business world is left in a state of *under*-indebtedness. Then the Debt Cycle (or cycle tendency) will be, so to speak, at the zero hour, ready for a recovery which may merge again into a Boom phase, similar to that from which it fell. At this zero hour the world is full of bargain prices—including, of course,

[6] In Appendix I will be found a schedule covering some of the complex chronology of the nine factors.

investments, and including interest rates for those who would borrow in order to invest. And since each dollar of debt no longer grows during the life of the debt, the nominal interest is not belied by the real interest, but both are, for the time being—for short-term loans—one. All that is then needed for an upswing is some left-over individuals, still possessed of resources enough to enable them to take advantage of these bargain prices.

The downswing has itself tended to produce such individuals. They are the prosperous residue of the creditor and salaried classes—the unharmed bondholders and the unharmed salaried folk. To them, as already noted, a higher dollar spells a lower cost of living, and encourages the buying up of the wreckage after the storm. Moreover, the hoarders, when convinced that the bottom has been reached and that they are safe in returning their hoards into circulation, become important buyers.

THE BOOM PHASE AGAIN

The upswing is helpful at first. It begins as a recovery all along the line, reversing each of the nine factors. Distrust and gloom gradually give way to confidence and then to enthusiasm. Hoards come out of hiding. Deposits cease to be idle. The rush includes commodity investments and new loans. For this very reason the nominal rate of interest rises; but it does not check the tide because the real rate falls. That is, the new buying and borrowing *reflates* the deposit currency, that is expands and speeds it, thus raising the price level (that is, shrinking the dollar), so that debts, though nominally increasing, diminish in real burden per dollar. The burden per dollar may even diminish faster than the nominal amount of the debts increases, thus diminishing the total real burden of the debts, despite their accumulating numbers. Thereafter, buying and borrowing become still more aggressive. The buyers rush still faster, so that their purpose may be accomplished while the buying is good. At the same time, the reflation, by raising prices, raises net worth, thus dispelling fear of business failure. Profits, too, are raised, thus encouraging the profit-takers to increase their out-put, their construction, and their pay-roll. Trade grows.

A VICIOUS SPIRAL UPWARD

If only the movement would stop at equilibrium! But our narrative in the last paragraph already implies a vicious spiral upward, the counterpart of the vicious spiral downward. It involves, like the downward spiral, three of the nine oscillatory factors, namely, Debts, Circulation, and Real Dollars. As reflation lightens the real burden of the debts, the debtors, including new and weaker borrowers, are lured into further extending their enterprises, and, for that purpose, into incurring more debts, which further dilute the real dollar and so further lighten the real debt-burden, and so still further tempt the business world (including new and still weaker borrowers) to incur still more debts, and so on and on—until again, after the number of dollars of debt grows faster than each dollar grows smaller, there comes an awakening to the fact that there is an over-indebtedness which must be corrected. Then borrowing diminishes, liquidation sets in; and once more we are headed for depression.

CHAPTER IV

STARTERS

UNPRODUCTIVE DEBTS

We began the discussion at the crest of the wave, with a state of over-indebtedness presupposed. But what started the debts?

First, as an approach to the problem of the origin of over-indebtedness, let us classify our debts.

Chiefly, there are two general classes of debts: productive and unproductive.[1]

An unproductive debt is incurred after some misfortune has cut a hole in the borrower's income-stream; and the loan partially fills up the hole, while the borrower awaits better times. Thus, if a workman falls ill and cannot, for a while, earn wages, he gets a loan to tide him over; and with its proceeds he ekes out the straitened family income, repaying the debt later when that income is increased by the resumption of wages. Occasionally, of course, such mischances may affect great numbers of people at one time, and so result in general over-indebtedness. A great earthquake, conflagration, flood, drought, pestilence, or war may result in unproductive debts on a large scale. Farm depression is often aggravated, if not caused, by drought, and crop failures. A war will create huge debts which are not only unproductive but devoted to destructive purposes.

[1] For fuller discussion, see *The Theory of Interest* by Irving Fisher (Macmillan, 1930).

44

Unproductive debts, however (except in war), are likely to be sporadic; and, since the borrowing in each case is reluctant and often cautious, it is likely to be limited by the available security. On the whole, therefore (except in war), this kind of indebtedness is not apt to be greatly overdone.

PRODUCTIVE DEBTS

As an explanation of economic crises, or of most economic crises, productive debts are far more important than the unproductive—except war debts. In the case of productive borrowing, as in unproductive, there has been a hole cut in the income, but this hole is no accident. It has been deliberately cut by the borrower. A man who sees an opportunity to invest at a tremendous profit would be quite willing, if he could not get a loan, to sacrifice the enjoyment of a large part of his present income, in order to invest in the supposed bonanza, even if, for a while, he must live on bread and cheese. That is, he saves instead of spends. But if he *can* get a loan, he may fill up the hole which he cut in his enjoyable income. That is, he will sacrifice little if at all on his current spending. And if he finds that he can borrow very freely, he may be tempted to go still further into debt, and spend even more than before the loan, relying on the expected returns from his investment to repay both his investment and his extravagance. His psychology is not that of the unfortunate. His mood is not fear, gloom or caution. It is enthusiasm and hope.

Often, if not usually, the opportunity to invest is the result of new inventions, new discoveries, or new business methods. When inventors, or their backers or exploiters, think they can, by borrowing at (say) 6 per cent, make profits of 100 per cent, why should they hesitate to borrow, and keep on borrowing? Examples of such lures are the opening of the Erie Canal, the building of new railways, the exploitation of the Bessemer steel process, new uses of electricity, and new industries, such as automobile, airplane and radio.

SOME HISTORICAL ILLUSTRATIONS

In 1792–93, in England, the lures were canals, real estate and machinery. In 1814–16, when Napoleon's interference with international trade had been broken, the lure, in England, was the prospect of renewed trade with the Continent. English speculation in exportable commodities became a stampede. In 1825, in the same country, there were various lures: mines and other commercial enterprises in Mexico, South America, and other foreign parts—what G. H. Powell calls "exaggerated views of coming prosperity," through the profits to be had by investing. Says Tooke:

"This possibility of enormous profit by risking a small sum was a bait too tempting to be resisted; all the gambling propensities of human nature were constantly solicited into action; and crowds of individuals of every description—the credulous and the ignorant, princes, nobles, politicians, patriots, lawyers, physicians, divines, philosophers, poets, intermingled with women of all ranks and degrees (spinsters, wives, and widows) —hastened to venture some portion of their property in schemes of which scarcely anything was known except the names."

In America, the chief depressions were 1819, 1837, 1857, 1873, and 1893. In most of these there was inflation beforehand and then deflation through contraction of the currency and bank credits. In 1819 and 1837 there had been wildcat banking causing inflation. In all cases there was speculation in real estate; for, as Victor Clark points out, a new country like America offers its opportunities for big profits largely in connection with the exploitation of new areas of land. In 1819 the land boom and collapse was in the east. In 1837 it was in the west and southwest. Whenever and wherever new lands were opened there was land speculation, the latest case being the Florida land boom of 1926. The crisis of 1837 followed land and cotton lures, and the lure of canal building, steamboats and turnpikes. The speculation was led by Biddle, the great Philadelphia banker of that day. The result was to open up each side of the Appalachians to the other. The opening of the Erie Canal had profound economic effects. The investments in these internal improvements were made possible by large loans from Europe.

The crisis of 1857 followed the exploitation of the California gold discoveries and the beginnings of railways, the extension of internal improvements, and the opening of the Northwest.

The panic of 1873 followed the exploitation of transcontinental railways, and western farms through the Homestead Act. These new farms were mortgaged to Eastern lenders.

Preceding the panic of 1893, in America there was an over-exploitation of farm implements resulting in overproduction of farm products, pointed out by Professor Bogart. But the main cause appears to have been distrust of the monetary situation due to the injection of too much silver into our currency. The gold base was too small.

THE SHADY SIDE

A genuine opening of new opportunities for profitable investment is only the first step. At first, it is the legitimate

leaders in the exploitation who are responsible for induc-
ing the public to invest, and to borrow for the purpose of
investing. Afterward some people, instead of investing for
earnings, merely speculate—buying in order soon to sell
again to others who want to invest or to other speculators. Afterwards come less scrupulous promoters; and
finally downright crooks. Probably no great crash has
ever happened without shady transactions. Indeed, the dis-
closure of these is often the last straw which breaks the
camel's back and precipitates the calamitous liquidation.
Fraud enters as one link or mesh in the net-work, being
both effect and cause—an effect of genuine opportunities
to invest, and a cause of over-indebtedness. No debt is so
excessive as one based on mistaken hopes, but when dis-
illusionment comes, the adventure is denounced as a
"bubble" that has been pricked, such as the Mississippi
Bubble and the South Sea Bubble.

MONETARY INFLATION ALONE

As debt starters, we have considered (1) Unusual Debts
of Misfortune, including War (that is, *decreased present*
income), and (2) Unusual Debts for Investing (when
there are prospects of *increased future* income). But we
also have to consider: (3) Monetary Inflation *without* any
unusual debts to begin with.

Such monetary inflation, whether designed or accidental,
begins directly on the currency, without unusual debts,
but presently reacts on the debt situation, by pouring
into business such unwonted profits that business men begin
to extend themselves in new enterprises, requiring *more*
debts. There are many historic instances of this sort of
thing. In 1849 California flooded the world with gold.
Again, between 1896 and 1913, new gold mines poured

out their injurious treasures from South Africa, Colorado, and Alaska; and at about the same time, the weaker mines were revived by a cheaper process of extracting gold from low grade ores. The world has suffered also from many great paper inflations, especially in war time. These inflations have all led to debt over-extension, which has thereupon set in motion the eight other cyclical tendencies.

COMBINED STARTERS

Sometimes we find Inflation and Great Expectations joining forces. Such was the case in the crisis of 1857. Men had been over-borrowing in order to invest in mines. This would have been bad enough if the mines had produced only copper; but the mines produced gold, whose inflationary out-pour was added to the influence of the debts; that is, the inflation of gold currency and the inflation of credit currency interlocked.

On the other hand, instead of intentional or accidental inflation, there might be intentional or accidental deflation. After the Civil War, when the greenback inflation of the 60's was replaced by the resumption of gold payments in 1879, there was a case of intentional deflation; moreover, this was followed up by accidental exhaustion of gold mines in the face of expanding business. Such may have been among the important causes of the depression which culminated in 1893.

In the vicious spiral, the debt factor and the inflation-deflation factor pursue each other, and either may be the starter of the pursuit. The greatest of all starters is war, including the rebound from war. War is the greatest inflater; and war's aftermath is the greatest deflater, because war is the greatest of all debt-makers, both public and private—and of both productive and unproductive debts.

And, finally, war stimulates other starters, such as invention.

Sometimes, by coincidence we get all conceivable sorts of starters working in the same direction—such as war, gold discoveries and new processes, new banking systems, with capacity for great credit expansion, great inventions and the rebound from a recent depression. Many of these coincided in the United States in the period 1913–19 and many also in 1926–9.

CHAPTER V

"THE" BUSINESS CYCLE?

THE DEVELOPMENT OF THE CYCLE IDEA

ORIGINALLY, people were content to refer to any given case of Boom and Depression as a "Business Crisis." Then the given cases seemed to recur with some regularity and to show an apparent family likeness. This fact is brought home, for instance, by the eloquent words of Leonard Bacon in 1837, quoted in the beginning of this book and applying almost equally to 1932. As a result of these family likenesses, and of the recurrence as well of the phenomena preceding and of the phenomena succeeding the "crises," the term "cycle" became more popular than "crisis." [1]

In 1867, before the Manchester Statistical Society, John Mills of Manchester, read a very able paper on "Credit Cycles and the Origin of Commercial Panics" [2] in which he stated that Booms and Depressions definitely repeat themselves "about every ten years." In 1894, Palgrave's *Dictionary of Political Economy* spoke rather more loosely of a "ten or twelve" year period; citing 1753, '63, '72, '83, '93; 1815, '25, '36, '47, '57, '66, '78, and '90. Recently, the favorite average seems to be nearer to 3½ years. More recently Professor Hansen has said: [3]

[1] This has been largely through the influence of Wesley Clair Mitchell.

[2] *Transactions of the Manchester Statistical Society*, December, 1867.

[3] *Economic Stabilization in an Unbalanced World*, by Alvin H. Hansen (Harcourt, Brace & Co., 1932), p. 93.

51

"The first great achievement of the scientific study of crises and depressions was the discovery that business *moves in cycles*. The first cycle to be discovered was the major cycle, which runs its course usually in from seven to eleven years. This cycle was firmly established by the great work of Clement Juglar in his *Des crises commerciales*, first published in 1860. Only in the last two decades was it established (notably through the work of Warren M. Persons and Wesley C. Mitchell) that there is, at least for the United States, a much shorter minor cycle of about forty months' duration. That it should be especially prominent in the United States is perhaps due to the fact that her domestic market is so vast that internal minor fluctuations can develop here that are not reflected in the outside world. Historically, in the United States every second or third minor depression develops into a major depression. Finally, it remained for Professor N. D. Kondratieff of Moscow, Russia, to point out the existence of 'long waves,' each extending over a period of from forty-five to sixty years."

"FORCED" CYCLES

Certainly there are in economic affairs cyclical *tendencies;* and these are of two sorts: those imposed upon the economic organism from the outside, or what may be called "forced" cyclical tendencies, and those inherent in it.

Those imposed from the outside are largely of astronomical origin. It is not impossible that among these there may be economic rhythms longer than a year. W. Stanley Jevons thought he detected a ten year economic rhythm produced by sun spots. H. S. Jevons seemed to uncover a three and a half year economic rhythm which he supposed to be the effect of solar radiation. Prof. H. L. Moore imputed an eight year economic rhythm to the conjunctions of Venus. More recently, Dr. Abbott of the Smithsonian Institution has been studying what appear to be long time cycles in solar radiation. It is, of course, quite possible that these cycles may have some obscure effect on the economic affairs of earth. All these tendencies may possibly exist—and exist consistently with one another, and with many more— although they seem as yet to lack sufficient proof.

There are, however, shorter rhythms in human affairs, indubitably caused by astronomical forces. These rhythms are yearly and daily. The swing of the earth around the sun causes variations of light, heat, and moisture, and these determine the seasons, thereby causing rhythmic tendencies in planting and reaping, and in certain resulting phases of commerce and of banking. These yearly rhythms have come to be called, not too happily, "seasonal variations"; they might rather have been named seasonal cycles or cyclical tendencies. So, also, the turnings of the earth around its own axis cause the alternation of light and darkness, thus producing, in all human activity (business included), rhythmic tendencies every twenty-four hours.

There are other cyclical tendencies imposed from outside the economic mechanism. These are customary or institutional rhythms. For instance, the religious and traditional observance of Sunday sets the weekly rhythm of payrolls; and the still more arbitrary month sets the rhythm of salary checks and billings.

All these "forced" rhythms, that is rhythms imposed upon the economic mechanism from the outside, are permanent, or at any rate as long-lived as the customs or astronomical or other outside influences which impose them.

"FREE" CYCLES

No one denies the existence of these "forced" rhythms; but none of them seems clearly to coincide with booms and depressions. To find the causes of booms and depressions, we must step *inside* the economic mechanism and consider rhythms relatively "free" of outside control.

But when we have done that, we find that clearness ends and debate begins. We find fairly clear "trends" or progressive changes, but these are not rhythms. And we find much evidence of rhythmic tendencies, but these are not clear; and their name is legion. This book has dealt with only one group of nine cyclical tendencies closely inter-related, and even their inter-relations are not simple, but form a tangled network of permutations and combinations. All their possible interactions by pairs would come to over 360,000 and this number could be multiplied indefinitely by sub-classifying our nine factors and adding others.

ANY UNBALANCE MAY CAUSE CYCLICAL TENDENCIES

The dis-equilibrium of any factor, theoretically at least, may start up oscillations in many or all of the others. The starting point may be not the two we have discussed (over-indebtedness and deflation) but some over-production or under-production, some over or under-consumption, some over or under-investment, over or under-saving, or any other sort of "over" or "under"—that is, any temporary deviation from balance causing a tendency to return to the point of equilibrium, and to pass beyond it, with subsequent swings back and forth.

Economic forces are not, as the classical economists once seemed to imagine, so simply related as a row of blocks, each acting on the one ahead; but rather, as Walras long ago pointed out, these forces consist of numerous variables, each affecting all the rest, so that a change in one tends to cause changes in all. Economic forces might be likened to a dozen agates in a bowl, a push on any one of which will set them all rocking back and forth. This being so, we need not look for one single or simple explanation of economic disturbances, though we may hope to find some of the factors—some of the agates—bigger and more dominating than the rest. Over-indebtedness, for instance, and deflation may—to change the simile—make big waves in the economic pond, while over-production, or a short wheat crop or even a Florida land boom may, in comparison, produce mere ripples.

BUT THESE TEND TO DIE DOWN

But, unless restarted by some outside force, any ordinary disequilibrium eventually gives place to restored equilibrium.[4]

Moreover, in every type of known action and reaction, there is a progressive deterrent called friction. This is true of mechanical devices like a pendulum; and it seems reasonable to think that in all economic movements there is something analogous to mechanical friction which, for convenience, may be called "economic friction," tending to stop economic movements in whatever direction. If this is true, when any economic pendulum has swung in one direction, it tends to swing less in the other direction. All of this is purposely stated as a tendency. It will be actually true only in the absence of a new jolt, which, however, is very likely to occur, in economics as in mechanics.

"THE" BUSINESS CYCLE A MYTH?

The proponents of "the" business cycle seem often to overlook other interfering cyclical tendencies and interfer-

---

[4] That is, we assume most equilibrium to be stable. Unstable equilibrium, *ipso facto*, destroys itself and is not repetitive.

ing "friction," and expect the actual resultant fluctuations to form well marked cycles—at any rate after eliminating secular trend and seasonal variation—and without any successive reductions in these waves. Yet, so far as I know, they have never been able to diagram any successive economic swings that had a reasonably similar shape, or covered reasonably equal spans, or did not start with some unrhythmic outside cause, such as discovery, or invention, or the opening of new markets, the development of new areas or of new resources in old areas; or such causes as war, pestilence, fire, flood or earthquake. As a matter of history, it always seems to be a case of one or more of these hap-hazard starters colliding with some price, prices, price level, income, production, consumption, stocks of goods, debts, or some other factors in the economic mechanism. It would be still more difficult to find any rhythmic tendency among the starters themselves. It is true that the misery of a depression often stimulates invention, and that one invention often leads to another, and that one war does not exhaust the causes of war; and it may be true that inflation tends to incubate war-preparations and that war tends to promote invention; but who can as yet discern any real rhythm in these? They are nothing if not miscellaneous. The capture of Napoleon in 1815 and the railway boom after the Civil War seem scarcely a part of a cycle, much less of "the" cycle.

Recent and intensive studies have pretty well dispelled the idea of *actual* periodicity; but the undoubted fact of rhythmic *tendency* in many if not all economic factors continues to make the search for periodicity—or at least for self-perpetuation—at once enticing and baffling. Sometimes the starters follow each other so fast that, before the rocking initiated by one has died away, another is in action, and this continuity lures on the searcher. Then sometimes, by good luck, several oscillations may complete themselves without the interrupting of a new starter, further corroborating the cycle idea. By still better luck, the initial pushes themselves may sometimes show an apparent periodicity, as if they operated like the escapement mechanism in a pendulum clock. Such a coincidence occurring in (say) half the cases will be very striking; and in the other half, the fading rhythm will stay sufficiently visible to satisfy the theorist, who wants to believe in its periodicity or power of self-perpetuation.

I am open to conviction, if and when evidence shall be presented of self-starting and self-perpetuating economic rhythms, but thus far I have been able to see only a tangle of coincidence and contradiction, which may be illustrated by a rocking chair, or a sea craft, in surroundings which furnish both rhythmic and erratic influences. The chair, when tipped, certainly has a tendency to keep rocking— but not forever. And perhaps it is either restarted or put out of rhythm by a new jolt from the dusting housewife.

The seacraft, when tipped by a wave, tends to return upon itself and to rock on regularly; but its rhythm is constantly put out by the buffeting of additional waves. The waves themselves act under laws of rhythm which are unfailing; yet the actual rhythm will fail, through the buffeting of cross winds. Imagine, then, a rocking chair on the deck of a rocking ship, on a rolling sea. The ultimate chair is subjected to so many influences that its motion will not conform with any simple rhythm. The net motion will be made up of many rhythms and non-rhythms, and will, therefore, appear sometimes rhythmic and sometimes completely unrhythmic. At all events, no one would think of referring to it as "*the* rocking chair cycle."

In short, it appears that "free" cycles tend to die down, while "forced" cycles do not, and that in any actual case we find a composite of both the free and the forced cycles as well as trends and starters.

CYCLES AS FACTS OR TENDENCIES

The main point, however, is to acknowledge the distinction between cycle as fact and cycle as tendency.[5] It is one thing to say that, under certain simplified conditions, business *would* oscillate according to a certain repeating curve, just as, under simplified conditions, the rocking of the chair would make a perfect repeating rhythm. It is quite another thing to say that business *did* actually oscillate on that curve, in the years 1929–32, or in any other historical case. A tendency is conditional; a fact is unconditional. A tendency is relatively simple; a fact will always be complex—the resultant of a great number of tendencies, some of which are cyclical and some—like the housewife's duster —not cyclical at all.

For these reasons, I deprecate the use of the term "cycle" as applied to any actual historical event. I would reserve the cycle concept for a tendency, or at the utmost a specified combination of tendencies.

But I am not disposed to deny the value of any real knowledge that can be gathered from the study of the cyclical tendencies behind the composite and jerky motions which finally emerge. In fact, it is precisely when the rhythms of the ship are most shaken by the pounding of a score of non-cyclical forces from both sea and sky, and only a series of short looks ahead are possible, that a sailor's knowledge of action and reaction is most important. When the ship is poised on the crest of a wave, it may be subject

---

[5] See "Business Cycles as Facts or Tendencies," by Irving Fisher, *Economische Opstellen* aangeboden aan Prof. Dr. C. A. Verrijn Stuart, Haarlam, 1931.

to any or all of a dozen possible disturbances; but, in another second, its movement will be determined and will be apparent to the sailor, who will then know approximately what actions to expect for the next five or ten seconds. And it avails him to know. Likewise it will avail us to know all we can of cyclical tendencies in business, even though, to use such knowledge, we need also to know the other components which are not cyclical.

The whole picture then contains these four elements: forced cyclical tendencies; free cyclical tendencies; starters; trends.

CHAPTER VI

OTHER THEORIES

MANY THEORIES MUTUALLY CONSISTENT

In this tangle, which includes factors that can oscillate and starters that can touch off the oscillations, it would be strange indeed if any two students of the boom-depression sequence should emerge with just one theory. A variety of searchers is pretty sure to chance upon a variety of approaches, and therefore end with a variety of conclusions. Yet those conclusions are often supplementary rather than inconsistent. Indeed, the regrettable feature of this subject is that some students become so enamored of one factor as to reject all others. Moreover, those who think there must be but one secret for all the phenomena of a boom-depression sequence, are sometimes too ready to greet any new contribution as a candidate for the coveted office of sole explanation. For myself, in various writings which bear only obliquely on the specific problem of the present work, from time to time, I have mentioned several oscillatory factors,[1] and afterwards found to my surprise that I was promptly pigeon-holed with each in turn as if I had tried to offer a full explanation of booms and depressions.

A brief glance at some of the theories that have been propounded will show that they are largely consistent with

[1] See, for the rôle of "lag in interest" my *Theory of Interest*, Macmillan, 1930, and, for the rôle of "price-change," "Our Unstable Dollar and the So-called Business Cycle," *Journal of the American Statistical Association*, June, 1925, pp. 179–202.

60

one another and with the theory of over-indebtedness—
although in none of them is over-indebtedness explicitly
given a leading rôle. Wesley Clair Mitchell, whose careful studies of business cycles are accepted as classics, makes,
in his review of cycle theories, apparently no specific mention of a debt cycle. In fact, neither in the index of his
"Business Cycles" nor in that of Hansen's "Business Cycle
Theory" is the term "debt" to be found. In Hansen, the
only reference to debt (which is under "credit") is: "See
Bank Credit," and this, of course, is only a part of the debt
picture.

In mentioning below some of these theories, the purpose
is not primarily to point out their inadequacy (for it should
go without saying that no one theory can be adequate),
but rather to concede whatever of truth they contain and to
show that, through the endless interactions of the economic
mechanism, they usually seem to be not unrelated to the
factors of over-indebtedness and deflation which form the
chief subject-matter of this book.

PRICE-DISLOCATION THEORY

1. There is, for instance, the "price dislocation" theory.
This holds that when among prices (of commodities, rent,
interest, and taxes) some are unduly low and others unduly high, the exchange of goods is retarded; and that
this involves the retardation of production and employment.

Evidently the deflation stressed in this book dislocates
prices, and when it arrives, it finds some prices, such as
rent, interest, taxes, salaries and wages, more unyielding
than others. If we add principal as well as interest, we may
think of the increased debt and interest burden as a sort of
"dislocation" due to inflation. Doubtless, any other sort of

price-dislocation will cause disturbances. Moreover these dislocations often tend to be cumulative. The more unyielding one group of prices the more other prices must yield. In the depression of 1932 some writers maintain that the area of "rigid" prices was the largest in history. If, as seems likely, there is going on a gradual progressive freezing of large parts of the price structure, the instability of the rest will become greater and greater, and will tend more and more to bring about a crash from time to time.

INEQUALITY-OF-FORESIGHT THEORY

2. Then there is the theory of inequality of foresight as between lender and borrower. In "The Theory of Interest," [2] I have worked out some of the oscillatory tendencies resulting from such inequality. During inflation, the borrower sees (or feels), better than the lender, the fact that real interest is low; and this tempts him to borrow too freely, and leads him into over-indebtedness.

CHANGES-IN-INCOME THEORY

3. Some theories stress the changes in income. The fluctuations of real income and the re-distribution of income are, of course, of supreme importance; and some of these changes have been included in the analysis of this book, especially as to their bearing on profits and unemployment.

FLUCTUATIONS-IN-DISCOUNT THEORY

4. There is the theory of fluctuations in the rate of discount at which income is capitalized. Such fluctuations are

[2] *The Theory of Interest*, by Irving Fisher, Macmillan, 1930.

important in many ways. A changed rate of discount affects the value of collateral against debts, and so affects solvency.

VARIATIONS-OF-CASH-BALANCE THEORY

5. Then there is the theory of the variation of people's cash balances in the banks. This is already included, to some extent, in the analysis of the present book, under the head of velocity of circulation. The variations of cash balances are especially important in relation to bank reserves. Hawtrey has pointed out that the lags between depositors' balances and the reserves of the banks make for instability.

OVER-CONFIDENCE THEORY

6. There is also the theory of over-confidence and over-optimism. These factors are clearly embodied to a large extent in the analysis of this book. They are especially important in an industrial society, with its long lags between production and consumption. Each producer has to guess about the future—future consumption and future competition; and he cannot always be right. His miscalculations and mistakes cause disturbances, one of which is over-indebtedness. Perhaps over-indebtedness is the chief disturbance resulting from over-confidence. Certainly, without over-indebtedness, over-confidence could scarcely produce bankruptcy!

OVER-INVESTMENT THEORY

7. The theory which, perhaps, comes nearest to covering the same ground as the one set forth in this book is the over-investment theory. But, if over-investment be ac-

complished without borrowing, there would seem to be no reason to imagine that it would be followed by anything so severe as a stock market crash, or an epidemic of bankruptcies, or vast unemployment. Doubtless, however, over-investment, even *without* borrowed money, would tend to set up some appreciable oscillations.

OVER-SAVING THEORY

8. The same applies to "over-saving." In fact, saving is usually preliminary to investing. Over-saving leads to over-investment and to over-indebtedness.

OVER-SPENDING THEORY

9. Instead of over-investment and over-saving, there are theories of *under*-investment and *under*-saving, or (what amounts to the same thing) over-*spending*. The oscillations set up by over-spending would naturally be opposite, in their initial direction, from those set up by over-investment. Why, then, do we find both saving and spending accused of the same thing? It is true that we do, in boom periods, encounter both over-investment and over-spending at one and the same time; but what reconciles the two is over-indebtedness. Nor is it easy to see any other way of reconciling them. If a man borrows enough, he can both over-invest and over-spend, whereas, without borrowing, he could scarcely make *both* mistakes at the same time.

DISCREPANCY-BETWEEN-SAVINGS-AND-INVESTMENT THEORY

10. The *discrepancy* between savings and investments has by some students been emphasized as causing trouble—and very likely it does, especially by investing out of borrowed money instead of out of savings. The discrepancy is caused largely by debts.

OVER-CAPACITY THEORY

11. As to over-construction and over-capacity, these are natural consequences of over-investment, whether the over-investment be caused by too much debt or otherwise. And sudden cessation of construction, as Professor J. M. Clark so well shows,[3] causes very violent oscillations. These are still further magnified if the over-construction is financed with borrowed money.

UNDER-CONSUMPTION THEORY

12. As to the theory of "under-consumption," and changes in the demand for "consumer goods," these maladjustments must have at least some oscillatory effects. But under-consumption appears to be much the same thing as over-production.

OVER-PRODUCTION THEORY

13. The over-production theory, despite the skepticism of most economists, seems to me to have, at least in the boom period, some theoretical possibilities. I do not accept the hoary tradition that "general over-production is impossible and inconceivable." But the point need not be debated here.

According to the important statistical researches of Carl Snyder, production seems to have progressed with such steadiness that it seems difficult to imagine how it could become a leading cause of major depressions; and the large inventory accumulations which have characterized many depressions (like that of 1920–21) seem to be rather

[3] *The Economics of Overhead Cost*, by J. M. Clark, University of Chicago Press, 1923.

symptoms of depression, or incidental *consequences*, than important causes.

Certainly many debts are contracted for production purposes; and if the judgment of the debtor is wrong as to what is a safe margin for his debts, this may be because his judgment was first wrong as to how much of his commodity would find a profitable market. Over-production can scarcely be itself the lasting force which keeps a depression going year after year. Were it merely a matter of over-production, it would seem to me to be likely to correct itself more promptly and almost automatically.

But it may still be true that over-production may precipitate liquidation of debts. The borrower's disappointment in the market for his goods may be one of the first symptoms to alarm both him and his creditors, as to the state of his debts. Perhaps that is why, in 1929, as we shall see, production and payroll and transportation began to slacken two or three months before the debt-structure crumbled. But thereafter the *wisest* producers were hit— not by over-production, but by the liquidation-spiral into which they were sucked; so that they were compelled, for the sake of liquidation, to turn *all* production into *under*-production.

CONCLUSION

The foregoing theories have been but barely mentioned, and are only a few of the theories which relate themselves to over-indebtedness, or deflation, or both, and which may, of course, contain important truth independently. I have devoted my effort in this book to nine tendencies—merely "some" of the "first principles" underlying business disturbances. Others may be shown to have an equal right to be called "first principles." It remains a question of fact how important the truth may be of the few principles here presented as compared with those in other theories. Any decisive conclusions must await intensive statistical and historical studies. Further studies are also needed to complete, in quantitative terms, even the picture of the ninefold cyclical tendencies here discussed. These studies should cover such fundamental questions as the duration of a typical cycle-tendency of any type; and whether upon recurrence, its amplitude tends to diminish as I have supposed; and if so, how fast. Also, what are the distinctive shapes of the nine or more curves, and what are the lags between them? [4]

The next two chapters are to be a very brief study of the facts of 1929–32, with special, but not exclusive, reference to the principles selected for study in this book.

[4] In Appendix II are suggestions for such studies, under about 70 heads.

PART II

FACTUAL

CHAPTER VII

THE OVER-INDEBTEDNESS THAT LED TO THE WORLD DEPRESSION

THE WAR AND THE NEW ERA

To support the most colossal of all wars required prodigies of finance. And after the cost of the war came the cost of reconstruction. In both destruction and reconstruction, private financing as well as public was involved; for, in modern war, non-combatants exist only in name. Almost every private industry is, in effect, drafted into the service. Many of these must borrow, and, after the war, many of them require readjustments which also involve borrowing.

After the World War, there was a joyful rebound. Europe appeared to be recovering. There were to be no more wars. Everybody was encouraged about everything. The war, moreover, had promoted endless new inventions, some of which were not merely destructive but could afterwards be applied to peaceful service. So the war gave a great new impulse to the spirit of invention. In America, invention became almost a trade, and something like mass production was brought to bear upon it. Captains of industry who had held the academic life in low esteem began to install laboratories exceeding the wildest dreams of universities—and hired university professors to run these laboratories. A questionnaire which was sent to some 600 industrial concerns brought back replies indicating that a majority had such installations. Accordingly, in the decade

71

1920–1929 more patents were granted in America than in its entire first century—the peak years being 1926 and 1929.

There were also innumerable technological improvements not recorded in the patent office. Great strides were taken by the electrical, chemical and transportation industries. Road building became active. Scientific management struck a new tempo. Efficiency engineers came into their own. People began to talk of a New Era.

INVESTING IN EQUITIES ON BORROWED MONEY

Meanwhile, there was a new trend in corporate financing. From 1921–29, as the boom developed, the new corporate issues took more and more the form of stocks instead of bonds. This policy of reducing the proportion of bonds had one good effect: It left the corporations less encumbered with debt; so that, despite the depression, many corporations kept in a strong position throughout the whole of the depression. This advantage, however, was more than offset by shifting the debt burden from the corporations to the stockholders. That is, in order to buy the stock, many persons borrowed, so that, instead of being indebted collectively in the form of a corporation, they became indebted individually. Moreover, their borrowing was of the most dangerous type: largely margin accounts with brokers, whose loans were call loans. Thus, upon the corporate equities represented by common stocks was superimposed a structure of equities represented largely by margin accounts and brokers' loans.

This preference for investing in equities instead of bonds was fostered by a number of statistical studies, published in books and articles, which showed that almost always in the past, bonds had produced less income for the investor than had been (or could have been) produced by a diversified assortment of common stocks.[1] Had the idea stopped at that, the effect of these studies would have been wholly good, for the total burden of debts would have been less than if bonds had continued to be the favorite investment; but, as things turned out, the volume of debt was made greater in size and more unstable in kind.

The new trend was further intensified by the formation of investment trusts whose express business was to invest the money of their clients in diversified stocks. These trusts began to spring up like mushrooms, and presently became a mania. Many of them operated on borrowed capital, leaving precarious equities; and the individual owners of these equities borrowed in turn, thus still further pyramiding the debt structure—equity upon equity.

MISCELLANEOUS INFLUENCES

Among the chief inciters to over-indebtedness for investment were the high-pressure salesmen of investment bankers, including bank-affiliates. One of the best informed students of this aspect of the problem writes me as follows:

"I should make American investment banking the chief villain of the piece. In just what proportion inexperience, incompetence, negligence, and bad faith have figured in the ballooning of debts by them I am not prepared to say, but I incline to think they are all well represented in the financings through American houses throughout the post war years. In seeking new issues to feed to a ravenous public, disregard for the debtor's ability to pay, for the possibility of effecting payment by willing and able foreign debtors, and for the existing interests of security holders in concerns to be reorganized or

[1] Edgar Lawrence Smith's excellent book, *Common Stocks as Long Term Investments*, had a great influence.

consolidated, mark a major portion of the financing during the period. The governing consideration seems to have been 'can the issue be sold at a handsome profit?' "

And, of course, there was an admixture of fraudulent enterprise, characteristic of boom periods.

Moreover, the inexperienced American public had been prepared for an investment fever by the financing of America's share in the World War. Unlike previous wars, this one was not financed exclusively by bankers and people of wealth. Nearly everybody had invested in it, even if only to the extent of a "baby bond," which was also a new idea. Millions of people, who before the war had never known what an "investment" was, suddenly became the proud possessors of securities, often bought with borrowed money.

Then there was the capital gain tax, improperly included in the income tax. During the rising market, this capital gain tax deterred many a holder of rising stocks from selling them and reinvesting the gains; for the holder knew that if he sold, he would be penalized by having a large share of his increased capital taken away from him by the Internal Revenue office. He therefore hung on to his stock; and, in order to invest the increased worth, he borrowed—using his appreciated stock for security.

The effect of this borrowing fever was steadily and enormously to inflate the deposit currency. Corporate profits rose, and the price level in the stock market rose. These were ominous signs.

THE STEADY COMMODITY PRICE LEVEL

One warning, however, failed to put in an appearance— the *commodity price level did not rise.*

The index of wholesale commodity prices, therefore, is not always an infallible index of monetary and business trends. In 1923–29, an index half-way between the level of commodity prices and the steep up-tilt of stock market prices would have been nearer the truth. Dr. Carl Snyder has devised a "general index" which embodies all available price categories, including stock and bond prices, wholesale commodity prices, retail food prices, rents, and wage rates. This is an excellent index but, necessarily, for the present, it is based on somewhat unreliable data and "weighting." For the present, therefore, the wholesale price index, despite its theoretical imperfections is generally accepted as the best. During and after the World War, it responded very exactly to both inflation and deflation. If it did not do so during the inflationary period from 1923–29, this was partly because trade had grown with the inflation, and partly because technological improvements had reduced the cost, so that many producers were able to get higher profits without charging higher prices. For instance, from the third quarter of 1925 to the third quarter of 1929, the quarterly profits of 163 industrial and miscellaneous corporations rose by 75 per cent. In such a period, the commodity market and the stock market are apt to diverge; commodity prices falling by reason of the lowered costs, and stock prices rising by reason of the increased profits. In a word, this was an exceptional period—really a "New Era."

INVESTING ABROAD

Meanwhile, the investing and speculating Americans were by no means content with the home market. Foreign countries, European and South American, in the throes of reconstruction and elated like ourselves, were soliciting capital; and Americans furnished much of it—to governments, to municipalities and to private corporations. Already, in the 60 years preceding 1931, according to a member of the British Parliament, British investors had lost 10 billion dollars by such loans.[2] Yet, after the World War, American investors, with inadequate experience, marched into this field and took the lead. During the war, Americans had lent a great deal to the Allies. After the war, we kept on lending and included Germany, who, in effect, borrowed to pay reparations.

In this way, America promoted or aggravated abroad the same unhealthy boom which was putting both our neighbors and ourselves in position for a slump. The reconstruction to which we contributed included much extravagance. Even though the municipal stadiums and swimming pools of Central Europe were not, as often charged, specifically financed with borrowed money, they necessitated borrowing for the other municipal purposes. In 1927, the reparation agent for the Allies, S. Gilbert Parker, protested Germany's excessive borrowing and the raising of governmental salaries; and Dr. Schacht, the head of the Bank of Germany, scolded his countrymen. "With borrowed American money," he said, "you live like rich people. With borrowed dollars you go every winter to the Riviera. If you borrow to improve productive equipment it is all right, but when you use American dollars for luxury expenditure, you act like fools. It would bankrupt private individuals, and it is just the same for the country." [3]

But lending can be an extravagance, too; and, in this sense, America was extravagant, and our bankers and in-

[2] *United States Daily,* March 16, 1931, "Foreign Lendings in 1930."
[3] See *What Makes Stock Market Prices,* by Warren F. Hickernell. Harper & Bros., 1932.

vestors might well have been scolded for it; instead of which our financial and political leaders proudly boasted that New York was supplanting London as the world's financial center.

MISCELLANEOUS BORROWING MOVEMENTS

The American farmer had long been over-extended. Already, on the slogan "Win the war with wheat" and on the tide of war inflation, he had financed his growing operations with borrowed money; and then, on the tide of post-war inflation, he kept on buying machinery and otherwise extending himself with borrowed money.

Finally, installment buying was promoted on an unprecedented scale by dealers in houses, automobiles, radio sets, furniture, refrigerators, vacuum cleaners, washing machines, and even fur coats and other clothing.

REPARATIONS [4]

After the armistice in 1918, as the time approached for the peace conference at Versailles, the plan most popular among the Allies was to take all that the defeated powers could pay; and "defeated powers" meant, to all intents and purposes, Germany, whose wealth and resources were so much greater than those of Austria, Bulgaria and Turkey. It was rumored that one British financier predicted a German indemnity of between 100 and 200 billion

[4] Debt figures are given more fully in Appendix III, with graphs and tables and the sources. On German reparations, see Keynes' *Economic Consequences of the Peace* and *A Revision of the Treaty*; James W. Angell, *The Recovery of Germany* (Yale University Press, 1929); *New York Times*, June 14, 1931, "German Reparations and Allied War Debts" by Edwin L. James; and November 1, 1931, "The War Debt Puzzle" by Charles Merz.

dollars.[5] Even after the treaty, but before the assessment by the Reparations Commission, Allied finance ministers talked of 75 billions.[6] The actual assessment (in 1921) was 33 billions—still a mammoth amount and one which, according to Mr. Keynes, involved a breach of the armistice agreement. It proved unmanageable; and after several conferences between the Allies and Germany, and then after the several consultations of the Dawes and the Young Commissions, a schedule of payments was drawn up to begin with 1930 and last 58 years. The total payments, if made, would come to about 27½ billion dollars. At 5 per cent the discounted value would be about 9 billion dollars as of 1930.[7] Down to 1932 Germany borrowed in order to pay; and even so, a moratorium was required.[8]

INTER-GOVERNMENTAL DEBTS PAYABLE TO AMERICA [9]

Up to 1920, the loans by the American government to 22 nations aggregated nearly 10 billions. In 1929, the principal and arrears (counting out five nations with which no debt "settlements" have been made) amounted to about 11.6 billions. By spreading both the principal and interest—22 billions—over a period of 62 years (and also by reducing the interest), we have, in effect, reduced the debt to a

[5] See Keynes, J. Maynard, *Economic Consequences of the Peace*, p. 141 (American Ed.).

[6] Keynes, J. Maynard, *A Revision of the Treaty*, p. 39 (American Ed.).

[7] Large confiscations and payments in kind had already been taken from Germany.

[8] On July 12, 1932, at Lausanne (See Part III) this situation was changed (after the Reparations had helped to build the crisis).

[9] See *Annual Reports* of the Secretary of the Treasury, 1927, p. 630, and subsequent reports; also in *New York Times*, June 14, 1931, the article by Edwin L. James on "German Reparations and Allied War Debts," and *New York Times*, November 1, 1931, article by Charles Merz on "The War Debt Puzzle."

much smaller present value—about 5.9 billions, if discounted at 5 per cent. But nominally the principal remains unchanged, at about 11.6 billions, as of 1929.

The reparations and these inter-governmental debts could be paid only in goods; but America deliberately and intentionally made such goods-payments enormously difficult, if not impossible, by erecting special tariffs against them—and then granted a moratorium!

The condition in 1932 was that American private interests had lent Germany the money with which to pay the Allies the money with which the Allies were supposed to be paying the American government.

INTERNATIONAL PRIVATE DEBTS

These were loans made by American private interests to foreign borrowers, both private and public. American foreign investments of this sort began their phenomenal growth about 1912, increasing eight-fold from 1912 to 1931, and 89 per cent from 1922 to 1931. The total growth of these foreign debts did not stop with 1929. In 1931 they passed 15 billions. In 1929, however—the crisis year —the amount was about 14 billions, which, added to the lendings of our government, made a total foreign investment in 1929 of well over 25 billions.

PUBLIC DEBTS IN THE UNITED STATES

These not only grew but went on growing after 1929. The total of federal, state and local debts increased from 1915 to 1919, 5½ fold, and then, up to 1932, they further increased by 14 per cent.[10] At the end of 1931, the sum was nearly 34 billions, or over $271 per capita. But in 1929, the

[10] Measured per capita, however, the increase was finished in 1919.

crisis year, it was about 30 billions: the state and local debts amounting to 13.4 billions; the federal, to about 16.9 billions.

Other countries also had great public debts, largely left over from the war. Even the neutral countries were not free of such debts.

PRIVATE DEBTS IN AMERICA

From 1910 to 1928, farm mortgages rose over 2⅔-fold; and in spite of a net increase in farm valuation for that period (including an inflation as well as a deflation period) the net equity of both the mortgaged and the un-mortgaged farms descended from 90 per cent of the gross valuation, in 1910, to 78 per cent in 1928; the aggregate burden being (in 1928 and 1929) about 9½ billions.

Other agrarian debts in 1929 came to about 1.9 billions.

As roughly estimated on the basis of incomplete data, urban mortgages, from 1920 to 1929, increased more than three-fold, reaching, in 1929, about 37 billions.

Debts on life insurance policies in 1929 were about 2.4 billions.[11]

Corporate long and short term debts in 1929 came to about 76 billions.

As to installment buying, only the roughest guesses are available. Professor Seligman guesses about 2.2 billions outstanding in 1926. The 2.2 billions would be about 3 billions by 1929.

Bank loans and discounts for all banks in the United States increased from June, 1914, to October, 1929, by nearly three-fold; from June, 1917, two-fold; from 1922, 50 per cent; from 1926, nearly 15 per cent. Deducting

[11] Based on an estimate for 1932 by Dr. W. A. Berridge of the Metropolitan Life Insurance Company.

brokers' loans from the total loans and discounts reported by the Comptroller of the Currency, we have 39 billions for the peak of commercial bank loans, in 1929.

BROKERS' LOANS

The year 1921 was the trough of a short depression. The stock market was full of bargain prices. About 1923, the bull market began its unprecedented climb. An ideal investor, buying an average assortment of stocks in 1926 and holding them till September 7, 1929, could have turned every $100 invested into $200—all in three years. By starting in 1913, he could, by the same policy of holding on, have turned every $100 into $400. It was during substantially this period that investment trusts, having been a mania, became a full blown bubble. During the first nine months of 1929 they rose from 200 to 400 in number, taking in a billion of their clients' money, to add to the two billions previously absorbed. During July they issued 222 millions of securities; during August, 485 millions; and September, 643 millions.

Naturally, brokers' loans kept pace with these opportunities. From October, 1928, to October 4, 1929, they increased by 50 per cent, reaching the record peak of nearly 9½ billions. This included "bootleg" loans which at the peak were by far the larger part.[12]

TOTALS IN 1929

Brokers' Loans	9.5 billions
Commercial Bank Loans	39

[12] All security loans increased from October 3, 1928, to October 4, 1929, by 36 per cent and reached on that date a peak just under 17 billions.

Total of all separable debts which
   (mostly) create credit currency   48.5 billions
Other domestic private debts   129.8
Total domestic private debts   178.3 billions
Our public debts and all foreign
   debts owing in America   55.6
Grand total owing in America   234. billions

As to the rest of the world, their domestic and international debts, including reparations, were vastly more burdensome than our own.

GOLD AND THE DEBTS

But mere totals do not tell the whole story. It will be remembered that over-indebtedness may be alarming to the debtors or the creditors (the chief creditors for our purpose, being commercial banks). The important signal that may alarm the debtors is a fall in the price level which limits his ability to pay; the important signal that may alarm the creditor-bank is a curtailment of the gold supply which limits the bank's lawful ability to extend the debtor's time. Gold is the only international money; and during the war the inflation of paper and credits drove gold out of these paper currency countries and forced them to abandon the gold standard, while a serious gold inflation was produced in the United States by the flood of gold driven from Europe by the "cheaper" paper currencies. The complaints of a gold shortage which began to be heard soon after the war really meant that the price levels had not sufficiently receded to permit a general return to the gold standard. Indeed, the attempts to return caused a "scramble for gold" which kept it scarce, or made it scarce, in many countries—especially in the debtor countries.

The creditor countries were more fortunate; and one of

them, at least—France—doubtless became possessed of a gold surplus. There is a prevailing opinion that the same was true of America. But this was only partly true, though it was fully believed by many Americans, including some American bankers. Gold came to America during the war because other countries were off the gold standard. But upon this gold we speedily built such a credit structure and raised the price level so high as to require almost all of the gold as a base. It is true that after the price level fell in 1920–2 there was temporarily an excess of gold in the United States, but soon both our business structure and our credit structure expanded so much as to make our unused or so-called "sterilized" gold more or less of a myth. The fact that we were a creditor nation was offset by the fact that we had collected very little from our debtors, and, on the contrary, had made new loans to them in excess of what they had paid us. Much of the gold in America was either ear-marked as belonging to Europe or was at any rate known to be subject to sudden withdrawal, as the result of short term credits held abroad.

If all this money, which had fled from Europe to America but was destined to return, could have been segregated as "refugee" money and sent home or even ear-marked, the myth of America's excess gold would not have arisen. We would not have done so much financing of Europe, to the disadvantage of both parties—or else we would have done it under contracts properly safeguarding us against gold withdrawals.

Thus, though our gold was great in quantity, the amount of it that was free was not great enough to justify much more than the credit currency erected upon it.

In 1924–5, the Federal Reserve authorities adopted a policy which had the effect of deliberately sending some of our gold away. Britain wanted to get back to the gold standard from which the war had forced her; and, to do this, the Bank of England tried to attract gold by raising its interest rates; and the Federal Reserve authorities obligingly cooperated by lowering the interest rates in this country. In this way, from 1925 to 1928, America lost 422 millions of its gold, and in the same period [13] increased its ear-marked gold from 13 to 35 millions.

Moreover, this lowering of our interest rates stimulated speculation on the New York stock market. In a word, we dismissed some of our gold foundation and at the same time built a debt structure over the place where the gold had been.

Billions of debts and a gold base that was slippery—these two conditions had now set the stage for the collapse of 1929.

[13] December 1925–December 1928.

CHAPTER VIII

THE WORLD DEPRESSION OF 1929-32

IN GENERAL

On the depression of 1929–32, Professor Hansen has said:

"Now the year 1930, as Professor Josef Schumpeter has pointed out, fell not only in the downswing of the long cycle (Kondratieff), but also formed a part of the down grade of the major cycle (Juglar), and at the same time a part of it (probably the second half) fell in the trough of the minor forty-month cycle (Persons-Mitchell). The convergence of all three cycles upon the years 1930–31 accounts in part for the severity of this depression." [1]

It is not the contention of this book that over-indebtedness is the sole explanation of the depression of 1929–32, nor even that over-indebtedness and the deflation caused thereby were the only factors. The revolutions in South America for instance, as well as the fighting between China and Japan and the Hitler movement in Germany were both cause and effect. Professor Hansen ascribes the severity of the depression chiefly to deflation, shifts in world trade, breakdown of great empires, internal capital movements and tariffs. And doubtless that list could be lengthened. But that over-indebtedness and deflation were strong and indeed the dominating factors seems to me highly probable.

[1] *Economic Stabilization in an Unbalanced World*, by Alvin Harvey Hansen (Harcourt, Brace & Co., 1932), p. 95.

Nor is it sure that the depression of 1929–32 is the greatest of all time. Any current depression is likely to be called the worst by its contemporaries. Such was the case in 1819, 1837, 1857, 1873, and 1893. Professor Victor Clark reports that in Philadelphia between 1816 and 1819 the number of employees in thirty leading branches of manufacture, principally cotton and woolen, decreased more than 75 per cent!

THE AMERICAN STOCK MARKET [2]

The first symptoms in America of the world depression of 1929–32 appeared in the summers of 1928 and 1929. In the summer of 1928, building activities began to decline. In the summer of 1929, production, trade and employment generally started a downward trend; and after July, the price level joined the down movement. These portents were quite generally overlooked as were the signs in Europe which were growing somewhat more marked. The first spectacular evidence that America was in for a depression was the crash of the New York Stock Market.

Charts 1 and 2 give a short and a long view of stock market history. Chart 1 shows that, while the commodity price level had been steady, the stock market price level had been persistently soaring. During 1928 the Federal Reserve Board tried to check the speculating fever by gradual advances of the re-discount rate, half of one per cent at a time, from 3½ per cent to 5; but in vain. On August 8, 1929, the rate was advanced more drastically from 5 to 6. This caused an ominous but temporary drop in the market; there was a quick recovery, and not till September 7 did the market reach its peak.

[2] See *The Stock Market Crash and After*, by Irving Fisher (Macmillan, 1930).

Brokers' loans—or, rather, the margin accounts on which these are based—are among the most unstable, because the creditors can call them without previous notice. Anxiety is always present, or should be, in the person who has a margin account. The pyramid of such accounts was both unstable and high. Only a nudge to the market values which secured the accounts would be needed to send both the loans and the price level crashing into the abyss.

Two nudges came—both from Britain; one on September 20 and one on September 26.

In Britain there had also been a bull market; and, on the tide of it Clarence Hatry had financed a group of enterprises so recklessly that presently he could go no further without forgery, and that expedient failed him on September 20, when his hopeless condition became known and seven of his issues were suspended from the London Stock Exchange. His subsequent failures involved 67 million dollars; and after the announcement of September 20, many of his stockholders had to fortify themselves by selling their American stocks. The bad news and these consequent English sales in New York, with a slight downward effect on the New York price level, constituted the first nudge.

Meanwhile, though Britain was now back on the gold basis, she was still bidding for the immigration of gold from America. On September 26 the Bank of England's discount rate was put up to 6½ per cent. This was when prices on the American stock market were so high that the yield on A1 stocks was very low; and it did not take a very high interest rate in Britain to induce British investors in America to sell their American holdings and to lend the proceeds in London. Accordingly, this action of the Bank of England produced a flurry of selling in the New York

147

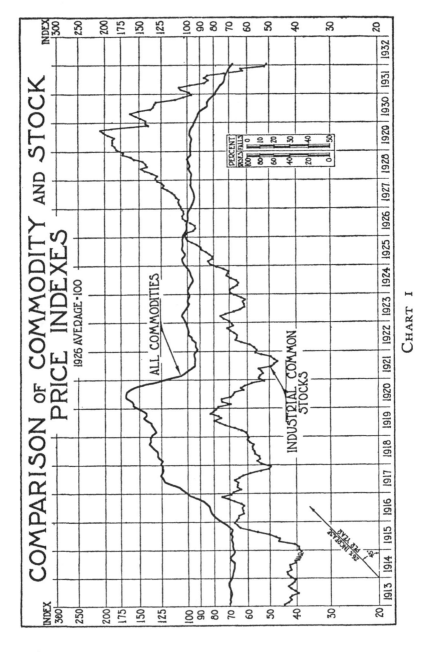

COMPARISON of COMMODITY and STOCK PRICE INDEXES

CHART I

148

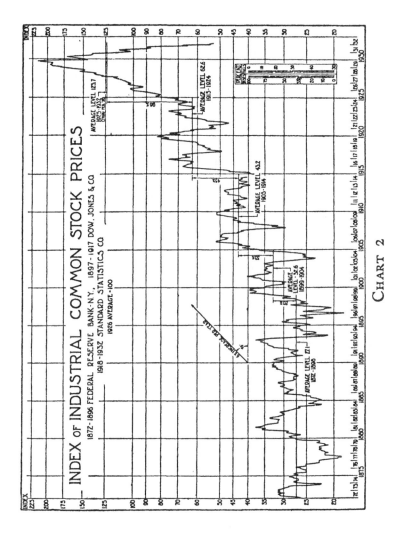

INDEX of INDUSTRIAL COMMON STOCK PRICES

1872-1896 FEDERAL RESERVE BANK-N.Y.   1897-1917 DOW. JONES & CO
1918-1932 STANDARD STATISTICS CO
1926 AVERAGE-100

CHART 2

149

Stock Exchange. And this was the second nudge. Then [3] it was that a retired New York broker said, "This marks the end of the New Era bull market."

THE PANIC

On September 29 the panic began. On October 24 nearly 13 million shares changed hands. Many people lost the savings of a life-time. Others bought up the bargains, and five days later were themselves wiped out. That 29th of October was the most sensational day of trading that the New York Stock Exchange has ever seen. It was said that a million persons were trading. Nearly 16½ million shares changed hands. The ticker was so late that when a man sold "at the market" he might, when his turn came, obtain 40, though, when he had put in the order, the ticker said 70. Billions of value were wiped out.

Then came the third and last spectacular day—November 13. The Federal Reserve System, by purchasing securities in the open market, tried to check the fall of prices; also it cut the rediscount rate on the 14th; but the effect was temporary. In the eight weeks brought to a close by November 13, the level of stock prices had fallen 42 per cent; and in October and November, 23 billions of value had gone. That was the end of the panic, though not the end of the descent of the stock market.

It was on October 4, 1929, that the brokers' loans began their crash; and then they went so fast that 3 billions, it was said, were wiped out in a few weeks.[4] By March,

[3] *What Makes Stock Market Prices?* (p. 173) by Warren F. Hickernell (Harper & Bros., 1932).

[4] The statistics exaggerate the initial speed at which brokers' loans went down because many hard pressed clients transferred their obligations to banks, and hung on a little longer, so that the time loans to which these transferred obligations were added continued to rise until December.

1932, after a few brief up-spurts, the level of industrial stocks had fallen by about 77 per cent, and brokers' loans had fallen by over 94 per cent.

Between the loans on the stock market and the stock market price level there could not be a better example of a vicious spiral. With every distress liquidation the price level fell; and every fall of the price level drove a new set of people into further liquidation, which still further lowered the price level, which compelled still further liquidation, and so on and on.

PRELIMINARIES IN THE COMMODITY MARKET

After the stock market crash, the great debt-liquidations began. I will not presume to dogmatize on why the American price level and the American production and employment had already started down before the crash of the stock market. Many people blame Europe for America's share in what is now understood to be a world depression. Europe was as over-indebted as America; and it is true that Europe's share in the depression preceded ours. This was made evident by the downswing of European price levels, both in the stock markets and in the commodity markets; and the interests of the two continents were so interlocked that what hurt one must sooner or later be felt by the other. But Europe, quite as plausibly, blames America for the depression. A part of Europe's economic trouble was due to internal political jealousies and a network of tariffs. These troubles were not entirely willful. They were really difficult to avoid; and instead of helping to settle them, we forsook Europe politically. We did not withhold financial assistance; but this, as we have seen, was sometimes harmful to both parties as well as helpful.

Economically, also, we aggravated Europe's handicaps, by accepting the doctrine that a government debt is like a debt at a grocery store. We demanded payment while erecting a tariff. In addition to this, Britain in 1922 began her disastrous deflation policy by retiring Treasury and Bank of England notes, preparatory to restoring the gold standard (in 1925) at the pre-war gold weight of the pound. Thus she depressed her price level, crippled her industries and increased her unemployment; and such was the importance of Britain in world trade and world finance that the fall of the British price level greatly aggravated the fall of other price levels, European and non-European.

In addition to these non-American influences to the detriment of America, we already had a case of over-production among some of our basic commodities, especially wheat, corn, cotton, petroleum, copper, iron and other raw products, agricultural and mineral. Certain lines of manufacture, too, were over-produced, notably automobiles, radios, and many luxuries.

But it matters little which factor in the vicious spiral (commercial bank liquidations or the fall of the price level) started first; nor what factor, remote or near, started either of them. They could even start together. But once started, they were doomed to continue in a vicious spiral, each accelerating the other. What seems sure is that the crash of the stock market helped to force the rest of our debt structure into liquidation, and that it was the hopeless magnitude of the debt burden which made it so difficult for the economic organism to right itself.

THE COMMODITY MARKET

Let us now take up what followed the stock market crash.

152

In the first place, many who were involved in both the stock and the commodity markets sold commodities in order to avoid selling stocks. In the second place, consumers took fright and reduced their purchases—in other words, reduced the turnover or velocity of their money. Deposit currency, as we have seen, grows out of the demand deposits in commercial banks. The demand deposits do not exactly correspond with the commercial bank loans, but the great majority of demand deposits are based on commercial bank loans; and, except for short periods, the movements of the two tend to run parallel. Immediately after the stock market crash, some demand deposits grew a little but all lost velocity. Nor did this loss of velocity apply to brokers' deposits alone. It was true of deposits outside of New York where brokers' loans are not a large factor.

And immediately after October, 1929, the commercial bank loans on which most demand deposits depend began to be liquidated. They were yielding, perhaps, to the already accumulated losses in the price level, perhaps to a sudden dearth of buyers, or to an anticipated dearth. These commercial bank loans (inclusive of brokers') [5] reached their peak in October, 1929; and then the progressive liquidation of these loans was soon proceeding. This could not happen without wiping out deposit currency. In the first half of 1930 the demand deposits and the loans joined each other in the down turn, but there appeared an *increase* of *time* deposits [6] which was little short of hoarding; and, savings bank deposits increased still faster in the same period. But after the middle of 1931 even the time deposits began to be depleted by the hoarding of pocket money.

[5] "Bootleg" loans, however, not being included.

[6] Reporting member banks: time deposits increased 570 million and demand deposits decreased 627 million.

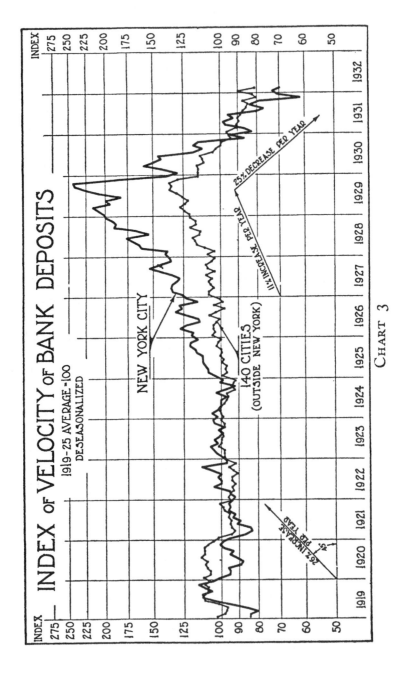

CHART 3

154

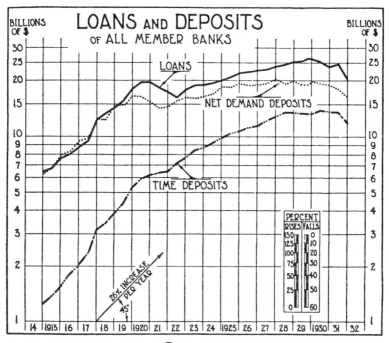

CHART 4

THE CURRENCY

Charts 3 and 4 illustrate these reactions of volume and velocity quite clearly. From October, 1929, to February, 1932, the deposit currency of the member banks of the country (in 141 cities including New York City) fell from $18,726,000,000 to $14,789,000,000. This was a fall of 21 per cent, leaving only 79 per cent of the earlier amount; and the velocity in the same period [7] fell 61 per cent—that is, to 39 per cent of the earlier rate, so that the efficiency of deposit money for sustaining the price level and the levels of production, trade and employment became, in 1932, only 31 per cent of what it had been in 1929.

Other elements in the currency have, of course, suffered less; but the statistics are not detailed enough to tell us exactly what happened to them. The phrase "money in circulation" simply refers to money which exists in the United States but is not in the Treasury, nor in the possession of the Federal Reserve Banks nor of the Federal Reserve agents. More or less of it could, so far as is revealed by the figures for this so-called "circulation," be in stockings or in other hoarding places and not circulating at all. In this misleading sense, 1930–31 saw an increase in cash "circulation," including increased quantities of Federal Reserve notes. A study of over two months indicated that hoarding was going on at the rate of 2.6 billions a year.

Thus the retardation of velocity through fear and the contraction of volume through liquidation kept the price level going down; and this so crowded the commercial debtors that more liquidation was necessary, resulting in a further fall of the price level, resulting in still more liquidation and hoarding, resulting in a still further fall of the price level, and so on, through the downward vicious spiral.

[7] 1919–25, as the base, equals 100.

TRADE AND PROFITS

Chart 5 shows the descent of some of the trade factors, beginning in the summer of 1929. The preliminary figures for 1930 showed that the corporate profits ratio was already nearly as low as in 1921.[8] In the last quarter of 1931, a reporting group of 163 industrial and miscellaneous corporations (whose quarterly profits between 1925 and 1929 had increased by 75 per cent) took a loss of a million dollars. These and other examples of the behavior of corporate profits are shown in Table 1.

TABLE 1

CORPORATION NET PROFITS *

(Millions of dollars)

Year and Quarter	Grand Total, 10 Groups (500)	Telephone (103)	Other Large Public Utilities (63)	Class I Railroads (171)	Industrial and Miscellaneous (163)
1925					
1	603	44	165	205	189
2	660	46	148	234	232
3	767	45	138	359	225
4	781	51	181	334	215
Quar. average	703	47	158	283	215
1926					
1	710	51	189	224	246
2	772	52	170	272	278
3	884	52	156	394	282
4	826	57	200	342	230
Quar. average	799	53	179	308	259

* Compiled by the Federal Reserve Bank of New York from quarterly reports of net profits of 500 companies, including 103 telephone, 63 other public utilities, 171 Class I railroads, 24 motor and motor accessories, 18 oil, 13 steel, 22 food, 20 metal and mining, 15 machine building, and 51 miscellaneous companies. The numbers have declined from a total of 531 to 500 for the last quarter of 1931.

[8] "Corporate Earning Power" by Prof. W. L. Crum in *Corporate Practice Review*, January, 1932.

TABLE 1—*Continued*

Year and Quarter	Grand Total, 10 Groups (500)	Telephone (103)	Other Large Public Utilities (63)	Class I Railroads (171)	Industrial and Miscellaneous (163)
1927					
1	745	59	206	227	253
2	779	59	185	247	288
3	819	56	169	336	258
4	739	54	214	276	195
Quar. average	771	57	194	272	249
1928					
1	769	63	226	217	263
2	837	66	204	245	322
3	953	60	192	358	343
4	984	64	246	373	301
Quar. average	886	63	217	298	307
1929					
1	937	70	263	260	344
2	1,031	68	245	304	414
3	1,080	66	224	397	393
4	945	72	275	314	284
Quar. average	998	69	252	319	359
1930					
1	778	67	270	176	265
2	805	70	259	200	276
3	775	65	223	283	204
4	683	68	273	226	116
Quar. average	760	68	256	221	215
1931					
1	382	69	81	107	125
2	441	72	78	132	159
3	390	67	59	167	97
4	267	64	79	125	− 1
Quar. average	370	68	74	133	95

UPTURNS

Just before 1930, at the beginning of the stock market crash, Mr. Hoover assembled some of the leading bankers and business men. Mr. Morgan and Mr. Ford were among them. Mr. Ford ascribed the stock market crash to a busi-

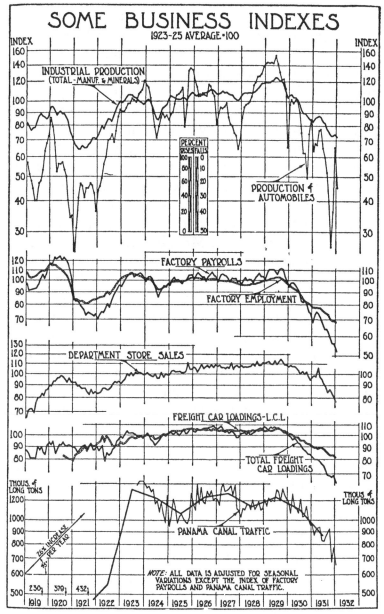

CHART 5

ness slump. He proposed that prices be not lowered and that wages be raised. Mr. Hoover proposed that constructions be pushed, both public and private. At the outset of 1930, the stock market began to do better, and hopeful prognostications abounded. The commodity price level turned up a little (from the last quarter of November to past the middle of January) [9] but almost at once resumed its descent, and never stopped again, except for a slight retardation (not an upturn) in the third quarter of 1930. Other business factors at the beginning of 1930 also registered upturns; stocks, velocity of deposits, production, and pay-roll, but not employment. Cities, states, and the Federal government took Mr. Hoover's advice; Mr. Ford took his own advice. But presently Mr. Ford had to discharge many thousands of his men and later to lower his wage rates; and, despite all the efforts of cities, states, and the Federal government, the upturns were promptly ended. Quite possibly the subsequent downswing was accelerated by way of reaction to falsified hopes.

Just before 1931, hopeful prophecies were again in the air, though the tone was not quite so confident. This time there was no response from the price level; but in January 1931, upturns were registered by the same factors as before: stocks, turnover of deposits, production and pay-rolls augmented this time by loans and department store sales. For five months employment stopped going down but did not go up.

INTERNATIONAL ACCELERATORS OF THE VICIOUS SPIRAL—1931

The Hawley-Smoot tariff, enacted in June, 1930, had aroused the bitter resentment of other countries and started reprisals in Canada and elsewhere.

[9] Not shown on the monthly chart, but shown by a weekly index.

In December, 1930, the so-called Bank of United States, a relatively small bank on the outskirts of New York City, had closed its doors. Many Europeans had mistaken this for a failure of the Federal Reserve System, which was regarded as the American equivalent of the Bank of England and the Bank of France. This shook the confidence of Europe.

March, 1931. Germany and Austria, being almost bankrupt, sought, in March, 1931, to establish a Customs Union (Anschluss); but this sound economic measure was blocked by the political opposition of France, Italy and Czechoslovakia, who feared a political union of Germany and Austria and argued that the Anschluss, by threatening Austria's independence, would violate the terms of a recent loan granted to Austria by the League of Nations.

May, 1931. This failure of national economics at the behest of international politics precipitated a severe crisis in Austria, whose leading bank, the "Credit Anstalt," being encumbered with frozen assets, could not meet its obligations and became insolvent in May, 1931. It was a great bank and its collapse embarrassed both Germany and England.

June, 1931. Austrian banks were now subjected to runs which spread to other countries. There were international gold withdrawals, until the gold standard was jeopardized for all southeastern Europe. American banks and investors were involved to the extent of 100 million dollars. A group of international bankers came to the rescue with a two-year extension of their short term loans, and the Austrian government agreed to guarantee the liabilities of the Credit Anstalt.

Meanwhile, however, Germany had been hard hit by Austria's plight, and being hard hit, she was raided of her gold by the French. The Reichsbank lost thus 227 million dollars; and at the same time, German capital, to the extent of 200 million dollars, fled from the uncertain mark. Mr. Hoover came forward in June, 1931, with his proposal for a moratorium on all intergovernmental debts. But once more France and the French bankers balked, precipitating a long and acrimonious discussion of terms, and robbed the moratorium, which was eventually granted, of much of its good effect. Some observers have even thought that Mr. Hoover's proposal, by calling attention to the extremity of the world's plight, scared the world into making its plight still more extreme.

July, 1931. The Bank of England now came to the rescue of the Reichsbank. In July the failure of the Darmstädter und Nationaler Bank, one of the large banks of Germany, frightened the French banks into withdrawing large amounts of gold from the Bank of England which was heavily involved in supporting German credit and industries.

August, 1931.[10] The Wiggin Committee—an international committee of bankers, meeting in Basle—reported on August 18 that, among other things, permanent prosperity could not return to the world until Germany's debts were put on a workable basis. But nothing happened, except that the financial troubles of Britain, due largely to financial troubles of Germany, caused the raids on British gold to continue.

September, 1931. Britain became so hard pressed that, in spite of large gold shipments from the Transvaal and in spite of large credits from the Bank of France and the Federal Reserve Bank of New York, she stopped her gold payments by going off the gold standard on September 21, 1931. Her example was quickly followed by 23 other na-

[10] See *What Makes Stock Market Prices?* by Warren F. Hickernell, Harper & Bros., 1932, p. 186.

tions, including Denmark, Sweden, Norway, Egypt, Greece, Finland, Rhodesia, Bolivia, Colombia, and Japan. Then, to prevent panic-sales of British sterling exchange and of British securities, the world's exchanges, except in America, Canada, France, and Spain, were closed.

In this same September, a sudden large scale raid—apparently intentional in part—was made on America's gold by European banks, led by the Bank of France. The fact that America was the chief lender to Germany and to Austria seems to have started the raid. Deliberate attempts were made to discredit the dollar. Rumors were circulated and believed to the effect that America was going off the gold standard and that the gold dollar was to be "devalued," or superseded by the silver dollar. In the last part of September, by the exportation and earmarking of some of our gold, the Federal Reserve Banks were depleted of 347.6 million dollars in gold. Ever since the failure of the Bank of United States, the world had been losing confidence in America. America now lost confidence in herself and in the world. We all knew that billions of foreign loans (the sum was over 25 billions) were likely, in large part, never to be repaid. Already there had been many American bank failures. It was known that other American banks were getting weak and that their "affiliates" had lost heavily in the stock market.

Despite the fact that the European raid did not prove really disastrous, American bankers and American depositors were now so scared that hoarding became a menace. Gold and Federal Reserve notes were withdrawn from circulation. The Federal Reserve System, from February to December, 1931, increased its issues of Federal Reserve notes by 80 per cent. These issues were due to bank failures which made necessary a larger use of cash. Yet, after a wave of bank failures, beginning in the

west and coming east, both banks and their depositors began raiding each other in a cut-throat competition which
more than defeated the new issues of Federal Reserve
notes.

October, 1931. Mr. Hoover now proposed a National
Credit Corporation, designed to help the smaller banks.
This was formed by bankers. He also proposed the Home
Mortgage Corporation under government auspices to
stimulate residential building which proposal was later
adopted. Premier Laval visited Mr. Hoover. For these or
other reasons, or for no reason, hope revived in October.
Stock prices made a weak spurt for a month (October–
November).

BALANCING THE BUDGET

In December, Mr. Hoover started his more elaborate
and largely commendable program for relief,[11] but, to
meet the rapidly developing emergency, each step was
too small and, by the time it was enacted into law, it was
too late.

And at least one possible error (as it seems to me and to
many other economists) was included in the program. This
was the attempt at balancing the budget (for the goal was
not really reached). "Balancing the budget" *annually*
sounds well to the man in the street and helps float bonds
with bankers, but the budget of a government affects the
currency and the requirements vary enormously at different
times—war, peace, boom, depression. To balance the budget
in a depression by forcing economy and increasing taxes
reduces government spending and (what is far more
important) reduces the spending of the public by taxing
away part of their income. In both ways it tends to reduce
the price level.

[11] See Appendix VII.

The purpose of balancing the budget was to prevent further borrowing by the government and thus to keep the public debt from growing. Actually, however, the deflation involved in this policy did increase the *real* debt of the government by increasing the burden of every dollar in it. All deflation does this, and the directors of fiscal policy cannot afford to leave out of account the deflationary or inflationary effects of their policies. Taxation tends toward deflation; borrowing tends toward inflation.

During the World War the government borrowed, even though the effect of borrowing was inflationary in a period of inflation; but in 1932, instead of borrowing and inflating in a period of deflation, the government taxed and deflated when each dollar [12] was already 60 per cent more burdensome to the debtor than in 1929. The government should have borrowed and spent, thus contributing to reflation and to a higher price level. And every climb in the price level would have lowered the *real* debts, public and private, by lightening the real dollar. This would have stimulated business; and, by checking the decline of prices, would have enabled corporations and individuals to pay increased taxes in later years much more easily, when there would have been something substantial to tax. You cannot tax a vacuum.

An economist who has made special study of this problem writes me:

"High tax rates, economy in expenditures, and retirement of debts should characterize boom periods. Low tax rates, large public borrowings, and increased public expenditures should characterize periods of stagnation."

Psychologically, the slogan "balance the budget" had a wide appeal; but on the other hand, the psychological ef-

[12] Third week of June, 1932.

fect of new taxes to come in the near future was like an additional debt burden to the tax payer.

Finally, the deficit was largely mythical, due to charging off capital expenditures as expenses. If the Government were to use in its own accounts the same methods which it requires for income tax schedules, the Fiscal year ending June 30, 1931, would have shown not a deficit but a surplus of $109,000,000, according to computations of Dr. Lubin of the Brookings Institution. The following year would show only a slight deficit.

SUMMARY AS TO THE NINE MAIN FACTORS [13]

From 1929 to 1932, the nine main factors which have been discussed in this book behaved as follows:

1. *Debts:* The liquidation of brokers' debts had cut the figures by 94 per cent; of commercial bank loans, by 22 per cent; of all debts due in America, by 23 per cent, except those (like public debts) which increased.

2, 7, 8. *Money; its velocity; pessimism:* Judging by the records of the Federal Reserve member banks, deposit currency had lost 21 per cent of its volume and 61 per cent of its velocity; the remaining efficiency for business purposes being only 31 per cent of its efficiency in 1929. The growth of pessimism is sufficiently indicated by this record.

3. *The price level:* industrial stocks had lost 77 per cent; and the descending commodity price level, instead of righting itself, lost 35 per cent. By the third week of June, 1932, this loss had become 38 per cent.

4. *Net worths:* Their behavior is best indicated by the record of commercial failures, including bank suspensions. In 1929, 1.04 per cent of our firms had failed (22,909 in

---

[13] More details will be found in Appendix V.

number); in 1931, 1.33 per cent (28,285 in number)—an increase of 28 per cent in the yearly rate of failures. Bank suspensions, in 1929, were 642 in number, in 1930, 1345, and in 1931, 2,550.

5. *Income:* the net profits of 163 industrial and miscellaneous corporations became a loss.

6. *Production, trade and employment:* All kept falling. According to a Federal Reserve index, industrial production [14] having fallen from June, 1929, to October, 1929, by 5.6 per cent, instead of righting itself, registered 39 per cent additional fall from October, 1929 to January, 1932.

The indexes show that construction fell earlier than output and much faster, just as indicated in Part I.

9. *Interest:* The various rates acted according to type. For instance, the rediscount rate, the call loan rates, and the 60 to 90 day time loan rates on mixed collateral, all rose with the boom and fell with the depression. The chief misfortune is that the rediscount rate rose too late to restrain those who borrowed in order to speculate on the bull market, and fell too late to check the stampede of liquidation by the same borrowers. That is, the real rate had been allowed to get so far away from the money rate —so light on the way up and so heavy on the way down— that the borrowers were insensitive to the nominal rates.

THE REAL DOLLAR

The whole tragedy is summed up in what happened to the Real Dollar. From 1929 to March 1932, by reason of the lowering price level, the real dollar, measured by 1929, became $1.53—later (third week of June, 1932) $1.62.

Thus all the liquidation that had been accomplished down to 1932 left the unpaid balances *more* burdensome

---

[14] Adjusted for seasonal changes.

(in real dollars of 153 cents apiece) than the whole debt burden had been in 1929, before liquidation began. Only one category of debt seems to have been reduced in fact as well as in name. This was brokers' loans, which were reduced, in name, 94.4 per cent, and in fact, 91 per cent. On the commercial bank debts of 39 billion, though 8½ billions had been paid up to 1932—nominally a reduction of 21.8 per cent—the burden had not decreased but actually increased by 20 per cent. On the intergovernmental debts of 11.6 billions, 400 millions had been paid up to 1932—nominally a reduction of 3.4 per cent, yet the real burden had increased by 48 per cent. On farm mortgages of 9½ billions, 1.9 billions were paid—nominally a reduction of 20 per cent; yet the real burden had increased by 22 per cent.[15] If we exclude public and other debts which grew even nominally after 1929, the total is 187½ billions on which the payments of 43¼ billions were made— nominally a reduction of 23 per cent; yet the real burden had increased by 17 per cent. If we take everything, the grand total is 234¼ billions, on which net payments of nearly 37 billions were made—nominally a net reduction of 15.7 per cent; yet the net real burden had increased 29 per cent.

In a word, despite all liquidations, the 234¼ billions of 1929 became over 302 billions in 1932, if measured in 1929 dollars.[16] By the third week in June, 1932, the business dollar had grown to $1.62 in terms of the 1929 dollar, and the debts expressed in this inflated dollar would have grown correspondingly. If there was no decrease in dollar debts, the total would be equal to 319.8 billion of 1929 dollars, or an increase of 36 per cent. Even assuming liqui-

[15] If we used a farm-commodity dollar, the increase would be greater.
[16] Of course, the figures merely compare valuations at two specific dates. They do not and cannot compare the various dates when loans were contracted and the dates when they were paid.

TABLE 2

ESTIMATED TOTAL DEBTS IN THE UNITED STATES

Change from 1929 to 1932

| | Debts | | | Changes from 1929 to 1932 | | | |
| | 1929 In 1929 Dollars (millions) | 1932 In 1932 Dollars (millions) | 1932 In 1929 Dollars (millions) | NOMINAL | | ACTUAL | |
				In Dollars Unadjusted for Changes in Value (millions)	Per Cent Change	In 1929 Dollars (millions)	Per Cent Change
Brokers' loans	$9,500	$ 530	$ 811	—$8,970	—94.4	—$8,689	— 91
Commercial bank loans	39,000	30,500	46,665	— 8,500	—21.8	+ 7,665	+ 20
Consumers' credits	3,000	2,000	3,060	— 1,000	—33.3	+ 60	+ 2
Loans on Life Insurance policies	2,379	3,400	5,202	+ 1,021	+42.9	+ 2,823	+119
Corporation debts (long & short term)	76,096	64,682	98,963	—11,414	—15.0	+22,867	+ 30
Farm mortgages	9,500	7,600	11,628	— 1,900	—20.0	+ 2,128	+ 22
Other agricultural loans	1,875	1,800	2,754	— 75	— 4.0	+ 880	+ 47
Non-Farm mortgages	37,000	26,000	39,780	—11,000	—30.0	+ 2,780	+ 8
Private foreign loans	14,000	15,200	23,256	+ 1,200	+ 8.5	+ 9,256	+ 66
State and local debts	13,400	16,000	24,480	+ 2,600	+19.0	+11,080	+ 82
Federal debt	16,931	18,508	28,317	+ 1,577	+ 9.5	+11,386	+ 68
War loans	11,600	11,200	17,136	— 400	— 3.4	+ 5,536	+ 48
TOTAL	$234,281	$197,420	$302,052	—36,861	—15.7	+68,291	+ 29

Computed and compiled by Dr. Royal Meeker from estimates by Dr. Carl Snyder, Dr. Lionel D. Edie, Professor E. R. A. Seligman, Professor John H. Gray and others, and reports of the Departments of the Treasury, Commerce, and Agriculture. The figures in some cases are little better than shrewd guesses, but in most instances they are based upon accurate statistical records. No attempts have been made to estimate small loans such as are made by individuals, credit associations, pawn-brokers, and "loan sharks." The decline in consumers' credit is assumed to be nearly equal to that in the automobile ingredient.

All conversions from 1932 to 1929 dollars are expressed in terms of the purchasing power of the business man's dollar over commodities at wholesale. One business man's dollar in March, 1932 equals $1.53 in 1929. By the third week of June, 1932, the business dollar had grown to $1.62.

dation by failure and foreclosure amounting to 10 billions, the real debts would have remained stationary at 302.9 billion dollars of 1929. The details are given in Table 2. It is this growth of *real* debt burden, despite huge efforts at liquidation, which, in my opinion, constitutes the master fact of the depression of 1929–32.

PART THREE

REMEDIAL

CHAPTER IX

PALLIATIVES VS. REMEDIES

A FRIENDLY critic has taken exception to the emphasis here placed upon the varying dollar—"a mere unit of measure, instead of the things measured." He is more impressed by the concrete dislocations of business. But a unit of measure which enters into practically every transaction and then starts growing and dwindling by turns (while it goes on looking the same to the contracting parties) will, of course, produce dislocations—dislocations in everything—dislocations in price, quantity, distribution, and all else that concerns the contracting parties, and all other parties in the world. Such dislocations (it seems to me) are bound to be more radical and more wide-spread than any that would be likely to result, for instance, from a blight on one crop or the over-production of another, or from any coincidence of such causes.

Within a stone's throw of my home is the plant of a great arms company. Early in the World War it entered into prodigious contracts with foreign countries to produce munitions; but the prices to be paid, though incredibly high, were fixed by the contracts; and no sooner had the wheels begun to grind out the goods than war inflation (1914–19) sent current prices sky-rocketing, including the prices of raw-materials and labor needed but not yet bought for the fulfillment of the contracts. So the profits, which had looked so large to start with, got squeezed out,

113

between fixed income and rising costs. Then, after the war, finding itself burdened with more floor space and more tools than could be used in peace times for war commodities, the company decided to devote its extra equipment to diversified hardware. Accordingly, it planted stores all over the country and put on a heavy advertising campaign. No sooner had interest and rent and wages become relatively fixed than post-war deflation (1920–21) began to force down the prices of all their products, old and new. So again the profits were squeezed out, this time between the relatively fixed costs and the lowering income. And before it could fight its way out (1921–29) came the price slump of 1929–32. Then, having been caught both going and coming, this great victim of a tricky unit of measure at last gave up the ghost. It sold out; and its former owners still wonder what hit them. No doubt they believe it was an epidemic of business dislocations; and it was—but all of them, or nearly all, were due to one sort of cause—price inflation (a shrinking dollar) and price deflation (a swelling dollar).

A monetary disease involves a profit disease. This is the core of the diagnosis; and on that diagnosis depends the remedy.

Before describing the currency reforms which, according to the diagnosis of this book, go to the root of the disease, I will run over briefly the leading "substantive cures"—not to disparage them as unimportant, but in the conviction that their importance is secondary. They are, it seems to me, palliatives, but not inconsistent with the currency reforms which do go to the roots.

FIRST AID

The most tragic sequel of impaired profits is unemployment. No doubt charity for the jobless man is desirable, but charity is everybody's business and therefore nobody's. As one means of taking up the slack in labor—a sort of half charity—the proposal has been put forward, that, in times of depression, the government extend itself as an employer. This would be done by means of an arbitrary program of public works, productive or unproductive or both. But in the depression, for instance, of 1929–32, hundreds of millions were spent in this way, which helped feed a few men but had little or no effect on the steady progress of the depression; and Mr. Hoover [1] estimated that the further efforts proposed along the same line could hardly accommodate more than 40,000 workmen the first year. To give out 40,000 jobs to millions of jobless men, without affecting the profits on which employment ultimately depends, would be of little avail—if we are to continue the private profit system at all. Indeed, an arbitrary program of public works might divert resources from more useful outlets.

In 1932, an ingenious *modus vivendi* for unemployed men was developed in Gary, Indiana, when the steel furnaces had become idle for part of the time. Industry, the relief agencies, and the University of Indiana helped some 20,000 families to cultivate their own food by reclaiming extensive swamp lands.[2]

Various forms of insurance against unemployment have been suggested. There is the plan proposed by Mr. Gerard Swope of the General Electric Company which embodies, in a measure, the insurance principle but aims less at paying for the loss of jobs than at keeping the jobs alive in the lean years through the cooperative action of industry. The plan is worthy of careful consideration, and the electrical industry, after a good deal of delay, adopted it in 1932.[3] But a depression is not caused by unemployment—

[1] *New York Times*, May 23, 1932.
[2] Associated Press dispatch, July 31, 1932.
[3] *New York Times*, Jan. 3, 1932.

quite the other way; and no plan for perpetuating employment could be long continued by industries drained of their profits. Congressman David J. Lewis is developing and pressing the idea that, though the World does not "owe everyone a living," yet there should always be, for those who are able and willing to work, a chance to work. This is a fine ideal, but attainable, it is to be feared, in a private-profit society, only when that society stops permitting its monetary unit to vary, and wipe out by billions the profits which should insure the chance to work.

REDUCING COST

Efficiency, like charity, is good for good times as well as bad. Business has long been efficient. But, in a depression, a new dose of efficiency would at least have the merit of operating directly on profits. One of its methods would doubtless be to relax by amendment the anti-trust laws, so. that costs might be reduced by further combination. Wasteful armaments should be cut, thus reducing the tax burden; also, the tariffs which hinder the exchange of goods should be reduced. And increased efficiency would embrace more system and more invention. But all these expedients, important as they are, work on a relatively small scale, while the dollar is jumping 50 per cent.

RETARDING THE DEBT DISEASE

We have seen that over-indebtedness may cause the liquidation which expands the dollar which raises the costs which ruin the profits. Any expedient should be adopted, therefore, which would retard the pyramiding of the debt burden—or (if the pyramid succeeds in getting itself erected) would retard its distress liquidation. In anticipation of booms, some of the superfluous and non-productive lures to over-indebtedness might be withdrawn—for instance, speculative temptations like the capital gain tax. And the so-called bank affiliates, which are suspected of undue speculation, might be held in check by laws exposing their accounts to the same publicity that is applied to the banks with which they are affiliated. Also, American banks might show less hospitality to stock market collateral and press still further the policy which they have in recent years copied from abroad and are already using—the policy of lending on balance sheets—being careful, of course, to check balance sheets with income statements. Also, in the interest of small corporations and other modest borrowers, more facilities might be made for the function of lending intermediate amounts for intermediate periods. At present the nearest approach we have to a loan for an intermediate period is usually a sort of gentleman's agreement on the part of a commercial bank to *renew* a *short* term loan. This is a perversion of commercial banking; and the result is that, when an emergency arises, the commercial bank must either break its promise or be handicapped by a "frozen" loan.

REPLACING INFLEXIBLE BONDS

Since rash maturity dates are a chief factor in over-indebtedness, corporate finance might go further with the present tendency toward selling more preferred stock and less bonds, since the bondholder can force liquidation, and the stockholder cannot. We want a debt system which, unlike the present one, will bend and not break. So far as bonds are still used, they might be so drawn as to be more easily refunded. For instance, a bond might well contain an option to refund after five years as a matter of course. It might even be drawn to run indefinitely, becoming a perpetual annuity without a due date. As bonds are now drawn, if a due date falls in a depression, refunding on any reasonable terms usually becomes impossible. Thus bad matters are made worse.

OTHER MEASURES OF DEBT FLEXIBILITY

The banks, too, might organize cooperatively for more lenient liquidation—as to borrowers and as to one another. Branch banking would be an improvement. It would enable the banks to support one another when runs occur. Receiverships intended to defer or avoid liquidation might be more freely used. The laws which compel certain agencies of trust, such as savings banks, to dump their securities on a falling market might be relaxed when there is a depression—since this dumping defeats collectively the very safety which is the purpose of each individual liquidation. The American Stock Exchange might adopt a rule approximating that of the English Stock Exchange which requires settlements only once a fortnight instead of daily.

DEBT SCALING

Profits are the spread between receipts and expenses; net worths are the spread between assets and liabilities. In a depression, profits (and, of course, net worths) are pinched by a fall in money values. If, then, expenses and liabilities could be forced into a parallel fall, the pinch would be avoided. This parallel action could be largely accomplished if wages and debts could be scaled. Such a procedure, moreover, would be entirely just to workmen and to creditors. In other words, since, in terms of *real* wages and *real* debts, a depression virtually gives the workman and the creditor more than the agreed amount, they ought to be willing to surrender some of the unintentional loot. Possibly, labor might sometimes be educated into accepting a temporary reduction; but, in general, the money illusion would stand in the way. No creditor would adjust his debt to the price level.

However, in 1932, the "Penn Zone Property Owners Association" issued a bulletin entitled "Stop Foreclosures." In this document, the point was made that foreclosures are an unduly expensive means of collecting debts and hurt the values of the property foreclosed as well as that of neighboring property. It was proposed that mortgagors and mortgagees cooperate during hard times and that interest be reduced proportionately with the fall of rents. In Gary, Indiana, in 1932, a still more radical plan was proposed, and, according to a news dispatch,[4] it won the consent of many mortgagees: that is, both interest and principal were reduced, and loans renewed.

THE INTERNATIONAL DEBTS IN 1932

Debt regulation, if based on an index number and made automatic, would practically amount to the same thing as the regulation of the price level. Debt regulation is, in general, out of the question. But the depression of 1932 is unique in that a large part of the debt burden is scalable, because a large part of it consists of inter-governmental debts. To these, scaling has already been applied in a measure, by means of the various reparation and other intergovernmental debt settlements.

Cancellation, or a large scale reduction, should, if properly coordinated with other remedial measures, raise the price level the world over; and one result of a higher price level would be to lighten the American debt burden

[4] *New York Times*, August 4, 1932.

and, by stimulating business and increasing incomes, indirectly lighten the burden of American taxes. On the other hand, to insist, even successfully, on full payment would only aggravate the process of deflation and make our taxes more, as measured in *real* dollars.

The greatest remedial effort yet proposed along this line is the Lausanne Accord between Germany and her creditors, reported in the press on July 12, 1932. Having long since reduced Germany's debt from 132 billion marks to 34 billion without satisfactory results, the Allies have, at last, almost released Germany altogether, by coming down to 3 billion marks, or 714 million dollars—a reduction to about 1 cent on the dollar.[5]

But, generally speaking, even large palliatives are not cures—at any rate not preventives. Nor will it ever be possible to forestall the debt disease by direct regulation of debts until we have better debt statistics and also a criterion as to how much debt is too much debt. Here is a need which is basic and must, in due time, be met.

[5] Germany is to deliver to the Bank of International Settlement at Basle (the "World Bank") 5 per cent bonds in the amount of 714 million dollars. These bonds are not to be negotiated until three years from the signing of the settlement; and such of them (if any) as the bank shall not succeed in negotiating in fifteen years are to be cancelled altogether.

CHAPTER X

REMEDIES

CREDIT CONTROL

BUT the lack of debt statistics does not bar us from forestalling the debt disease by a direct attack upon the dollar or price level disease. True, the debt disease is often the precipitator of the dollar disease; but, under the operation of the vicious spiral, the debt disease soon becomes the effect, and the dollar disease, the cause. In the boom period, for instance, the really gross over-indebtedness usually springs from the upward movement of the price level, which, by expanding profits unduly, over-excites the profit maker so that he expands his undertakings unduly, with too much borrowed money.

Invention or discovery *alone* need not carry up the aggregate indebtedness very high, if the price level promptly refuses to follow up the lure of invention or discovery with the lure of profits *not due to the invention or discovery* but to credit inflation. The point is to quell the inflation as soon as the price level is even slightly affected by it.

Even in cases (like 1923–29) in which the commodity price level fails to register the inflation, there is still the stock market as an indicator; and even if inflation altogether escapes observation or is neglected, then to prevent the sequel, deflation will become all the more important.

THE MANDATE TO TREAT THE DOLLAR DISEASE

The Constitution of the United States, in Article I,

section 8, clause 5, reads as follows: "The Congress shall have power: . . .

"5. to coin money, regulate the value thereof . . . and fix the standard of weights and measures."

Units of measure other than the dollar were standardized long ago. Their nature made them easy to standardize. They could be determined once for all, and then some of them put under a glass case for protection against changes of temperature and humidity. On the other hand, the dollar had to be defined before there was any instrument available for measuring its value apart from its weight,—that is, before the science of index numbers had developed; so that, though the dollar was called a standard of value, or purchasing power, it became really a standard of weight. Now that we possess index numbers we can, if we will, make the dollar more truly a standard of purchasing power. This can be understood by reference to a simple equation, of which the price level (that is, the reciprocal of the purchasing power of the dollar) is one factor.

THE EQUATION OF EXCHANGE [1]

According to this "equation of exchange," the price level, multiplied by the yearly volume of trade, is equal to the money in circulation multiplied by the number of times it circulates in a year.

Expressed in the simplest algebra, this means that, in any given year,

$$PT = MV$$

where

P is the index number measuring the price level (a percentage figure, relative to a base year—say 1913),

[1] See *The Purchasing Power of Money*, by Irving Fisher (Macmillan, 1931).

T, the volume of trade (the total value of the year's trade in terms not of current prices but of the base year prices),

M, the quantity of money in circulation (including deposit currency), and

V, the velocity at which this money circulates (that is, the yearly turn-over of the entire mass of money).

It is statistically possible to ascertain each of these items.

What happens to the price level (*P*) depends largely on what happens to the other three factors. What happens to the trade factor should (within certain well-recognized lines of regulation) be left to the laws of supply and demand, and could safely be left to those laws, if the dollar in which they register did not unsettle their natural behavior. But, though trade should thus be left to nature, the other two factors, especially *M* (the quantity of money), are proper subjects for human control. The problem, therefore, is: by regulating the quantity of money and also by influencing its velocity, to keep the price level essentially steady.

Dr. Carl Snyder has shown that the velocity of money on one side of the equation tends, of itself, to keep pace with the short-time changes of trade on the other side of the equation. Thus, there is little disturbance of the price scale from short-time changes in the volume of trade. So if money, on one side of the equation, were kept in pace with the long, steady progress of trade, on the other side, *P* (the price level) would remain fairly constant.

THE QUANTITY THEORY

Though the control of *M* has here been presented in terms of the "equation of exchange," this has been done for simplicity and not because we can safely assume that

T and V are constant, or even that the ratio of T to V is constant, or that this ratio is subject only to a constant progressive change—though the last is approximately true. The presentation could have been made without any recourse to the "quantity theory of money,"—that is, the "equation of exchange." We need only to assume that an increase in the quantity of the circulating medium has *some* tendency to raise the price level, and *vice versa*. Nor need we take seriously the common objection that any control must be futile because "other factors besides money and credit" also have an influence. According to this reasoning the use of a rudder in steering a ship is futile because, besides the influence of the rudder, there is the influence of wind and wave!

ADJUSTING CREDIT TO BUSINESS

A plan to make money keep step with trade (or rather with the ratio of trade to velocity) has been suggested by Dr. Carl Snyder, Dr. Lionel D. Edie, and Professor James Harvey Rogers. Under this plan, the previous growth of trade would be watched and its behavior for the preceding ten years taken as a guide. If the ten year growth had been, say, 3 per cent, the supply of money would then be increased at the rate of 3 per cent per annum to meet the expected requirements of business.

This adjustment of money to the requirements of trade will appeal to the business man to whom the idea of a stable price level or a stable dollar seems academic. But the proposed adjustment is the same thing as stabilizing the dollar, and we can get a more exact adjustment if we take the price level, or the purchasing power of the dollar, as our guide.

REFLATING AND STABILIZING THE PRICE LEVEL

Suppose that the price scale has recently jumped up or down so as to impoverish lenders to the advantage of borrowers, or borrowers to the advantage of lenders. In that case, the price level should be first *corrected* by reflation and thenceforward *safeguarded*.

How much reflation is right? In other words, how far back by way of correction should we put the price level before starting to safeguard it?

The answer is: far enough back to repair, as nearly as possible, the injustice to the creditor or the debtor, as the case may be. But, alas, there is no "the" creditor and no "the" debtor. There are many of each class, and they date from different points on the down- or upswing. Standing at 1932, let us look back upon the downswing of the price level from 1929 to 1932. Some debts were contracted in 1929, some in 1930, 1931, or 1932. By putting the price level back from the 1932 level, we would do injustice to the creditors who lent in 1932. By not putting it *all the way back to the 1929 level*, we would do injustice to the debtors who borrowed in 1929.[2] By putting it back to 1930, we would do exact justice to the debtors and the creditors of 1930, but we would leave the debtors on one side of 1930 and the creditors on the other side to suffer something less than justice, according to the respective distances of their contracts from the 1930 price level. Yet we cannot let things alone. In 1932, injustice rested on one group—the debtors. If the price level were put part way back, the injustice would be shared by two groups—

[2] Sir Arthur Salter, in *Recovery—The Second Attempt*, recommends the 1929 level. The minority report of the League of Nations Gold delegation recommends 1928, practically the same as 1929. Gustav Cassel recommends halfway back to 1929—which appeals to me.

debtors and creditors; and this would be the only reasonable solution; for it would minimize the injustice to both groups taken together.

But, the chief purpose of the correction must be to secure the future, so that things can go on; to restore to a prosperity basis as many profit accounts as we reasonably can, so that the wheels of industry may move again, and the maximum number of the unemployed be put back to work. As a practical matter, we should feel our way to the most restorative price level, and stop when we find that business is sufficiently able to reabsorb unemployed labor. Thereupon, the price level thus reached should become society's vested interest, and be stabilized.

REGULATION THROUGH THE REDISCOUNT RATE

The regulation of M (the quantity of money) belongs to what Sir Josiah Stamp calls the "mechanics" of money. The regulation of V (the velocity of money) is more baffling because it is more psychological.

We shall begin, therefore, with what may well be called the mechanics of money—M.

Money, as the word is used here, is, in general, of two kinds:

1. Deposit currency, or bank deposits subject to check;
2. Hand-to-hand money, consisting of paper money, subsidiary coinage and gold.

Deposit currency, being nine-tenths of the country's currency, should be the first item on any program for sound money.

Inasmuch as deposit currency is borrowed, its volume can be more or less regulated by the rate of interest. A lowered rate increases the borrowing and a raised rate decreases it. Many people miss this point about interest. Even a former member of the Federal Reserve Board missed it when, in a public lecture, he averred that interest was too small an element "in the cost of production" to effect prices! The point, however, is not the cost of production but the quantity of currency. If, at a 5 per cent rate of interest, the quantity of currency were satisfactory to business, then a change to 4½ per cent would make money excessive and progressively so, and a change to 5½ per cent would make it progressively insufficient. The water in a bath-tub is kept constant when the outflow through the waste-pipe exactly equals the inflow through the supply-pipe; but the slightest turn of the spigot from this equilibrium point will, in time, fill or empty the tub. The interest rate acts like the spigot, to fill or empty the country's reservoir of circulating deposit currency.

The human race should forget its primitive notions about interest. One of the greatest of all economic reforms would be, on the one hand, to get rid of the popular prejudice against raising, promptly and drastically, rates of interest when conditions justify; and, on the other hand, to get rid of the inertia which keeps rates high when conditions call for reduction. In some places, the rate stays at 6 per cent through good times and bad. In a western town I saw "4 per cent" engraved in inflexible stone on the walls of a new bank building. Even in New York, where interest is more elastic than anywhere else in America, it is not elastic enough. Ideally, any trustworthy borrower should be able to get a loan *at a price;* and any lender to place one.

THE FEDERAL RESERVE SYSTEM

To make the regulation of interest effective, the banks must act in concert; and so far as concerns the Federal Reserve System, this requirement can easily be met. At the

center of that System is the Federal Reserve Board, which
sits at Washington. Next, there are the 12 regional banks
—the so-called Federal Reserve Banks—each operating as
a central bank in its region. Next come the member banks
for each region. The member banks, so far as lending is
concerned, make all the contacts with the public. The 12
Reserve Banks, besides performing other functions, lend to
the member banks by rediscounting for them the paper
which they have previously discounted for the public. The
Board at Washington keeps in touch with the 12 Reserve
Banks through 12 Federal Reserve agents, stationed in the
respective banks. Naturally, under this scheme of things,
the interest rates which the member banks can afford to
charge their customers are largely governed by the rediscount rates which the member banks expect to pay to
the Reserve Banks. These central banks, therefore, by
means of the rediscount rate, already regulate, to a considerable degree, the whole country's volume of deposit
currency—for good or ill.

But the reaction of the volume of deposit currency to the
rediscount rates, though great in the end, is relatively
slow, and the Reserve Banks have at their command a
supplementary instrument which works faster.

REGULATION THROUGH "OPEN MARKET OPERATIONS"

Every bank keeps a reserve against its deposits. In the
case of a member bank in the Federal Reserve System, its
reserve consists of its own deposit balance in its Federal
Reserve Bank. This balance must, under the law, be at least
equal to a certain percentage of the total outstanding deposits which have been granted by the member bank to its
customers. For time deposits the requirement is only 3
per cent; but for demand deposits, which chiefly interest

us, the reserve must be 7, 10 or 13 per cent, according to the location of the member bank,—the higher percentages being required in the larger and more active business centers.

The balance held by a member bank in a Reserve Bank may arise not only from rediscounting but from selling securities to the Reserve Bank, the proceeds being left in the Reserve Bank on deposit. It follows that the 12 Reserve Banks, can, by *buying* bonds from member banks, enlarge the reserves of these member banks, and, by *selling* bonds to them, can lower their reserves. True, if a member bank is indebted to the Federal Reserve Bank, it may use its deposit balance (in excess of its existing reserve requirements) to pay off the debt. It thus deprives itself of the privilege of using the enlarged balance as a reserve for new credit issues. But after its indebtedness is paid off, any further excess in its balance is pretty sure to be used as reserve for further loans to the public.

WHAT IS TRADED IN OPEN MARKET OPERATIONS

This buying or selling of bonds is the "open market policy."

Practically the only articles in which the Federal Reserve can legally deal by way of open market operations are government bonds and "commercial bills." Accordingly, these operations have aroused the complaint that they interfere with the bond market. Theoretically, any other property or commodity might be made the subject of open market operations. Silver, for instance, might be bought or sold—by the government if not by the Federal Reserve. Buying silver from or through the member banks, like buying bonds, would enable the banks to put purchasing power into circulation, and thus tend to raise prices generally. The trouble is, however, that this operation would raise the price of silver in particular and put it out of line with other prices. Buying wheat or cotton would be subject to the same objection. Nor could we expect to buy or sell all goods impartially and in the right proportions. As to perishable goods, for instance, there would be the objection that they would perish. Durable goods, on the other hand, would be unduly held out of use. Similar objections apply to bonds; nevertheless, bonds are the most suitable class of goods in which to deal for stabilization. The range of selection might, of course, be extended to include other bonds than those of the government.

Thus, by operating not only the rediscount rate but also the open market policy, the 12 Reserve Banks can powerfully regulate the volume of the country's deposit currency—for good or ill.

If the Federal Reserve System should decide to exercise its enormous power over deposit currency with the acknowledged purpose of affecting the price level, the exercise of this power ought to keep close on the heels of the price level; for, if once a rapid up-movement of the price level (say over 10 per cent per annum) were allowed to get started, it would make the *real* interest rate [3] so low that a very high nominal rate would be powerless to check the borrowing; for even 10 per cent nomimal interest would then leave the real rate at zero. On the other hand, if once a rapid down-movement of the price level (say over 20 per cent per annum) were allowed to get started, it would make the real rate so high that a nominal rate of nearly zero would not tempt the borrower; for what is a nominal rate of zero, if the rate actually felt becomes 20 per cent?

But when such an up or down movement does get the

[3] See p. 38.

bit in its teeth, it is because the operation of these two policies (rediscount and open market) has been tardy.

In short, the dictator of "real" interest is the price level, but nominal interest can dictate the price level if it dictates in time.

AUTOMATIC REGULATION OF RESERVES

To be sure of being in time, the machinery of regulation must be flexible; and to that end the reserve requirements may sometimes need to be temporarily relaxed. The relaxation should be by administrative authority—without waiting upon the slow process of legislation. An ingenious plan for one kind of relaxation has been suggested by Mr. Winfield Riefler of the staff of the Federal Reserve Board. This plan would prescribe the amount of the reserve required of a member bank, not according to the location of the bank and the character of its deposits, but according to the daily *activity* of those deposits. The slower the deposits, the smaller the reserve to be required (thus stimulating lending power); the faster the deposits, the more the reserve to be required (thus retarding lending power).

This rule would have the advantage of applying not only between different places but also in the same place at different times. Whenever the turnover should exceed the speed limit, the brakes would go on automatically. On the other hand, if a depression should retard the turnover, an inducement to lending more freely would be created automatically.

ADJUSTMENTS TO FACILITATE OPEN MARKET OPERATIONS

The law also imposes a reserve requirement on each Reserve Bank. The reserve in such a case must be at least

35 per cent of the total deposit balances which a Reserve Bank grants to its circle of member banks—the 35 per cent consisting of gold or of "lawful money." Since a 35 per cent reserve supports nearly three times its own amount in the form of member deposits, and since each member bank can, on the average, issue to its own customers about ten times the amount of its deposit in the Reserve Bank, the final volume of deposit currency may become nearly 30 times the original reserve of gold and lawful money in the Reserve Bank.

The Reserve Bank has another currency function: it may obtain from the Reserve Board an allotment of Federal Reserve notes. In this transaction, the government is theoretically the issuer of the notes and guarantees them. The Reserve Bank obtains the notes from the government and then circulates them, making itself responsible, both to the government and to the holders, for the redemption of the notes. As security for the notes thus obtained from the government, the Reserve Bank deposits with the Federal Reserve agent 100 per cent of collateral, consisting either of commercial paper which it has rediscounted or of gold or (under the recent Glass-Steagall Act) of government bonds. All this precedes the actual issue of the notes by the bank. When the bank actually issues any of them, it must have, in its own vaults, or with the Federal Reserve agent, gold equal to 40 per cent of the face of the notes issued; which means that the gold thus used will support only 2½ times its amount in the form of Federal Reserve notes.

Thus gold, or other lawful money, may support nearly 30 times its face in deposit currency, and gold may support 2½ times its face in Federal Reserve notes. The Federal Reserve Act authorizes the Reserve Banks to reduce their reserve ratios in an emergency, and there should be some authority equipped with the power to relax or to stiffen, in emergencies, all or any of the requirements designed to secure the proper exercise of either the credit function or the function of obtaining or issuing Federal Reserve notes.

CONFLICTS OF FUNCTION

The Federal Reserve System might well exercise such diverse functions as the care of the commodity price level and the care of the stock market price level. To prevent these from interfering with each other, a plan has been proposed by Mr. Luther Blake, President of the Standard Statistics Corporation of New York City. He would empower the Federal Reserve Board to put special obstacles in the way of loans to brokers (or to any other class of borrowers), whenever such loans were, in the judgment of the Federal Reserve Board, about to become excessive. Mr. Blake suggests that, for this purpose, the reserves required of the member banks should be allocated among the various classes of loans, and the reserve requirement against each class varied from time to time, according as any class should be found to be over-extended or not. This plan might make it feasible, as it has not been hitherto, to keep "separate pools of credit."

A UNIFIED BANKING SYSTEM

Before the organization of the Federal Reserve System, in 1913, American banking was little better than a jungle; and outside of the system, the jungle is still very incompletely reclaimed. Almost any inexpert person is still free to call himself a banker and try his luck at the art of surviving or perishing—along with his clients. It is absurd to think that there can be 30,000 bankers in the United States really competent to operate in splendid isolation. A run on an American bank is likely to be fatal, whereas, with due cooperation, the whole system of banks would come to the rescue of the individual bank, and "tide it over." In most other first class countries—England, France, Belgium, Germany, Holland and the Scandinavian countries—co-operation among banks is made secure, either by an inclusive system of "central banking" or by the system known as "branch banking." Accordingly, in the depression of 1929–32, France had only one large bank failure, Austria one, Germany one, Britain and Canada none at all, while the United States in 1931 alone had 2,550 bank suspensions.

The Federal Reserve System is sound within itself, and even with the present set-up, its credit policy (when it has one) affects, to some extent, directly or indirectly, all banks. But a unified credit policy is not enough. Those who exercise it should also be fortified against sheer bank failures. Most of the small state banks could be brought into the Federal Reserve System by branch banking. To this end, something could perhaps be accomplished by making it disadvantageous for state banks to stay out. Perhaps a service charge might be imposed for clearing their checks. In 1865, the Federal government, by taxing state bank notes out of existence, induced many state banks to become national banks. Some analogous tax might be tried now in order to tax the deposit currency of non-member banks out of existence.

STABILIZATION PROPERLY A GOVERNMENT FUNCTION

All that the law now requires of the Federal Reserve System is "the accommodation of business and commerce." But sometimes the accommodation of this or that partial interest of business conflicts with the accommodation of the whole country's price level. It should not be left to the

discretion of a semi-private banking interest, coupled with
wholly private but enormously powerful bankers, to regulate or not to regulate, and even for illicit ends (if cor-
ruption enters) to *un*regulate, the whole country's basic
unit of measure. Mr. M. K. Graham of Graham, Texas,
has written a book [4] in which he develops the thesis that
"since deposit currency (that is, bank credit) is money, that
part of it made by state banks is made in violation of the
Federal Constitution, and will in time be so declared."

At any rate the mandate of the law should not only make
the integrity of the price level paramount,—it should take
it wholly out of irresponsible, chance controls and put it
under responsible controls, guided by an exact, scientific
and openly published criterion determined by the Index
Number.

The government puts all its strength behind its legal
tender money; yet deposit currency does ten times the
business of legal tender and has ten times the power to
wreck our most basic unit of measure—the dollar. Already,
by having its representatives on the Federal Reserve
Board, the government has indirectly acknowledged its
responsibility toward the country's deposit currency, but if
the government is to fulfill completely that responsibility,
it might well add to its present operations a policy analogous to the "open market policy" of the Federal Reserve
Banks—for which purpose the following plan has been
worked out: [5]

A BOND SECURED DEPOSIT CURRENCY

First, a Stabilization Commission would be set up. This
commission, in case of a depression, would, on behalf of the

[4] *Continuous Prosperity* by M. K. Graham (The Parthenon Press,
Nashville, Texas, 1932).

[5] By James H. Rand, Jr., Ragnar Frisch, and Irving Fisher.

government, sell to all the banking institutions that are willing, a large number of Treasury short term bonds—the distribution to be in proportion to the existing deposits of the respective banks. By way of payment, each bank would give the government a time deposit for, say, a year, in the absence of earlier termination by mutual consent. The interest running from the government to the banks and the interest running from the banks to the government would be equal, so as to cancel.

The banks would thus have an additional quick asset without an additional quick liability. They could sell the bonds or hypothecate them with the Reserve Banks, obtaining additional deposit credit, against which they could grant to the public additional deposit currency—10 dollars of money (on the average) to one dollar of hypothecated bonds. Even if a bank chose not to sell or hypothecate the bonds, the fact that bonds were on hand, ready like a fire extinguisher for emergency use, would so strengthen the bank's position as to encourage it in a more liberal lending policy. After the depression, this same method could be used or reversed; that is, it could be operated either to discourage or encourage lending, according as the existing tendency was toward inflation or deflation.

This mechanism would work fast. The government could supply 10 billions of bonds almost over night. The only lag in enlarging the deposit currency would be the time required by the banks to negotiate the additional loans to their customers.

Already, this method has, in effect, been used very quietly on a small scale and found salutary.

GOLD CONTROL

Credit control has its limitations, due to the relation of the credit superstructure to the gold base. The only real importance of gold lies in its function as a reserve; and the smaller and more precarious the reserve, the greater the importance of the gold. In short, we have the paradox that, just because gold is so small a part of our circulating system it plays a large rôle. In general in the United States, the gold base is about 10 per cent of the total money. Therefore, for adjusting the total money to the needs of business and the price level, the chief prerequisite is to adjust the gold base, which supports the other currency, including credit.

THE SURPLUS RESERVOIR PLAN

There are three chief methods of adjusting the gold base.

The first is to maintain a margin of safety; that is, to have *more* gold available for the base than the indispensable minimum, but keep the surplus impounded or "sterilized," drawing upon it or adding to it according as the price level calls for enlarging or diminishing the credit superstructure.

This plan of enlarging or diminishing can be operated so long as we really have a surplus of gold, the surplus of gold enabling us to accomplish stabilization by credit control.[6] But the instant the surplus is wiped out, credit expansion is precluded by law.

To make sure of a surplus of the metal base, we might enlarge the gold base by supplementing it with silver or otherwise.[7]

[6] Provided (and this is only of academic interest) the gold surplus is not so excessive as to require, to prevent inflation, the wiping out of all credit.

[7] See *Rand Plan*, Appendix No. VII.

THE LEHFELDT PLAN

The second method is to control the production of gold. For this purpose, a nation acting alone would be handicapped; and the late Prof. R. A. Lehfeldt,[8] therefore proposed a syndicate of nations including, in particular, the United States and the British Empire. The syndicate would act through a commission having both an administrative bureau and a scientific bureau. All over the world, monetary and price statistics and mining laws and geology would be studied, and the production of gold would be encouraged or discouraged according to the world's monetary needs. In an emergency, some of the less productive mines might even be closed. In that case, the commission would buy the mines in order to compensate the owners (compensating also the workmen thus put out of work), and thereafter re-open or close mines according to the world's monetary needs. In case of insufficient gold, the commission, having prepared itself in advance with surveys of new gold regions, would purchase or subsidize whatever mining facilities might be required to sustain the price level.

But this plan, too, has a breaking point; that is, it would fail if and when it became impossible to secure enough gold.

THE "COMPENSATED DOLLAR" PLAN [9]

In the absence of such international control, each country could use the plan which (if characterized in terms of American money) may best be called the "compensated

---

[8] See *Restoration of the World's Currencies*, by R. A. Lehfeldt (P. S. King & Son, Ltd., London, 1923).

[9] See *The Purchasing Power of Money* (Macmillan 1931), *Stabilizing the Dollar* (Macmillan 1920), *The Money Illusion* (Adelphi Company 1928), by Irving Fisher.

dollar" plan. That is, if in spite of all other efforts to regulate the price level, the purchasing power of gold over goods should fall, the weight of the gold dollar would be correspondingly increased; or, if the purchasing power of gold should rise, the weight of the dollar would be correspondingly reduced.

Under this plan, the actual coinage of gold would, of course, be abandoned, and, instead of gold coins, gold bars would be used to redeem the gold certificates. Only the gold certificates would circulate, and the price of the bars in terms of these certificates would be varied from time to time. But, between the buying and selling prices, a small spread would be provided. Otherwise, when a change in price was announced, speculators might buy of the government at today's prices and sell back at tomorrow's, or *vice versa*, making a profit at the expense of the government.

This plan need not be embarrassed by the gold clause in some private contracts; for such clauses could be virtually abrogated by taxing their execution.

A simple application of the compensated dollar plan would be to rely principally upon credit control, and only at long intervals regulate the weight of the dollar when other means proved inadequate.

One advantage of the compensated dollar plan would be that any nation could operate it alone. The only inconvenience would be that each alteration in the dollar's weight would cause a corresponding alteration in foreign exchange. But this is a small matter. The Lehfeldt plan, on the other hand, would necessarily affect all nations; and no one country could operate it without having also to control the price levels of all the other countries which had the gold standard.

But as world-wide stabilization is highly desirable, all plans should include international cooperation. The realization of this fact has led to the calling of an international conference on the problem of price levels.

We turn now from the volume of money (M) to its velocity (V). When velocity misbehaves, it misbehaves in the same direction with volume. We have already seen, for instance, that, in the depression of 1929–32, while the volume of deposit currency in member banks was falling 21 per cent, the velocity of it was being reduced by 61 per cent. In the case of a rising price level, the remedy for the velocity must perhaps be looked for in the volume of money, by taking the surplus M out of the overflooded circulation; for people cannot spend what they do not have. The price level would come down, and V would come down. On the other hand, people *can* hoard what they *do* have; so that, in the case of a depression and a falling price level, a mere new supply of money, to replace what has been liquidated or hoarded, might fail to raise the price level by failing to get into circulation. If, for instance, there is fear of going off the gold standard, the very effort to expand credit may, by increasing that fear, defeat itself, the new money being more than offset by withdrawals for hoarding. For a prompt boost of the price level, therefore, a mere increase in M might prove insufficient, unless supplemented by some influence exercised directly on the moods of people to accelerate V—that is, to convert the public from hoarding.

The authorities charged with the duty of rescuing confidence in a depression would have to be careful not to make bad matters worse by raising false hopes, or by using suggestions which automatically induce counter-suggestion. But wise measures whose wisdom the public can be made to see should be made public with all the enthusiasm they deserve.

CONFIDENCE IN BANKS

The banks, if they are enabled to re-capture the hoards (and also to re-capture their own confidence, so as to quit hoarding on their own account), are better equipped than any other agency to put the re-captured money to work, because banks can use this money as the basis of many times its face in the form of credit currency. Therefore, anything that will restore and justify confidence in the banks is eminently desirable. If, for instance, deposits in banks were guaranteed by an authority satisfactory to the depositing public, some of the hoards would melt and flow back into the banks and help support credit currency. In America, this guaranty expedient has been tried; but, I regret to say, with poor success, due usually to the failure of the guarantors to justify confidence by excluding "bad risks" from their guaranty. Abroad, guaranty policies have apparently served a useful purpose.

For a successful guarantor of properly selected banks there might be a coalition of banks, or the Federal Reserve System, or the government. Preferably, the government; for, in a depression, the banks themselves are as badly scared as the public, and only the government is strong enough to handle such a scare. The Canadian government, in 1930–31, in order to facilitate the marketing of grains, guaranteed to the several chartered Canadian banks certain credits granted by those banks to the grain industry. This transaction was accomplished by an Order of Council under specific statutory provisions.[10]

I have already suggested that the Federal Reserve

[10] *Budget Speech* of Hon. Edgar N. Rhodes, Minister of Finance in the House of Commons, April 6, 1932. (F. A. Acland, Ottawa, 1932.)

System be enlarged and that the government take a more direct interest in credit currency by depositing bonds to support it. Few things would go further toward dispelling the hesitations of both banks and borrowers.

STIMULATING BORROWERS AND BUYERS

The government could, for the duration of the emergency only, offer subsidies which would have the effect of negative interest.[11]

But there is one more cause for the hesitation of the borrowers. Business does not wish to borrow until it is sure of buyers; and in a depression, the buyers wait for business to inspire confidence, and business cannot inspire confidence till it gets back on a normal borrowing basis. If only buying could be started first, business borrowing would follow. For the purpose (of directly stimulating the buyers), a unique "stamped dollar" plan has been devised —a sort of stamp tax on hoarding.[12] This plan did not come to my attention until after this book had been finished. The plan offers the most efficient method of controlling hoarding and probably the speediest way out of a depression.

In this chapter, we have seen the main methods available for credit control, gold control, and velocity control. The last named is badly needed only in emergencies. In ordinary times, credit control through open market operations would suffice, reinforced at long intervals by gold control, or otherwise.

---

[11] See *Appendix VII* for proposals of Col. Malcolm C. Rorty, H. B. Brougham, E. F. Harvey, and Byron DeForest.

[12] See *Appendix VII* for the anti-hoarding plan of Silvio Gesell. In the same *Appendix* will also be found fuller details, including a number of stabilization and reflation methods not mentioned in this chapter.

CHAPTER XI

THE WORLD MOVEMENT FOR STABLE MONEY

NOT ALTOGETHER NEW

TWENTY-ONE hundred years after Pythagoras, and a century after Copernicus, Galileo was still afraid to tell people that the earth was round, not for fear of religious persecution (as commonly supposed) but for fear of public ridicule.

French peasants who have tuberculosis still shut their windows lest fresh air be allowed to get in and make them worse; and a generation ago, all the rest of us refused to believe that "a bad cold" (as tuberculosis seemed to be) could be cured by the air, which we had always been taught to shut out—what else were houses for?

Perhaps the lag between the acquisition of knowledge and its general acceptance was shorter in the case of tuberculosis than in that of astronomy, because its application was of practical importance. The question of stabilizing the dollar lies in an intermediate region. It is immensely important, since the instability of money is a major cause of poverty and of the diseases (including tuberculosis) which go with poverty; but, as in the case of astronomical truth, the disposition to see the truth about the dollar is forestalled by a very definite illusion. On the whole, the progress of the movement for a revamped and safeguarded monetary unit (dollar, franc, pound, mark) has been

143

gratifying. We haven't yet arrived, but we have been going for only about a hundred years!

In 1824, John Rooke [1] proposed that the price of gold be so regulated as to counteract variations in the wages of farm labor (which were visible even without an index number).

In 1879, in *The North American Review* for September, Simon Newcomb, the famous astronomer who was also the author of an excellent treatise on economics, published an article called "The Standard of Value." In this he proposed with considerable detail what has since been called the "compensated dollar" plan.

In 1888 Knut Wicksell,[2] a Swedish economist, proposed an elaborate scheme for regulating discount rates; and he cited on this point a still earlier work by Weiss. The compensated dollar plan and other plans for stabilization were described by the distinguished English economist, Alfred Marshall in 1887. One of these was in principle the same as the "Open Market Policy." In 1898, Alfred Russel Wallace, the naturalist, made a plea for stabilizing money by means of a managed currency. Many famous economists, such as Carl Menger, Charles Gide, and E. Benjamin Andrews, anticipated the "managed currency" proposals which Professor Keynes is now urging with so much ability.

Today, though there is not yet full agreement as to methods, the necessity of stabilizing the world's monetary units is affirmed by such economists and business men as:

(in England) Sir Josiah Stamp, once professor of economics and now chairman of one of the largest railways in England, and a director of the Bank of England; Reginald McKenna, who has been chancellor of the British

---

[1] In *Inquiry into the Principles of National Wealth*, Edinburgh, 1824.
[2] In *Geldzins und Gütepreise*.

Exchequer and is now Chairman of the Joint City and Midland Bank; Lord D'Abernon, a banker—once Britain's minister to Germany; John Maynard Keynes, the economist who represented Britain at Versailles and who foretold the economic consequences of the treaty made there; and the Honorable Pethick-Lawrence, formerly a member of Parliament; (in Germany) Professor Schulze-Gaevernitz; (in Sweden) Professor Gustav Cassel, who was an official adviser to the League of Nations; (in Norway) Professor Ragnar Frisch; (in America) Professor E. W. Kemmerer, Professor John R. Commons, and many others.

In 1919, in America, a Stable Money League was formed which later became the Stable Money Association.

THE PRESENT WORLD MOVEMENT

During the World War, there began to be a demand to put theory into practice. A committee of the American Economic Association on the Purchasing Power of Money in War Time (including E. W. Kemmerer, Royal Meeker, Wesley Clair Mitchell, and Warren M. Persons) reported as follows: "The Committee regards the stabilizing of the value of monetary units under international agreement as desirable and economically feasible. The details of the plan, the time of its introduction and the question whether international agreement is indispensable should receive the immediate attention of statesmen and economists."

After the war, in 1922, at Genoa, the representatives of 35 nations unanimously adopted a resolution, reading in part as follows: "The essential requisite for the economic reconstruction of Europe is the achievement, by each country, of stability in the value of its currency," and suggested specific steps "to avoid those wide fluctuations in the purchasing power of gold which might otherwise result . . ."

The Dawes Reparation Plan contained a provision (due chiefly to Sir Josiah Stamp) for varying the amounts to be required of Germany, according as the price level might vary. Unfortunately, this was not incorporated in the Young Plan.

The Central Bank of Sweden is reported to have adopted a definite stabilization policy for Sweden, making use of a new index number for their guidance, and, an, article in a Swedish Journal,[3] applauding the movement, bespeaks a similar declaration by Britain.

Both Sweden and Britain and many other countries are, at this writing, off the gold standard, and Honorable Pethick-Lawrence asks their cooperation, remarking that many of them have already chosen to link themselves to the paper pound rather than gold as an international standard. He testifies to the benefits of a regulated currency in England since she was forced off the gold standard, in so far as a rise of prices followed, and predicts that Britain may not return to gold, unless gold, too, shall submit to regulation—or, as he puts it, become "a constitutional sovereign which shall no longer possess arbitrary power, but shall guide the destinies of nations according to the people's will."

In the opinion of many, it has been Britain's intention "to institute a system of stabilization of the price level, when prices have reached a position at which they yield an adequate margin of profit and when unemployment has fallen well below a million." [4] Indeed, in 1931, in a report made to Parliament by the Macmillan Committee on Finance and Industry, headed by Lord Macmillan, it was said: [5] "Our objective should be, so far as it lies within the

[3] *Skandinaviska Kreditaktiebolaget*, No. 4, October 1931, article on "The Suspension of the Gold Standard."

[4] From a private letter to the present writer.

[5] June, 1931, pp. 117–8.

power of this country to influence the international price level, first of all to raise prices a long way above the present level, and then to maintain them at the level thus reached with as much stability as can be managed. We recommend that this objective be accepted as the guiding aim of the monetary policy of this country. The acceptance of such an objective will represent in itself a great and notable change. For, before the war, scarcely anyone considered that the price level could or ought to be the care and preoccupation, far less the main objective, of policy, on the part of the Bank of England or any other Central bank."

Once in the Taft Administration a resolution for the purpose of calling an international conference on price levels passed the Senate but reached the House too late to be acted upon before the expiration of the Congress in 1913.

On May 14, 1932, a sub-committee of the House Committee on Coinage, Weights and Measures recommended that the President call an international monetary conference. In June, Premier MacDonald inquired of our State Department (which replied favorably) whether the United States would consider an international conference on raising and stabilizing commodity price levels. Later the official invitations were received and accepted, the conference being called by the League of Nations, and the subjects to be discussed including almost all the problems of world economics including price levels.

THE AMERICAN LEGISLATIVE MOVEMENT

The Federal Reserve Act was first known as the Glass-Owen bill, and in 1913, in one of its first drafts, there was a stabilization clause which originated with Senator Owen. This, however, was taken out by the conferees who represented the House.

Congressman Husted in 1919 introduced a bill for stabilization; and afterwards similar measures were proposed by Congressman Dallinger, Congressman Goldsborough (1922) and Congressman Strong (1926). On both of these last two bills there were extensive hearings, public interest in which, though slight at first, has grown with remarkable speed.

There has recently been in America a degree of genuine popular pressure for legislative action along these lines. The American Farm Bureau Federation has had a stabilization committee for several years. This society and the other two leading farm organizations (the National Farmers' Union and the National Grange) have given active support to stabilization proposals; and the same is true to some extent of the labor organizations, including the American Federation of Labor.

THE FEDERAL RESERVE EFFORTS

Meanwhile some actual, though quiet—almost secret—efforts toward stabilization have been made through the Federal Reserve System. The late Benjamin Strong, Governor of the New York Federal Reserve Bank, formed an unofficial committee, consisting of himself and the heads of four other Reserve Banks, for the purpose, among other things, of using the open market policy to prevent the inflation which then threatened. Mr. Strong's committee was later taken over by the Federal Reserve Board and enlarged into a conference including the heads of all the Federal Reserve Banks. But, except Governor Strong, the members of this conference have never very definitely accepted the basic idea of stabilization.

Governor Strong himself was loth, publicly and specifically, to favor stabilization, and is even on record as opposing a bill in Congress for that purpose. But before he died, he privately expressed his acquiescence and helped frame the last draft of the bill. He also declared himself as willing to avow his approval publicly, provided the Federal Reserve Board would avow theirs, which, however, they withheld. The bill was that of Congressman James C. Strong (not a relative of Governor Strong).

THE GOLDSBOROUGH BILL OF 1932

Nevertheless, for ten years, Congressman Strong and Congressman T. Alan Goldsborough have kept an educational movement alive in the House of Representatives; and, at last, in 1932, the Goldsborough bill, designed principally to requisition the rediscount and open market policies for the express service of the country's price level, was brought to a vote.

Of course, the Goldsborough bill was only a first step. A perfect monetary system for America would not rely solely on the Federal Reserve System. It would put the currency as a whole—not deposit currency alone—under the control of a permanent agency, say a commission devoted to that single purpose. The duties of such a commission would not be complicated by personal side-issues, such as those which beset a bank manager. On the other hand, it would have the cooperation of bank managers and of all those government agencies whose functions bear on the currency. There would be the cooperation of the Bureau of Labor Statistics for computing the index number of prices, and also for studying wages and other matters. There would be the cooperation of the Treasury and the mint, and, above all, of the Federal Reserve System. The commission would also cooperate with local, foreign and international banks. Further details for such a commission will be found in Appendix VI.

The House passed the Goldsborough bill by an overwhelming vote: 289 to 60. But despite powerful support, including that of Farm and Labor organizations, the bill failed in the Senate when it came before the Committee on Banking and Currency. Senator Glass, whose influence when he was in the House, in 1913, had eliminated the stabilization clause from the Glass-Owen bill (which became the Federal Reserve Act), was chiefly responsible for the failure of the Goldsborough bill.

The bill aroused opposition and a fear that it would force the United States off the Gold Standard and embark on unrestrained German inflation. This fear was especially evident abroad. It was due partly to real reason, the precarious gold situation, and the seeming impossibility of raising the price level as high as the 1921–9 level specified, but partly and chiefly to misunderstanding and consequent misrepresentation which unduly excited a public mind already rendered over-excitable by the prolonged depression.

OPPOSITION TO THE GOLDSBOROUGH BILL

The opponents of the Goldsborough bill said that it sought to regulate prices contrary to the "law of supply and demand." Those who glibly used this phrase did not realize that supply and demand presuppose a price level,[6] nor did they understand the distinction between individual prices and the scale of prices.

Even less reasonable were those who denounced the Goldsborough bill as "inflation." When the bill was introduced, the country's malady was *de*flation; and deflation

[6] See, for instance, *Elementary Principles of Economics*, by Irving Fisher, Macmillan, 1928.

can be cured only by a certain amount of "reflation"; that is, inflation justified as counteracting recent, rapid and great deflation. But "inflation" is a word with a bad history; and the economic illiteracy betrayed by those who used it was all the more dangerous because they used an historic word.

Many of those who decried the Goldsborough bill as inflationary were themselves explicit champions of what Mr. Ogden Mills, Secretary of the Treasury, has described (and proposed) as "controlled credit expansion." Controlled credit expansion and controlled inflation (or reflation) are one and the same thing. Controlled inflation was the very purpose of the open market bond purchases which the Federal Reserve Banks had been carrying on, and these open market operations had the support of many conservative bankers. The official publication of the National City Bank in May, 1932, said, "the effort to revive business and raise the price level should have support everywhere. The Reserve System is giving the lead."

Finally, some held that the Goldsborough bill would put too much power in the hands of a small committee sitting in Washington. But the Federal Reserve Board already has the power and already has done sufficient harm, both by exercising it and failing to exercise it, inasmuch as they exercised it and failed to exercise it without due reference to the price level. The Goldsborough bill would commit them to the price level expressly; and the price level would serve at any rate as a limit to their power, which is now *unlimited* so far as concerns credit expansion and contraction—that is, inflation and deflation. A former member of the Federal Reserve Board has characterized the Federal Reserve System as "rudderless." It is a case of power without direction.

OUR DOLLAR'S BAD RECORD

The greatest absurdity of all, however, is the claim (implied in all this obstruction) that sound money is the kind of money we have been having for all these tortured generations. The first requirement for soundness is stability; and the purchasing power of a dollar is stable in proportion as the price level is stable. How stable that has been may be judged from the following chart of its history from 1860 to 1932 (chart 6).

This crooked line should some day serve as an inscription on the gravestone of unstable money. It is largely responsible for countless actual gravestones of children starved and of men killed in the wars between capital and labor; for these wars were generated in large part by this crooked line. Every dip in the line, including the numberless minor jogs, means thousands of debtors cheated (unconsciously) by their creditors; and every climb of the line means thousands of creditors cheated (unconsciously) by their debtors. In both the debtor and the creditor camps there have been both rich and poor. A poor debtor, for instance, builds a cabin with the help of a mortgage. He borrows $1,000 in 1865; and in 1896, having paid all the interest, he pays the principal—$1,000 that are worth over 3,000 of the 1865 dollars which he had borrowed. And for an example of a poor creditor, take a person who in 1896 put $100 in the savings bank, and in 1920 draws out (including compound interest) $256 that are worth 77 of the 1896 dollars which he had deposited.

If we treat the 1913 dollar as 100 cents, then the follow-

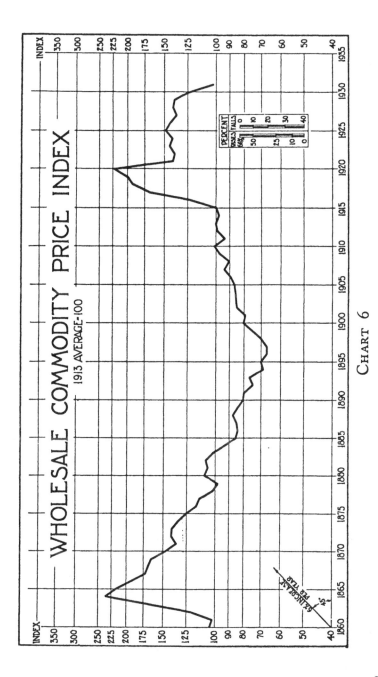

CHART 6

213

ing schedule shows the various buying powers which the
dollar has had at various times since 1860.

in	1860,	it	was	96	cents
in Jan.	1865,	"	"	47	cents
in	1896,	"	"	150	cents
in	1913,	"	"	100	cents
in May	1920,	"	"	45	cents
in	1922,	"	"	72	cents
in	1923,	"	"	69	cents
in	1924,	"	"	70	cents
in	1929,	"	"	71	cents
in	1930,	"	"	81	cents
in	1931,	"	"	98	cents
March 19,	1932,	"	"	111	cents
the third week of June,	1932,	"	"	118	cents

Or, if the 1929 dollar was 100 cents, then the dollar of
the third week of June, 1932, was $1.62.

Nor does this take into account what happened abroad,
in and after the World War, in the way of "calamity
booms," as the Germans called them—which wiped out
the middle classes—many by death, including suicide, because their incomes (consisting of salaries or of interest on
bonds) did not rise when the price level did. In Britain,
between 1913 and 1920, the price level rose more than
3 fold; in France, more than 5¼ fold; in Italy, more
than 6½ fold; in Austria, between 1914 and 1922, more
than 17,000 fold, which, in 1925, became more than
21,000 fold; in Russia, by 1922, over 4,000,000 fold, and
this, in 1923, became more than 6,000,000,000 fold. In
Germany, for 1920, the rise was only 15 fold, but at the

peak of inflation in 1923 it went far above the astronomical figure of a trillion fold.[7]

In its relation to monetary derangements (which are themselves almost as cruel as war) war is the greatest obstacle to the movement for stable money. There is no money device which war will not wreck. War debts, war inflation, and post-war deflation are all on too large a scale to be checked by delicate machinery.

But there is no reason why the same cure that was effectively applied to frontier brawls should not be applied to war—that is, judicial machinery; for war, like frontier gun-play, is a crude form of litigation, which must always go on so long as there is anything to litigate and nothing else to litigate it with. War guilt is not in my department, but I believe that no scholar now assigns the entire guilt of the World War to any one nation. Some assign it almost or quite entirely to what G. Lowes Dickinson calls "The International Anarchy," [8] under which nations had to conduct their commercial rivalry. To avoid war, the balance of power became a sort of insurance policy; and, for a time, it did preserve the peace; but sooner or later it had to turn bad—no balance of power can stay put; and, when it began to slip, all the great powers of Europe, according to this view, reluctantly chose war as the less of two evils.

Since the international forms of litigation are a thousand years behind the municipal forms, the first step for the purpose of superseding war must, of course, be quasi-judicial—not yet fully judicial.

[7] December, 1923—1,261,560,000,000 fold. Another official figure (November 1923) 1,422,900,000,000 fold.

[8] In his book by that name.

The threat of Socialism (if it deserves to be called a threat) is, of course, often made by those who would stir people to the need of making things better. But the threat seems to become more logical every year; witness Russia since 1919, and Chile in 1932.

Both war and the unstable dollar (with its hunger and its strikes) play into the hands of Socialism. What we call the Capitalistic Sys⁺ might better be called the System of Private Profits; and a depression, being a profit disease, is one to which Capitalism is peculiarly liable. So typical an exponent of Capitalism as Nicholas Murray Butler has recently affirmed that the system is on trial today. His remark, if he is right, can only portend that, unless Capitalism shall clean house by taking the dirt of depression out of profits, some form of Socialism may tear the house completely down. For profits are always at the mercy of the unstable dollar,—always in danger of disappearing *en masse* whenever the price level shrinks, while debts and debt service do not.

Socialistic thinkers of all degrees make common cause against private profits, and add that, without such profits, crises would disappear. Accordingly, in 1929–32, the plight of the capitalistic world drew a good deal of derision from the Russians, who, though not prosperous, were apparently going up while we were going down. I shall not here debate the comparative merits of the two systems. Capitalism boasts of its rewards for initiative; Socialism claims a less selfish stimulus for the same virtue. But, for the present purpose, suffice it that each system has been compelled to borrow from the other. The capitalistic system, for instance, is not wholly capitalistic: witness government itself; witness public schools, the post office, and the Panama

Canal. On the other hand, Russia, which furnishes the only large-scale example of a socialistic experiment, has, in ten years, drifted perhaps as far toward Capitalism as we, in a thousand years, have drifted toward Socialism.

Meanwhile,—to close this book with the quotation with which it began—Sir Josiah Stamp, in the introduction which he was so kind as to write to the English edition of my little book, *The Money Illusion*, puts it thus: "Money, as a physical medium of exchange, made a diversified civilization possible . . . and yet it is money, in its mechanical even more than its spiritual effects, which may well, having brought us to the present level, actually destroy society."

POSTSCRIPT

As this book goes to press (September, 1932) recovery seems to be in sight. In the course of about two months, stocks have nearly doubled in price and commodities have risen 5½. European stock prices were the first to rise, and European buyers were among the first to make themselves felt in the American market.

These developments might be due to various causes, including an increase in the volume or velocity of currency, or both. In fact, velocity increased while volume (at first) slightly decreased. This paradox, signalling a rise in prices, is the opposite of the one that signalled the fall. Confidence was aroused, partly by the virtual cancellation at Lausanne of German Reparations, and partly by our announced preparations for reflation. These un-froze some of the hoards and raised prices; and the increased value of collateral encouraged some debtors, who had been hanging on, to liquidate, thus temporarily reducing the volume of credit currency. But the stage is set for further reflation through such measures as: the recent Glass inflation Act, allowing an increase in bank notes; the Glass-Steagall Act, in February, "freeing" gold; the consequent open market operations of the Federal Reserve System on an unprecedented scale; the credit operations of the Reconstruction Finance Corporation; the Home Loan Banks Act, and other reflationary measures. The banks had achieved "liquidity." Gold, also, has begun to flow back from Europe.

If the end of the great depression is really at hand, it will be the result, apparently, of human effort more than a mere pendulum reaction.

But the most noteworthy recent case of human effort to control the price level is that of Sweden. The programme mentioned on page 146 of this book has, according to Professor Cassel, "been carried through with complete success. The present purchasing power of the Swedish currency is, within the limits of unavoidable statistical error, just the same as it was in September last. This achievement is of great importance. It shows that a deliberate regulation of the purchasing power of a paper currency is possible and that a Central Bank actually can, by a suitable policy, control this value." [9]

[9] See *Quarterly Report* of the Statistical Department of the bank "Skandinaviska Kreditaktiebolaget," Gothenburg, Stockholm, Malnö, Sweden, July, 1932.

APPENDICES

APPENDIX I

APPROXIMATE TYPICAL CHRONOLOGY OF THE NINE FACTORS

The following table of our nine factors, occurring and recurring (together with distress selling), gives a fairly typical, though still inadequate, picture of the cross-currents of a depression in the approximate order in which it is believed they usually occur. (The first occurrence of each factor and its subdivisions is indicated by italics. The figures in parenthesis show the sequence in the original exposition.)

I (7) Mild *Gloom* and Shock to *Confidence*
   (8) Slightly *Reduced Velocity* of Circulation
   (1) Debt *Liquidation*

II (9) *Money Interest Falls* on Safe Loans
   (9) but Money Interest Rises on Unsafe Loans

III (2) *Distress Selling*
   (7) More Gloom
   (3) *Fall in Security Prices*
   (1) More Liquidation
   (3) *Fall in Commodity Prices*

IV (9) *Real Interest Rises*; REAL DEBTS INCREASE
   (7) More Pessimism and Distrust
   (1) More Liquidation
   (2) More Distress Selling
   (8) More Reduction in Velocity

161

V (2) More Distress Selling
(2) *Contraction of Deposit Currency*
(3) Further Dollar Enlargement

VI (4) *Reduction in Net-Worth*
(4) Increase in *Bankruptcies*
(7) More Pessimism and Distrust
(8) More Slowing in Velocity
(1) More Liquidation

VII (5) *Decrease in Profits*
(5) *Increase in Losses*
(7) Increase in Pessimism
(8) Slower Velocity
(1) More Liquidation
(6) *Reduction in volume of stock trading*

VIII (6) *Decrease in Construction*
(6) *Reduction in Output*
(6) *Reduction in Trade*
(6) *Unemployment*
(7) More Pessimism

IX (8) *Hoarding*

X (8) *Runs on Banks*
(8) *Banks curtailing Loans* for self-protection
(8) *Banks selling Investments*
(8) *Bank Failures*
(7) Distrust Grows
(8) More Hoarding
(1) More Liquidation
(2) More Distress Selling
(3) Further Dollar Enlargement

As has been stated, this order (or any order, for that matter) can be only approximate and subject to variations at different times and places. It represents my present guess as to how, if not too much interfered with, the nine factors selected for explicit study in this book are likely in most cases to fall in line.

But, as has also been stated, the idea of a single-line succession is itself inadequate, for while Factor (1) acts on (2), for instance, it also acts directly on (7), so that we really need a picture of subdividing streams or, better, an interacting network in which each factor may be pictured as influencing and being influenced by many or all of the others.

SORTS OF DATA AVAILABLE ON THE NINE FACTORS

To answer adequately the questions raised in Chapter VI, statistical studies are needed. For this purpose, the following series are today available in more or less satisfactory form as raw material:

Debts:
  Brokers' loans from banks
  Brokers' loans "by others" (corporations, etc.)
  Bank collateral loans
  Other bank loans
  Installment sales loans
  Corporation bonds
  Farm mortgages
  Non-farm mortgages
  Municipal bonds
  State bonds
  Federal bonds
  Loans to and from abroad—intergovernmental and otherwise
  (All the above debts may be sub-classified as to length, security, etc.)
Money—Volume and Velocity:
  Individual bank deposits subject to check
  Velocity of bank deposits
  "Money in circulation"
  Hoarding
  Loan-liability ratios
  Investments of banks

164

Prices:

Prices of stocks classified as {
common, preferred
rails, industrials, utilities
listed, unlisted
}

Bonds (See "rates of interest")

Prices of Commodities classified as {
consumers', produc-
ers',
raw, semi-manufac-
tured, finished
agricultural, non-
agricultural
}

Prices of real estate
Rent
Wages

Net Worth:

Bank failures (number and the values involved)
Commercial failures (number and the values involved)

Profits:

Dividend payments
Corporation profits
Profit and earning ratios

Trade, Production, and Employment:

Trade Volume
Shares traded
Unfilled orders
Car loadings
Panama Canal traffic
Net ton miles freight carried

Trade value (volume multiplied by price)
Department store sales
Chain store sales
Farm crops marketed
Imports, exports
Postal receipts
Railway freight traffic receipts
Railway gross earnings
New securities issued

Real estate transfers
Life insurance
Advertising
New York clearings (and debits to individual accounts)
Outside clearings (and debits)
Output
   Pig iron production
   Coal, iron, copper, wool, cotton (produced or consumed)
     automobiles, certain other important items
   Number of blast furnaces in blast
   Electric power consumption
   Farm crops
   Live stock
Equipment
   Building permits
     Residential
     Commercial
     Factory
     Public works and utilities
     All other
Employment
   Numbers
   Payroll
   In all industries
   In specified industries
Rates of Interest:
   Call rates
   Commercial paper rates
   Rates on acceptances
   Rates realized on bonds
   Industrial
   Railroad
   Government
   Reserve Banks' Rediscount rates

The only one of the nine cyclical tendencies not represented in the foregoing list is the psychological sequence—the sequence

226

of confidence and discouragement. But these moods are more or less definitely registered by some of the other statistics, for instance, statistics of: hoarding; deposits subject to check; time deposits; deposits withdrawn from either class; exports of gold; the so-called "money in circulation"; velocity of circulation of bank deposits; the changing spread between high grade and low grade bonds; changing proportions of bank notes, Federal Reserve notes, and gold certificates.[1]

---

[1] See *The Journal of Political Economy*, Vol. XL, No. 1, February, 1932, "Distrust of Bank Deposits as Measured by Federal Reserve Note Issue," by Harold L. Reed.

STATISTICS OF DEBTS LEADING TO DEPRESSION OF 1929–32

INTERNATIONAL PRIVATE DEBTS

TABLE 3

PRIVATE AMERICAN LONG TERM INVESTMENTS ABROAD *

(millions)

1912	$ 1,902
1922	8,020
1923	8,877
1924	9,135
1925	10,004
1926	10,876
1927	11,684
1928	12,656
1929	13,973
1930	14,764
1931	15,170

* United States Department of Commerce. *A New Estimate of American Investments Abroad*, pp. 24–25.

PUBLIC DEBTS

The federal debt, which, of course, grew enormously during the war, declined (in dollars) quite rapidly until 1931 when new borrowings to meet deficits have again brought an increase of about 2 billion. From June 30, 1914, to June 30, 1919, the gross federal debt grew 21 fold.

State and local debts, in the six years between 1922 and

168

1928, increased by 76 per cent, or about 12⅔ per cent per year. The amount in 1922 was $7,153.6 million, in 1928, $12,608.7 million, and in 1932, $15,017.2 million (estimated).

The debts of the 146 cities of the United States having more than 30,000 inhabitants have been increasing heavily since 1903; and the debts of all the states have been increasing since 1913. The debts of these 146 cities increased from $2,319 million in 1903 to $7,192 million in 1929. Bankers have grown cautious and have refused to lend money to Chicago, Philadelphia, New York, and other debt ridden cities until these cities give evidence that extravagant and wasteful expenditures are eliminated.

The per capita debt (federal, state and local) grew rapidly up to 1919 when it reached the maximum, $291.95. It then declined to $246.08 in 1930 since which it has increased to $271.18 in December, 1931. Table 4, which follows, gives the estimates made by the National Industrial Conference Board [1] for state and local debts down to and including 1928. Estimates of these debts since 1928, made by Dr. Royal Meeker, are rough approximations but can not be greatly in error. The Conference Board has calculated the ratio of state and local debts to total national tangible wealth from 1922 to 1928. These ratios are interesting, but there is too much guess work as to total national wealth to make them trustworthy. According to the Board's estimates, the total public debt "per capital," i. e., per thousand dollars of wealth, increased from 1917 to 1919 more than 2½ times while the per capita debt increased nearly 5¼ times. The "per capital" debt reached its first peak in 1922, when it was 3½ times that in 1915. It declined sharply to 1925, rose somewhat to 1927, then declined again until 1929, since which it has risen 9 per cent in 1930 and 67 per cent by the end of December, 1931. From 1929 to 1930, the per capita debt declined slightly; and from 1929 to December, 1931, it increased only 8 per cent. (See Table 4.)

The story of public debts is even worse in other countries. In Germany practically all domestic public debts were wiped out

[1] *Cost of Government in the United States*, 1928–1929, p. 43.

TABLE 4

COMBINED FEDERAL STATE AND LOCAL DEBTS

Fiscal Year	State and Local Debts (millions)	Federal Debt (millions)	Combined Federal State Local Debts (millions)	Population (millions)	Combined Public Debt Per Capita *	Total Wealth in Current Dollars (billions)	Combined Public Debt Per Thousand Dollars
1915	$4,357.4	$1,191.3	$5,565.7	99.3	$56.05	$200.2	$27.80
1917	4,917.6	2,975.6	7,893.2	102.2	77.23	351.7	22.44
1919	5,173.8	25,482.0	30,655.8	105.0	291.95	431.0	71.13
1922	7,153.6	22,964.1	30,117.7	109.9	274.05	320.8	97.19
1925	9,802.7	20,516.3	30,319.0	115.4	262.73	362.4	83.66
1926	10,702.7	19,643.2	30,345.9	117.1	259.14	356.5	85.12
1927	11,717.8	18,510.2	30,228.0	118.6	254.87	346.4	87.26
1928	12,608.7	17,604.3	30,213.0	120.0	251.78	360.1	83.90
1929	13,365.2	16,931.2	30,296.0	121.4	249.56	361.8	83.74
1930	14,033.4	16,185.3	30,218.7	122.8	246.08	329.7	91.66
1931 (End of Dec.)	16,061.2	17,825.4	33,886.6	124.9	271.31	241.2	140.50

The figures on State and Local debts for 1915 to 1928 inclusive are taken from *Cost of Government in the United States, 1928–1929*, by the National Industrial Conference Board. Figures for these debts since 1928 are rough estimates.

Figures for total wealth are taken from the Conference Board Bulletin No. 62, February, 1932. Figures for the end of December 1931 are estimated by Dr. Royal Meeker. The estimate of total wealth is made on the assumption that tangible wealth was the same as in 1929 and that its value in current dollars declined one-third through the increase in the purchasing power of the business dollar.

* *In current dollars.*

230

by the "devaluation" of the mark at a trillion to 1. In Italy, France, Poland, Austria, and Russia the "devaluation" amounted to the repudiation of by far the larger portions of the domestic debts.

The growth of the British national and local debts in pounds sterling are shown in Table 5.

TABLE 5

PUBLIC DEBTS OF BRITAIN

	Total Debt of the United Kingdom	Total Debt of the Local Authorities	Grand Total of National and Local Debts
1914	£706,154,110	£562,630,045	£1,268,784,155
1915	. . . .	. . . .	. . . .
1916	. . . .	565,556,617	. . . .
1917	. . . .	557,983,804	. . . .
1918	5,921,095,819	550,508,799	6,471,604,618
1919	7,481,050,442	544,184,848	8,025,235,290
1920	7,875,641,961	555,145,292	8,430,787,253
1921	7,623,097,128	657,760,895	8,280,858,023
1922	7,720,532,214	768,566,752	8,489,098,966
1923	7,812,562,525	803,880,725	8,616,443,230
1924	7,707,537,545	820,262,540	8,527,800,085
1925	7,665,880,145	864,882,330	8,530,762,475
1926	7,633,722,502	934,656,498	8,568,379,000
1927	7,652,687,904	1,027,857,547	8,680,545,451
1928	7,630,972,670	1,121,258,965	8,752,231,635
1929	7,620,853,547	1,174,984,992	8,795,838,539
1930	7,596,210,899	. . . .	. . . .
1931	7,582,899,661	. . . .	. . . .

Source: Statistical Abstract for the United Kingdom, 1932, pp. 140, 196–7.

AMERICAN FARM MORTGAGES

So far as there is truth in the theory of over-production as a cause of this depression, it applies particularly to our farms, though it must be borne in mind that over-production was an effect before it became a cause. But on the farms, its effects were real. Conveniences and luxuries you can buy forever, if you have the money. Food you buy only so far as you are hungry. In this respect, the present depression differs from that of 1921. In 1921 there was little agricultural over-production. True, in both cases, agricultural prices fell; but in 1930 they fell much more than they would have fallen had it not been for increased production. Increased acreage brought under the plough by the high prices of 1917–1920 and improvements in agriculture have hurt the farmers by driving prices below costs of production.

One other handicap was more or less peculiar to the farmer. When the time came to reduce acreage, he revealed his immobility. By sticking to his farm through thick and thin, he became further the victim of his debts. Between 1910 and 1928 (including an inflation as well as a deflation period) farm values rose, in the net, from $35.6 billion to $43 billion; but mortgage debts, during the same period, rose faster: from $3,600 million to $9,500 million. The net result was that, in 1910, farmers' equities were 90 per cent of the values of all farms, mortgaged and unmortgaged, and in 1928 only 78 per cent. (See Table 6.)

TABLE 6

FARM MORTGAGES *

Year	Amount (millions)	Value of Farms (millions)	Percentage of Debt to Value
1910	$3,599.0	$35,600	10 per cent
1920	7,857.7		
1925	9,360.6		
1928	9,468.5	43,000	22 per cent
1930	9,400.0		

* Compiled from *Year Book of Agriculture*, 1931; and mimeographed sheet, "Total Farm Mortgage Debts in the United States" prepared by the United States Department of Agriculture.
See Report of the Secretary of Agriculture for 1931, p. 31.

The results are worse in terms of the farmer's dollar than shown in the table. The real debt burden upon farmers has increased more than is shown by these figures. The prices of the products farmers sell have been reduced to 45 per cent of the prices in 1929,[2] whereas all commodities have declined only to 65 per cent. Since the "farmer's produce dollar" has become $2.20, this nominal "decrease" of 20 per cent in money mortgage debts is a real increase of about 75 per cent in the farmer's real mortgage debt burden. For other agricultural loans the increase in *real* debt is 111 per cent.

MORTGAGES OTHER THAN FARM MORTGAGES

The report made by Professors John H. Gray and George W. Terborgh for the Real Estate Research Committee of the Brookings Institution in Washington [3] presents the available information of the holdings of non-farm first mortgages by various institutions, roughly as follows: building and loan associations, $6.6 billion; mutual savings banks, $4.8 billion; life insurance companies, $4 billion; all other banks, $6.4 billion. The authors add: "How incomplete this calculation is, becomes apparent when we realize that no account whatever is taken of the mortgage holdings of mortgage companies, fire and casualty insurance companies, educational and other institutions, foundations, trustees, and individual investors . . . but it is certain that in the aggregate they are large. It seems indeed a safe conclusion that first mortgages on non-farm real estate in the United States total over 25 billions of dollars."

This estimate excludes all second mortgages and other junior mortgages. It surely is conservative to estimate the total non-farm mortgage debt in 1928 at not less than $29.5 billion and in 1929 at $37 billion.

If we can assume that the growth in total mortgage indebtedness has been equal to the growth in mortgages held by building and loan associations alone, then the total non-farm mortgage debt in 1920 was about $9.6 billion and the percentage increase up to 1929 was more than three fold. The decline

[2] See *Crop Reporter*, February, 1932, p. 87.
[3] *First Mortgages in Urban Real Estate Finance*, by John H. Gray and George W. Terborgh, Washington, D. C., 1929.

from 1929 to the beginning of 1932 in all types of non-farm mortgages is estimated to be $11 billion which probably errs on the side of conservatism.

CORPORATE LONG AND SHORT DEBTS

There is no dependable measure of total corporate indebtedness and the changes therein. New and refunding issues of all types of corporate securities are reported by the *Commercial and Financial Chronicle,* but there is no way of calculating the amount of long term and short term debts retired. Carl Snyder estimated total corporate bonds at 30 to 40 billion dollars in 1926. If this is accurate, it would seem to suggest a total of long term bonds and short term bonds and notes of about $65 billion in 1929. Professor G. F. Warren quotes Mr. E. White, Chief Statistician, Office of the Commissioner of Internal Revenue, as authority for the figure of $76,096 million for corporate liabilities in 1929. The decline in these corporate dollar debts since 1929 has probably been not less than $11,414 million or 15 per cent.

Corporate bonds, both new issues and refunding issues, were at a low of 23.1 per cent of all security issues in 1919. The proportion increased to 41.6 per cent in 1920 and to 79.1 per cent in 1921, when industry was at the bottom of the slump following the crash of 1920. The percentage of long term bonds declined continuously until 1926 and 1927 when it rose slightly to 66.9 and 68.7 per cent respectively. In 1928, when the stock market boom was fully under way, the proportion of long term bonds suddenly slumped to 45.8 per cent while the percentage of common stock shot up from 10.5 per cent to 30.2 per cent. In 1929 bonds fell to 25.3 while common stock skyrocketed to 53.9 per cent. In 1930, the first year after the big crash, the proportions had become reversed, 56.7 per cent being long term bonds and 22.3 per cent common stock, while in 1931 they were 68.7 per cent and 8.2 per cent, respectively.

The slump in the proportion of common stock and the increase in long term and short term bonds and notes has con-

TABLE 7

CORPORATE DOMESTIC SECURITY ISSUES 1919 TO 1931

(millions of dollars)

	Total Domestic Corporate Issues	LONG TERM BONDS		SHORT TERM NOTES		PREFERRED STOCK		COMMON STOCK	
		Amount	Per Cent of Total	Amount	Per Cent of Total	Amount	Per Cent of Total	Amount	Per Cent of Total
1919	$2,739.7	$ 633.7	23.1	$540.2	19.8			$1,565.8	57.1
1920	2,966.3	1,234.4	41.6	660.8	22.3			1,071.1	36.1
1921	2,419.8	1,915.2	79.1	226.4	9.4			278.2	11.5
1922	2,949.2	2,195.0	74.4	133.8	4.5	$ 332.8	11.3	287.8	9.8
1923	3,178.9	2,262.5	71.2	180.5	5.6	406.7	12.2	329.2	10.4
1924	3,520.8	2,319.5	65.9	335.7	9.5	346.1	9.8	519.6	14.8
1925	4,222.1	2,667.3	63.2	308.0	7.3	636.8	15.1	610.1	14.4
1926	4,573.7	3,059.1	66.9	294.5	6.4	543.6	11.9	676.6	14.8
1927	6,506.9	4,466.2	68.7	302.5	4.6	1,054.7	16.2	683.5	10.5
1928	6,930.2	3,174.1	45.8	264.9	3.8	1,397.1	20.2	2,094.1	30.2
1929	9,376.6	2,369.4	25.3	250.6	2.7	1,694.7	18.1	5,061.8	53.9
1930	4,957.1	2,810.3	56.7	620.3	12.5	421.3	8.5	1,105.0	22.3
1931	2,371.2	1,628.0	68.7	400.1	16.9	148.0	6.2	195.1	8.2

Compiled from statistics published in the *Commercial and Financial Chronicle*.

tinued in 1932 as is shown by comparing the January and February issues in 1931 with 1932. (See Chart 7 and Tables 7 and 8.)

TABLE 8

CORPORATE DOMESTIC SECURITY ISSUES, JANUARY 1931 AND 1932 AND
FEBRUARY 1931 AND 1932

	Total Domestic Corporate Issues	LONG TERM BONDS		SHORT TERM NOTES	
		Amount	Per Cent	Amount	Per Cent
Jan. 1931	460,706,279	392,235,000	85.1	23,168,750	5.0
Jan. 1932	48,163,750	41,345,000	85.8	2,400,000	5.0
Feb. 1931	88,225,944	48,420,000	54.9	13,040,100	14.9
Feb. 1932	44,550,775	30,138,000	67.6	10,600,000	23.8

	Total Domestic Corporate Issues	PREFERRED STOCK		COMMON STOCK	
		Amount	Per Cent	Amount	Per Cent
Jan. 1931	460,706,279	26,503,779	5.8	18,798,750	4.1
Jan. 1932	48,163,750	4,250,000	8.8	168,750	.4
Feb. 1931	88,225,944	7,509,000	8.5	19,256,844	21.8
Feb. 1932	44,550,775	2,312,775	5.2	1,500,000	3.4

BANK LOANS AND DISCOUNTS

Investments of all banks increased from $5,541 million in June, 1914, to the peak of $17,801 million in June, 1928, an increase of nearly 3¼ times. They declined to $16,634 million in 1929 which was a three-fold increase over 1914. Investments slowly increased after December, 1929, to a new peak of $19,637 million in June, 1931, since which they have slowly ebbed to $18,481 million in December, 1931, which is 18 per cent above October, 1929.

The loans by Federal Reserve member banks reached the

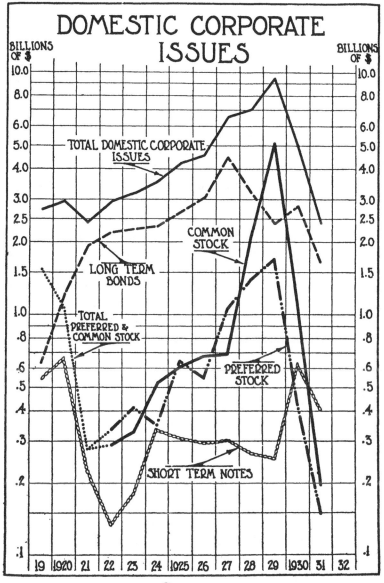

CHART 7

237

peak in October, 1929, at $26,165 million, a four-fold increase over December, 1914 ($6,419 million) and very nearly 50 per cent over December, 1922 ($17,930 million). The rates of increase correspond very closely to the rates for all banks combined.

The decline of 26 per cent to $19,261 million at the end of December, 1931, brought their loans to the lowest figure since June, 1924.

The percentage declines in loans for all banks and for Reserve member banks are nearly identical.

We may here note, in passing, that bank deposits (demand plus time), which are directly related to bank loans and investments, reached their maximum for all banks in December, 1928, at $56,766,000,000—an increase of three-fold since 1914 and of 50 per cent since 1922. No available figures exist for demand deposits outside of the Federal Reserve System. The net demand deposits of Federal Reserve member banks alone reached the peak in November, 1929, at $19,979 million which is an increase of more than three-fold over December, 1914, and nearly 24 per cent more than December, 1922.[4]

The trend has been steadily downward since 1929. The figure for November, 1931, was $16,358 million, a decrease of 18 per cent from the peak. Demand deposits had sunk in February, 1932, to $14,789 million, 26 per cent below the peak, the lowest figure since March, 1922.

The percentage increases and decreases in loans on the one hand and demand deposits on the other are almost identical.

Beginning in December, 1929, Reserve Bank credit fell until, from February to July, 1931, it was about $525 million below the average for October, 1929. This great drop in credit nearly counterbalanced the entire increase of $577 million in gold imports during this period. After July, 1931, Reserve Bank credit increased $996 million from July to December, 1931, but member bank reserve balances declined $338 million. This decline in reserve balances was almost entirely due to with-

[4] See "Reports of the Federal Reserve Board" for 1930, pp. 94 and 95, and "Federal Reserve Bulletins" for June, 1931 and for April, 1932.

drawals of gold for export and the increase of money "in circulation" which resulted from the large number of bank failures and the loss of confidence in the stability of the dollar, and in the solvency of our whole banking system both at home and abroad. (See Tables 9 and 10, also Chart 4 in Chapter VIII.)

TABLE 9

LOANS, INVESTMENTS AND TOTAL DEPOSITS

All Banks in the United States

(millions of dollars)

	Loans		Investments		Total Deposits Excluding Inter-bank Deposits	
	June 30	Dec. 31	June 30	Dec. 31	June 30	Dec. 31
1913						
14	15,248		5,541		18,566	
15	15,643		5,823		19,131	
16	17,961		6,626		22,759	
17	20,510		7,777		26,352	
18	22,392		9,421		28,765	
19	24,710		11,860		33,603	
20	30,824		10,861		37,721	
21	28,970		11,029		35,742	
22	27,732		12,224		37,615	
23	30,378	30,778	13,360	13,225	40,688	42,163
24	31,523	32,440	13,657	14,742	43,405	45,853
25	33,865	35,640	14,965	14,963	47,612	49,224
26	36,157	36,759	15,404	15,260	49,733	50,029
27	37,360	38,407	16,391	17,043	51,662	52,909
28	39,464	40,763	17,801	17,504	53,398	56,766
29	41,512	41,898	16,962	16,519	53,852	55,289
30	40,618	38,135	17,490	18,074	54,954	53,039
31	35,384	31,616	19,637	18,481	51,782	46,261

Source: Annual Report Federal Reserve Board, 1930, pp. 89–90, tables 42–43 and Federal Reserve Bulletin, April, 1932, p. 297.

TABLE 10

LOANS AND DEPOSITS OF ALL MEMBER BANKS

(in millions)

Call Date	Loans*	Invest- ments	Net Demand Plus Time Deposits†	Net Demand Deposits	Time De- posits‡
1914—Dec. 31	6,419	2,079	7,468	6,235	1,233
1915—June 23	6,720	2,044	8,163	6,811	1,352
Dec. 31	7,622	2,239	9,477	7,971	1,506
1916—June 30	7,964	2,351	10,001	8,226	1,775
Dec. 27	8,714	2,561	11,485	9,502	1,983
1917—June 30	9,370	3,083	11,993	9,690	2,304
Dec. 31	12,316	4,580	15,643	12,487	3,156
1918—June 29	13,233	5,274	15,612	12,217	3,395
Dec. 31	14,224	6,368	18,397	14,563	3,834
1919—June 30	15,414	6,827	19,069	14,725	4,344
Dec. 31	18,149	6,630	21,881	16,576	5,305
1920—June 30	19,533	6,026	22,333	16,422	5,911
Dec. 29	19,555	5,976	21,533	15,345	6,188
1921—June 30	18,119	6,002	20,688	14,321	6,367
Dec. 31	17,394	6,088	20,900	14,449	6,451
1922—June 30	17,165	7,017	22,714	15,539	7,175
Dec. 29	17,930	7,649	23,848	16,203	7,645
1923—June 30	18,750	7,757	24,444	16,066	8,378
Dec. 31	18,842	7,645	25,027	16,376	8,651
1924—June 30	19,204	7,963	26,042	16,838	9,204
Dec. 31	19,933	8,813	28,273	18,468	9,805
1925—June 30	20,655	8,863	28,650	18,277	10,381
Dec. 31	21,996	8,888	29,913	19,260	10,653
1926—June 30	22,060	9,123	29,977	18,804	11,173
Dec. 31	22,652	8,990	30,362	18,922	11,440

* Includes rediscounts and overdrafts; excludes acceptances of other banks and bills of exchange sold with indorsement.

† Deposits subject to reserve requirements.

‡ Includes postal-savings deposits, except that such deposits of State bank members prior to June 20, 1917, are included with demand deposits.
Source: Seventeenth Annual Report of the Federal Reserve Board, for the year 1930, pp. 94–5; Federal Reserve Bulletin, May, 1932, p. 296.

Call Date	Loans	Invest-ments	Net Demand Plus Time Deposits	Net Demand Deposits	Time De-posits
1927—June 30	22,938	9,818	31,460	19,250	12,210
Dec. 31	23,886	10,361	32,870	20,105	12,765
1928—June 30	24,303	10,758	32,629	19,191	13,439
Dec. 31	25,155	10,529	33,397	19,944	13,453
1929—June 29	25,658	10,052	32,302	18,977	13,325
Oct. 4	26,165	9,749	32,269	18,952	13,318
Dec. 31	26,150	9,784	33,030	19,797	13,233
1930—June 30	25,214	10,442	32,982	19,170	13,812
Dec. 31	23,870	10,989	32,516	18,969	13,546
1931—June 30	24,678	12,106	31,602	18,055	13,548
Sept.	20,301	12,199	28,218	16,358	11,860
Dec. 31	18,471	11,314	27,353	15,925	11,428

BROKERS' LOANS

The Federal Reserve System tried—in 1928 and 1929—to discourage the rash speculative boom partly by moral suasion and then by the exercise of its rediscount power to force member banks to discriminate against brokers' loans. There are those who think they would have succeeded if more skill and promptitude had been marshalled. But even so, lending is too fluid to be effectively stopped by a dam half-way across the stream. The desired result was circumvented by borrowing not from the banks but from corporations and individuals who preferred to get 10 per cent on call loans rather than to invest in enterprises which were paying only 4 to 6 per cent. A portion of "loans by others" were made by banks for out of town customers who carried large deposits which they instructed their banks to lend for them on call. During the frenzied boom of 1929 the "loans by others" exceeded greatly the loans by member banks to brokers.

Chart 8 and Table 11 show the growth of all security loans including brokers' loans during the boom and their sudden collapse since 1929.

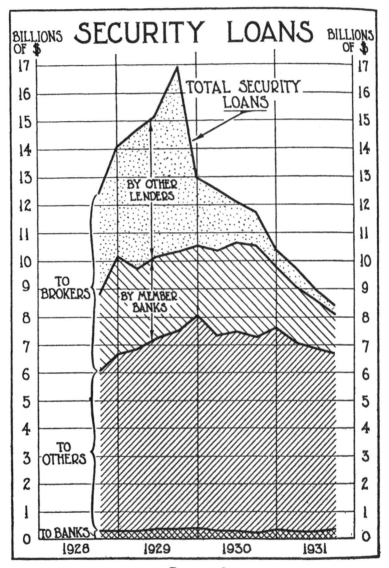

CHART 8

TABLE 11

TOTAL REPORTED SECURITY LOANS

(in millions of dollars)

Dates	Total Security Loans	BROKERS' LOANS			To Banks	To Others*
		Total	By Member Banks	By Other Lenders		
1928—Oct. 3	12,429	6,359	2,749	3,610	274	5,796
Dec. 31	14,052	7,411	3,531	3,880	269	6,373
1929—Mar. 27	14,643	7,843	2,893	4,950	274	6,526
June 20	15,144	7,996	2,946	5,050	335	6,813
Oct. 4	16,954	9,464	2,824	6,640	320	7,170
Dec. 31	12,955	4,913	2,463	2,450	357	7,685
1930—Mar. 27	12,544	5,260	3,050	2,210	260	7,024
June 30	12,085	4,614	3,184	1,430	230	7,242
Sept. 24	11,701	4,436	3,246	1,190	175	7,090
Dec. 31	10,364	2,783	2,173	610	315	7,266
1931—Mar. 25	9,752	2,685	2,205	480	219	6,848
June 30	8,943	2,112	1,732	380	229	6,602
Sept. 29†	8,378	1,724	1,444	280	312	6,333

Source: Federal Reserve Bulletin, Jan. 1932, p. 18.

* Commercial borrowers.
† Preliminary.

TOTAL DEBTS

Estimates of public and private debts have been made by Professors G. F. Warren and F. A. Pearson.[5] They have omitted all foreign debts due to American nationals and have included estimates of loans on life insurance policies and by pawn brokers and loan sharks. Some of their figures for other debts differ considerably from estimates made by other students. They make no estimate of the reduction in the total money debt since 1929 and of the amount of the real debt today in terms of 1929 dollars. They say in part:

"Extremely rough estimates of the total indebtedness are shown in table 3. The total debt is approximately $1,700 per

[5] *Farm Economics*, No. 74, February 1932, pp. 1667–1668.

capita, or about one-half of the national wealth in 1929. If the value of commodities is to drop one-third and remain at that level, the debt would become about 75 per cent of the value of the property. So much of this can never be collected that it is probable that the lenders would have a greater buying power if they were paid in full at a price level of 150. The usual argument for reducing wages is that a dollar has more buying power. This same argument might be applied to debts which are the most serious result of deflation.

"Table 3.—Rough Approximation of Public and Private Debts (from table 2)

	Amount (billions)	Per Cent	Per Capita
Corporations	$ 76	37.4	$ 618
Urban mortgages [6]	37	18.2	301
Bank loans	35	17.3	284
State, county and local	21	10.3	171
National	18	8.9	146
Farm mortgages	9	4.4	73
Life insurance policy loans and premium notes	3	1.5	24
Retail installment papers [7]	3	1.5	24
Pawn brokers' loans and unlawful loans of all kinds [8]	1	0.5	8
Total	$203	100.0	$1,649"

The estimate in the table prepared for this book by Dr. Meeker of 234,281 million for the total money debts in 1932 corresponds approximately with Dr. Edie's estimates ranging from a minimum of 120 billion to "more probably 150 billion." Dr. Edie excluded bank loans, 39 billion; consumers'

[6] Based on estimates furnished through the courtesy of George Terborgh of the Brookings Institute.

[7] Based on reports of the National Association of Finance Companies.

[8] Ryan, F. W. "Family Finance in the United States, *The Journal of Business* of the University of Chicago, Vol. III, No. 4, Part I, p. 404, October 1930.

credits, 2.2 billion, external debts, 25.6 billion and apparently life insurance loans, 2.4 billions, which would raise his totals to 189.2 billion as a minimum and 219.2 billion as a more likely figure.

GOLD BASE (AND GOLD SHORTAGE)
DEPRESSION OF 1929–32

Mr. Joseph Kitchin is the leading authority on gold scarcity, and based on his data the gold scarcity idea has been emphasized by Professors Gustav Cassel, J. Maynard Keynes and other economists of international reputations. These views have been endorsed in their several Reports in 1930 and 1931 by the Gold Delegation of the League of Nations and by the Report of the Macmillan Committee of Parliament in June, 1931. Meanwhile, the production of gold has increased somewhat beyond the estimates made by Mr. Kitchin and the metallurgical engineers. Instead of gold production falling one-half of one per cent, it increased by 5 per cent from $416.8 million to $438.4 million from 1930 to 1931 and it is still increasing. It is reported that large new fields of low grade gold ores have been discovered in Canada. India, the great gold absorbing sponge, is being squeezed and has become a leading exporter of gold. During 1931, she exported $95.7 million gold, whereas in 1930 she *imported* $57.7 million. During January and February 1932 she exported $51.4 million but in these two months in 1930 she *imported* $9,214,000 and in 1931, $727,-000.

The total world monetary gold supply increased in three-year periods as follows:

December,	1913—December,	1916,	34	per cent
"	1916	"	1919,	2.5	per cent
"	1919	"	1922,	23.6	per cent
"	1922	"	1925,	6.9	per cent
"	1925	"	1928,	11.8	per cent
"	1928	"	1931,	12.2	per cent

186

In the two months from December, 1931, to February, 1932, the increase has been one per cent. Beginning in 1929, there has been a tremendous falling off in production and trade, thus reducing greatly the demand for money.

There is great inequality in the distribution of gold. In the United States, until the Glass-Steagall bill released more "free gold," gold was virtually scarce because so much of it was technically tied up and unusable under our laws. Thus while statistically gold has been abundant, so far as usability is concerned, it has been scarce. The scarcity has been accentuated by the higher price level since the war.

See also "The English View" by Sir Henry Strakosch, in *Fortune*, April, 1932, pp. 52–55 and 104–108, and *America Weighs Her Gold* by James Harvey Rogers, Yale University Press, 1931.

Sir Henry attributes the persistent flow of gold to France and the United States to the Reparations and war debts. He attempts to show that the policy of debt collections in gold brought on liquidation and plunged the whole world into the disastrous plight of deflation.

Sir Henry says that from the beginning of 1925 to the end of 1927 countries other than France and the United States absorbed gold at a slightly greater rate than the rate of total world production. Early in 1929 an abnormal gold movement began which increased the gold holdings of France 76 per cent and of the United States 23 per cent from January 1, 1929, to June 30, 1931, while the rest of the world (excluding Russia) lost 15 per cent of their holdings.

The concentration of gold in France has continued unchecked. Between June 30, 1930, and March, 1932, the gold holdings of the United States have declined from $4,593,000,-000 to $3,985,000,000, a loss of 13 per cent, while the holdings of France have risen from $2,212,000,000 to $3,002,-000,000 or almost 36 per cent. The rest of the world lost about 1.8 per cent of their gold. In March, 1932, France held more than 26 per cent and the United States, about 35 per cent of the world's monetary gold.

Professor Rogers has shown that the accumulation of gold in the Federal Reserve Banks of the United States has not made money in circulation abundant, nor made the gold standard secure against the possibility of overthrow by raids from the French banks and other holders of short term credits. Our total gold holdings are misleading. Our "free gold," which is neither required as collateral and reserves against Federal Reserve Notes nor foreign owned gold masquerading as American gold, is not greatly in excess of our legitimate requirements. That is the reason for the apprehension of our bankers during the raid on our gold holdings in the fall of 1931.

Table 12 compiled from data published in the Federal Reserve Bulletins gives the distribution of gold at the end of December in each of several years from 1913 to 1931 and for February, 1932.

TABLE 12

GOLD HOLDINGS OF CENTRAL BANKS AND GOVERNMENTS

(millions of dollars)

	Total	United States	France	England	Germany	Italy	Japan	Spain	All Others
1913 Dec.	$4,933.4	$1,290.4	$ 678.9	$164.9	$278.7	$265.5	$ 65.0	$ 92.4	$2,097.6
1916	6,619.6	2,202.2	652.9	395.8	600.4	223.4	113.4	241.4	2,190.1
1919	6,788.1	2,517.7	694.8	578.1	259.5	200.1	350.0	471.5	1,716.4
1922	8,394.1	3,505.6	708.4	742.7	239.4	217.3	605.5	487.0	1,888.2
1924	8,947.9	4,090.1	710.4	748.2	180.9	218.4	585.7	489.2	1,925.0
1925	8,965.3	3,985.4	711.0	694.8	287.8	218.8	575.8	489.5	2,002.2
1928	10,018.7	3,746.1	1,253.5	748.4	650.1	265.7	540.9	493.8	2,320.2
1929	10,297.0	3,900.2	1,633.4	709.8	543.8	273.0	542.5	495.1	2,199.2
1930	10,907.4	4,225.1	2,100.2	718.4	527.8	278.6	411.8	470.5	2,175.0
1931	11,242.0	4,051.0	2,699.0	588.0	209.0	296.0	234.0	434.0	2,731.0
1932 Feb.	11,364.0	3,947.0	2,942.0	588.0	221.0	296.0	215.0	434.0	2,721.0
Percentages									
1913 Dec.	100	26.2	13.6	3.5	5.6	5.4	1.3	1.9	42.5
1916	100	33.3	9.9	6.0	9.1	3.4	1.7	3.6	23.0
1919	100	37.1	10.2	8.5	3.8	2.9	5.2	6.9	25.4
1922	100	42.0	8.4	8.8	2.9	2.6	7.2	5.8	22.3
1924	100	45.7	7.9	8.4	2.0	2.4	6.5	5.5	21.6
1925	100	44.5	7.9	7.7	3.2	2.5	6.4	5.5	22.3
1928	100	37.4	12.5	7.5	6.5	2.7	5.4	4.9	23.1
1929	100	37.9	15.9	6.9	5.3	2.7	5.3	4.8	21.2
1930	100	38.7	19.3	6.7	4.8	2.6	3.8	4.3	19.8
1931	100	36.0	24.0	5.2	1.9	2.6	2.1	3.9	24.3
1932 Feb.	100	34.7	25.9	5.2	1.9	2.6	1.9	3.8	24.0

Compiled from *Federal Reserve Bulletins.*

DEPRESSION OF 1929–32

STATISTICS OF CURRENCY VOLUME AND VELOCITY
(FACTORS 2 AND 8)

For the First Half of 1930

Federal Reserve Member Banks reported that time deposits increased by $570 million, and demand deposits decreased by $627 million in the first half of 1930.

Money in Circulation (nominally)

The total "money in circulation" in the United States normally drops abruptly every year from the end of December to the end of January. From December 1926 there was a slow downward trend to December 1930, when the amount was $4.9 billions, nearly 16 per cent below December 1926. The "money in circulation" during 1930 had been excessively low, reaching $4.4 billions in August. From that time the amount was sharply increased to December 1930. During 1931 the depressive effects of sagging prices continued despite large increases in Federal Reserve Notes in circulation. These increases were due largely to bank failures which led to the use of cash in place of bank checks. Total "money in circulation" reached $5.65 billion in December 1931—an increase of 16 per cent over December 1930 and 22 per cent over April 1931. Federal Reserve note circulation increased 80 per cent from $1.46 billion in February 1931 to $2.6 billion in December 1931. (See Chart 9.)

Meanwhile, deposit currency (demand deposits) for member

189

banks of the Federal Reserve System acted as follows (measured by a velocity index number based on 1919–25 as 100):

IN NEW YORK CITY

From October 1929 to March 1932

Volume fell 13 per cent (from $5,752 millions to $4,959 millions); velocity fell 72 per cent. The resulting efficiency (87% × 28%) was 24% of what it was in October, 1929.

IN 140 CITIES OUTSIDE OF NEW YORK CITY

October 1929 to March 1932

Volume fell 28% (from $13,373 million to $9,616 million); velocity 44%. Resulting efficiency (72% × 56%) 40%.

FOR ALL MEMBER BANKS IN 141 CITIES INCLUDING NEW YORK

October 1921 to February 1932

Volume fell 21% (from $18,726 million to $14,789 million); velocity fell 61%. Resulting efficiency (79% × 39%) 31%.

See Table 13 and Chart 9, also Charts 3 and 4 in Chapter VIII, p. 94.

STOCK PRICES (FACTOR 3)

From December 27, 1929, to April 10, 1930, the level of stock prices rose 20 per cent. From April 10, 1930, to December 1930, it fell 43.5 per cent; and this continued till it reached 48.8 at the end of January 1932.

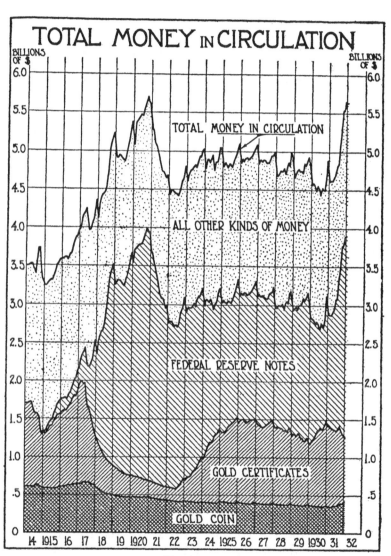

CHART 9

TABLE 13

FEDERAL RESERVE BANK OF NEW YORK
REPORTS DEPARTMENT
INDEXES OF VELOCITY OF BANK DEPOSITS

Daily basis.   Normal equals 1919–1925 average.   Seasonal allowed for
Velocity based on relation of debits to individual account to demand
deposits in weekly reporting member banks

I

NEW YORK CITY

Years	Jan.	Feb.	Mar.	Apr.	May	June	July	Aug.	Sept.	Oct.	Nov.	Dec.	Aver.
1919	84	84	80	85	94	104	111	112	106	110	115	105	99
1920	101	95	95	96	89	88	91	95	93	99	101	99	95
1921	95	87	83	84	91	89	93	92	96	95	96	94	91
1922	92	95	95	105	100	100	102	100	106	113	97	97	100
1923	99	103	105	107	102	105	101	99	102	98	104	105	103
1924	102	106	102	100	100	100	97	103	97	92	101	99	100
1925	104	108	108	100	112	112	112	116	117	121	120	115	112
1926	120	118	128	124	114	115	123	132	127	129	115	124	122
1927	127	134	135	134	131	128	135	145	153	144	135	136	136
1928	140	138	162	164	169	177	154	166	190	188	191	201	170
1929	202	210	216	195	201	182	208	228	242	244	189	139	
1930	129	143	159	150	143	146	118	112	118	115	87	95	
1931	83	87	97	99	93	96	80	77	84	80	62	71	
1932	73	70	68										

II

140 CITIES (OUTSIDE NEW YORK CITY)

Years	Jan.	Feb.	Mar.	Apr.	May	June	July	Aug.	Sept.	Oct.	Nov.	Dec.	Aver.
1919	103	98	97	96	102	111	112	111	108	108	111	107	105
1920	112	107	107	109	110	109	113	111	111	111	109	105	110
1921	102	94	92	94	95	94	96	95	98	99	101	94	96
1922	96	95	93	94	92	94	94	91	93	96	92	97	94
1923	98	98	98	102	100	100	99	99	102	98	98	100	99
1924	99	100	101	100	98	97	96	97	92	94	93	92	97
1925	100	97	98	97	100	99	101	100	100	103	102	100	100
1926	106	104	105	105	103	101	108	103	98	105	99	101	103
1927	108	108	105	107	108	106	110	104	109	110	106	104	107
1928	109	104	111	116	117	119	114	113	117	121	117	121	115
1929	121	125	128	124	123	126	131	136	135	137	130	115	128
1930	115	115	116	111	112	114	105	103	100	100	94	95	107
1931	97	91	91	90	91	89	88	86	85	88	81	83	
1932	90	81	77										

III

141 CITIES (INCLUDING NEW YORK CITY)

Years	Jan.	Feb.	Mar.	Apr.	May	June	July	Aug.	Sept.	Oct.	Nov.	Dec.	Aver.
1919	95	92	90	93	101	109	113	113	105	110	112	107	103
1920	105	99	100	102	100	97	101	101	101	104	103	103	102
1921	98	89	86	88	92	90	94	93	96	96	98	95	93
1922	94	95	95	101	99	97	99	96	99	104	94	98	98
1923	98	101	100	103	100	100	99	98	98	97	99	103	100
1924	100	102	101	101	99	100	99	103	98	95	98	100	100
1925	103	102	103	99	107	105	106	108	108	111	109	109	106
1926	113	110	117	114	108	108	114	116	110	115	104	113	112
1927	117	120	120	121	120	117	123	126	131	128	124	123	123
1928	128	124	141	143	146	148	134	140	154	150	153	165	144
1929 *	160	164	169	155	160	149	167	176	182	195	160	129	164
1930	120	126	136	131	127	130	110	106	108	109	90	97	116
1931	90	89	96	95	93	92	84	81	85	84	71	77	
1932	81	75	73										

* Decrease in 1929 in the 141 cities is probably due to revision in "net due to
banks" figures; therefore index is not exactly comparable to those in the past years.

Commodity Prices

Commodity price index (1926 equals 100) the peak 167.2 in May 1920, low 91.4 in January 1922, then 104.3 in August 1925, 93.7 in May 1927, 100.1 in September 1928, then down a little and relatively stable instability until July 1929. For what happened after that, see Chapter VIII with Chart 1; also see Charts 10 and 11 (as to both stock and commodity prices).

NET WORTHS AND FAILURES (FACTOR 4)

In 1919, (one year after the World War) the record was the best since 1890, not only in the percentage of existing firms that went to the wall, but in the absolute number and in the sum of their liabilities. Ever since then, though the record has varied a good deal, its trend on the whole has been to the bad. The year 1931 was the worst on record for the number of failures and for the liabilities of the failed firms, and the percentage of failures to firms in business. (See Table 14.)

Bank Suspensions

The failure or the suspension of a bank is of vastly more consequence than the failure of an industrial or commercial company, because banks are the custodians of the funds and the creditors of most industries.

Canada has long since come out of the banking jungle. She was as hard hit by the economic crisis and depression as we were, but not a Canadian bank or branch has closed its doors. Her banking system is much stronger than ours because her chartered banks are strong financially and serve the country by means of branch banks. There are 10 large banks with 4,000 branches. There have been only three bank failures in Canada during the past 22 years with total liabilities of $27.8 million. As for the United States, see Tables 15 and 16.

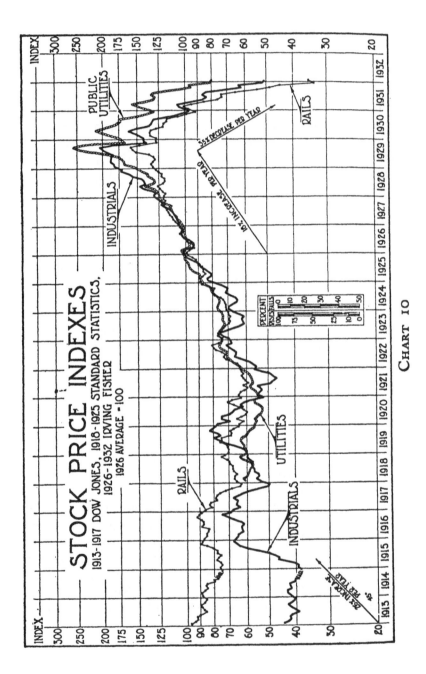

STOCK PRICE INDEXES

1913-1917 DOW JONES, 1918-1925 STANDARD STATISTICS,
1926-1932 IRVING FISHER
1926 AVERAGE = 100

CHART 10

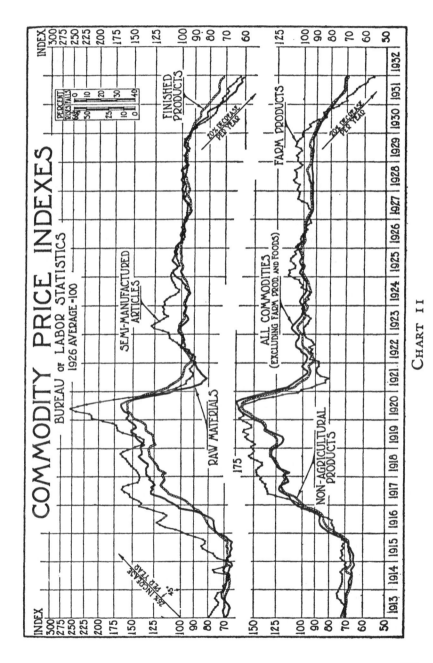

CHART II

255

TABLE 14

PERCENTAGES OF COMMERCIAL FAILURES TO THE TOTAL NUMBER OF
BUSINESS CONCERNS IN THE UNITED STATES

Years	No. of Failures	No. of Business Concerns	Per Cent of Failures	Years	No. of Failures	No. of Business Concerns	Per Cent of Failures
1891	12,273	1,142,951	1.07	1912	15,452	1,564,279	.98
1892	10,344	1,172,705	.88	1913	16,037	1,616,517	.99
1893	15,242	1,193,113	1.28	1914	18,280	1,655,496	1.10
1894	13,885	1,114,174	1.25	1915	22,156	1,674,788	1.32
1895	13,197	1,209,282	1.09	1916	16,993	1,707,639	.99
1896	15,088	1,151,579	1.31	1917	13,855	1,733,225	.80
1897	13,351	1,058,521	1.26	1918	9,982	1,708,061	.58
1898	12,186	1,105,830	1.10	1919	6,451	1,710,909	.38
1899	9,337	1,147,595	.81	1920	8,881	1,821,409	.49
1900	10,774	1,174,300	.92	1921	19,652	1,927,304	1.02
1901	11,002	1,219,242	.90	1922	23,676	1,983,106	1.19
1902	11,615	1,253,172	.93	1923	18,718	1,996,004	.94
1903	12,069	1,281,481	.94	1924	20,615	2,047,302	1.01
1904	12,199	1,320,172	.92	1925	21,214	2,113,300	1.05
1905	11,520	1,357,455	.85	1926	21,773	2,158,400	1.01
1906	10,682	1,392,949	.77	1927	23,146	2,171,700	1.07
1907	11,725	1,418,075	.82	1928	23,842	2,199,000	1.08
1908	15,690	1,447,554	1.08	1929	22,909	2,212,779	1.04
1909	12,924	1,486,389	.80	1930	26,355	2,183,008	1.21
1910	12,652	1,515,143	.80	1931	28,285	2,125,288	1.33
1911	13,441	1,525,024	.81				

Source: *Dun's Review*, Jan. 16, 1932, p. 6.

TABLE 15

BANK SUSPENSONS

	NUMBER OF BANKS										
Month	1921	1922	1923	1924	1925	1926	1927	1928	1929	1930	1931
Jan.	59	51	41	145	103	65	133	53	54	99	202
Feb.	27	43	41	92	61	52	81	50	60	85	77
Mar.	45	33	46	69	43	51	75	66	51	76	86
Apr.	44	28	28	74	48	56	49	43	29	96	64
May	39	25	30	81	54	68	47	29	112	55	89
June	20	17	32	51	34	77	41	28	48	66	167
July	27	14	36	47	29	140	37	24	69	65	93
Aug.	35	28	46	34	14	52	27	21	17	67	158
Sept.	31	17	51	36	30	37	36	20	39	66	305
Oct.	57	28	68	39	53	88	44	41	43	72	522
Nov.	61	35	110	47	74	154	43	72	68	254	169
Dec.	57	35	121	62	69	116	49	44	52	344	618
Total	502	354	650	777	612	956	662	491	642	1,345	2,550

Total Suspensions 1921–1931—number, 9,541.
Sources: Annual Reports of the Federal Reserve Board and the Federal Reserve Bulletin, Jan. 1932.

TABLE 16

BANK SUSPENSIONS

Deposits (in thousands of dollars)

Month	1921	1922	1923	1924	1925	1926	1927	1928	1929	1930	1931
Jan.	23,301	13,873	9,032	45,403	25,477	13,384	32,038	10,983	16,413	28,903	78,130
Feb.	25,202	20,024	9,240	26,501	15,593	11,763	25,157	18,352	21,746	32,800	35,123
Mar.	17,867	15,196	14,629	15,667	10,142	10,249	31,222	16,953	9,002	23,769	35,285
Apr.	9,653	9,404	7,887	17,843	16,055	12,512	11,750	8,190	7,790	33,388	42,417
May	13,957	8,430	7,961	29,861	15,930	16,324	13,198	6,394	24,090	19,315	43,963
June	17,543	4,389	14,110	9,033	10,368	34,229	10,784	13,496	19,219	70,566	195,951
July	12,315	4,071	13,353	16,620	5,882	48,618	12,162	5,368	66,161	32,333	41,334
Aug.	6,493	7,733	15,946	7,545	1,837	10,001	17,364	6,147	8,532	21,951	185,902
Sept.	4,804	3,223	11,367	6,081	14,141	12,050	8,988	7,888	10,050	23,666	236,511
Oct.	15,972	5,072	21,534	9,824	15,581	18,209	11,542	9,011	13,153	24,599	493,751
Nov.	18,825	10,105	30,617	10,418	19,791	45,983	11,210	24,784	22,646	186,306	83,409
Dec.	32,422	9,201	33,129	18,648	22,103	39,166	8,476	11,076	15,730	367,119	287,148
Total	198,354	110,721	188,805	213,444	172,900	272,488	193,891	138,642	234,532	864,715	1,758,924

Total Suspensions 1921–1931—deposits, $4,347,416,000.

PROFITS AND INCOMES (FACTOR 5)

Total dividend and interest payments by corporations are an imperfect index even of corporate earnings and they are often quite misleading as to changes in total net national income. No soundly managed corporation ever pays out in dividends during prosperous years all its earnings above fixed charges. Part of net earnings is set aside as surplus against the proverbial rainy day and part is turned back into the enterprise. When adversity comes, dividends are paid out of the accumulated surplus as long as possible or desirable.

The net profits of corporations are better indicators of business conditions. The Federal Reserve Bank of New York has compiled reports of quarterly earnings from more than 500 corporations including 163 industrials, 171 Class I railroads, 103 telephones and 63 other large public utilities. The averages for 1931 are not strictly comparable with other years.

The net profits of all reporting corporations increased 41 per cent from the third quarter of 1925 to the third quarter of 1929. They declined for the third quarter of 1931, 64 per cent, and for the fourth quarter 15 per cent.

Telephone net profits increased 41 per cent from the fourth quarter of 1925 to the fourth quarter of 1929. The decline the last quarter of 1931 is 11 per cent. Profits of other large public utilities increased 52 per cent from the last quarter of 1925 to the last quarter of 1929, the third quarter of 1931 showing a decline of nearly 80 per cent. The last quarter profits rose, reducing the slump to 71 per cent since 1929.

Net Profits of Class I railroads for the third quarter increased 11 per cent from 1925 to 1929 and declined 58 per cent to the same quarter of 1931, and sunk for the last quarter to nearly 70 per cent below the 1929 peak.

Net profits of industrial companies for the third quarter increased 75 per cent from 1925 to 1929 and slumped 75 per cent in that quarter in 1931, and more than 100 per cent in the fourth quarter to a net deficit.

258

Table 1 in Chapter VIII, pp. 97–8, shows these and other facts.

Inflation and over-borrowing swelled corporation profits inordinately from 1925 to 1929. Deflation and "liquidation" since 1929 have reduced these profits appallingly and have even transformed them into deficits in many leading industries.

Total and Per Capita National Income

The estimates of total national income and per capita income are better indicators of the amounts available for expenditure for consumption. These estimates of income give no measure of well being or ill being, because they cannot indicate anything regarding the distribution of the national income. Total national income has been estimated by the National Bureau of Economic Research, by the National Industrial Conference Board and by Mr. W. R. Ingalls.

All are but approximations, sometimes so rough as to be mere guesses, but they do show an astonishing degree of agreement.[1] The Bureau's figures [2] are reproduced here because they are based on much more careful research and the estimates in current dollars are converted into 1913 dollars. (See Table 17.)

Figures for the years 1929, 1930 and 1931 are added using the methods employed by the Conference Board in making their estimates for 1929 and 1930.[3] The decline in current dollar income in 1931 was estimated at $15 billion or 21.2 per cent. The amounts obtained in current dollars have been

[1] Mr. W. R. Ingalls compares the three series for 1920–1928 in his article, "The National Income for 1929 Tentatively Estimated at Eighty-Three Billion," in *The Annalist*, January 30, 1931, p. 270.

[2] *The National Income and Its Purchasing Power*, by W. I. King, National Bureau of Economic Research, Inc., New York, 1930, pp. 74 and 77.

[3] See *New York Times*, January 25, 1932, p. 30, and *Conference Board Buletin*, Feb. 20, 1932, No. 62, pp. 497–500.

TABLE 17

ESTIMATED REALIZED INCOME AND PURCHASING POWER IN 1913
DOLLARS OF THE PEOPLE OF CONTINENTAL UNITED STATES

(millions of dollars)

Year	Total Income in Current Dollars	Total Income in 1913 Dollars	Per Capita Income in 1913 Dollars
1909	$27,661	$29,221	$322
1910	29,345	30,207	327
1911	29,660	30,634	332
1912	31,755	32,373	341
1913	33,393	33,413	346
1914	33,227	32,841	335
1915	34,690	34,137	335
1916	40,585	36,996	367
1917	48,314	37,613	368
1918	56,658	37,261	360
1919	61,628	35,098	334
1920	68,442	34,348	322
1921	58,271	33,638	310
1922	61,187	37,623	342
1923	69,295	42,072	377
1924	71,905	43,577	384
1925	76,561	45,191	392
1926	80,284 *	47,261 *	403
1927	82,921 *	49,655 *	419
1928	84,119 *	50,692 *	423
1929	87,500 †	51,200	421
1930	72,900 †	44,500	365
1931	57,500 †	38,900	314

Source: The National Income and Its Purchasing Power, by W. I. King, pp. 74 and 77.

* Preliminary estimate.

† Estimates made by applying the methods used by the national Industrial Conference Board.

deflated into 1913 dollars by the United States Bureau of Labor Statistics cost of living indexes for those years.

The most striking comparisons brought out by these figures are that 1917 was the peak year in total "real" national income and that 1920, instead of showing an increase as is commonly assumed, shows a decrease in real income of $750 million, or 2 per cent compared with 1919.

The per capita buying power shows a continuous increase except for 1914–15 and 1918–21. The depression of 1914 cut down the buying power per person only $11 from 1913, or 3 per cent. The depression of 1921 cut it only $12 below 1920, or 3.7 per cent. The depression of 1924–25 actually increased the buying power per person over 1923 by $15, or 4 per cent. The present depression has for 1931 cut the buying power per capita by $107, or 25 per cent, below the 1929 peak and the trend is still downward.

Dr. W. I. King has shown that the crisis and depression of 1920 and 1921 took from some of the people of the United States $40 billion. This consisted mostly in transfer of ownership. The actual loss of national income in 1920 compared with 1919 was only $750 million, or $12 per person. The statistical estimates confirm the view that depressions transfer ownership of wealth and income but destroy little if any real values. The present depression has transferred ownership probably more sweepingly than ever before and at the same time has seemingly destroyed for the time being approximately 34 per cent of the money income, or 25 per cent of the real national income. The loss in real wealth cannot be estimated, but deterioration of plants and equipment has been disconcertingly great.

THE FARMER'S INCOME

The farmer, as usual, has been chief sufferer, next to the unemployed. In the first place, he did not fully recover from the depression of 1920 to 1922. Beginning with 1926, the slump in agriculture was caused by falling prices which were in turn caused by increased production in the United States, Canada, Australia, Argentina, Brazil, Cuba, Russia and Eastern Europe, coupled with diminished consumption due to debts and depression. Agriculture in 1929–31 was an easy mark for any monetary appreciation.

The greatest losses in commodity prices have hit farm products. According to the *Crop Reporter,* published by the United States Department of Agriculture, farm products declined from October 1929 to January 1932 by 55 per cent while the goods bought by farmers receded only 22 per cent. The ratio of the prices farmers received to the prices they paid in January 1932 was 53, which means that the farmers' "commodity dollar" will buy only slightly more than half as much as it would buy on the average in the period 1909–1915. The farmer who contracted a debt in 1929 must pay today about two and one-quarter times as much in produce as the original debt was worth.

The Department of Agriculture estimates that the total farm income for 1929 was $11,851 million, for 1930 $9,300 million, and for 1931 only $6,920 million—a decline in two years of 42 per cent in the dollar income of farmers, despite the fact that physical production has increased for most products. (See Table 18.)

The statistics of gross incomes from farm production in earlier years are somewhat inconsistent and confusing, but from 1924 the Department of Agriculture reported gross incomes as in Table 19. The loss in buying power of the farmer's commodity dollar, coupled with the loss in the number of dollars farmers receive, gives a startling statistical picture of the agricultural depression. The evils of deflation and liquidation through bankruptcy and default manifest themselves more malevolently in agriculture than in any other great industrial group.

TABLE 18

INDEX NUMBERS OF FARM PRICES RECEIVED BY COMMODITIES, AND
RETAIL PRICES PAID BY FARMERS

Year and Month	Index Number of Farm Prices (August, 1909–July, 1914 = 100) All Groups	Prices Paid by Farmers for Commodities bought *	Ratio of Prices Received to Prices paid
1919	209	205	102
1920	205	206	99
1921	116	156	75
1922	124	152	81
1923	135	153	88
1924	134	154	87
1925	147	159	92
1926	136	156	87
1927	131	154	85
1928	139	156	90
1929	138	155	89
1930	117	146	80
1930:			
January	134	153	88
February	131	152	86
March	126	151	83
April	127	150	85
May	124	150	83
June	123	149	82
July	111	148	75
August	108	147	74
September	111	146	76
October	106	144	74
November	103	142	73
December	97	139	70
1931:			
January	94	137	69
February	90	136	66
March	91	134	68
April	91	132	69

Source: Crops and Markets, June, 1932.

* These index numbers are based on retail prices paid by farmers for commodities used in living and production reported quarterly for March, June, September, and December. The indexes for other months are straight interpolations between the successive quarterly indexes.

TABLE 18—*Continued*

INDEX NUMBERS OF FARM PRICES RECEIVED BY COMMODITIES, AND RETAIL PRICES PAID BY FARMERS

Year and Month	Index Number of Farm Prices (*August, 1909-- July, 1914 = 100*) All Groups	Prices Paid by Farmers for Commodities bought	Ratio of Prices Received to Prices paid
May	86	131	66
June	80	129	62
July	79	127	62
August	75	125	60
September	72	123	58
October	68	122	56
November	71	120	59
December	66	119	55
1932:			
January	63	118	53
February	60	116	52
March	61	114	54
April	59	113 †	53 †
May	56	112 †	50 †

† Preliminary.

TABLE 19

FARMERS' GROSS INCOMES, EXPENDITURES AND BALANCE AVAILABLE FOR CAPITAL, LABOR AND MANAGEMENT

(millions of dollars)

Year	Gross Income	Total Expenditures	Balance Available for Capital, Labor, and Management
(1)	(2)	(3)	(4)
1924	11,337	5,853	5,486
1925	11,968	6,233	5,735
1926	11,480	5,939	5,541
1927	11,616	6,041	5,575
1928	11,741	6,263	5,478
1929	11,851	6,273	5,578
1930	9,300		
1931	6,920		

Source: *Yearbook of Agriculture*, 1931, p. 979.

For corporate profits, see Table 1, Chapter VIII, pp. 97–8.

PRODUCTION, TRADE AND EMPLOYMENT (FACTOR 6)

The decrease in department store sales under-estimates the loss of physical trade, because the figures come from the large department stores which, in the depression, took over smaller ones and so showed a gain when sales as a whole declined. On the other hand, the growth of the dollar made the money sales decline much more than the volume of goods. Department store sales reached the peak in September, 1929, and from then to January, 1932, fell 30 per cent [4]—the volume of goods probably fell only about 18 per cent.

The Federal Reserve Board and the several Reserve Banks, especially the Reserve Bank of New York have compiled most valuable index numbers relating to Trade, Production, Employment and Consumption. The Reserve Board's compilations are based on 1923–1925 equals 100. The index of total freight car loadings increased 38 per cent from 78 in May 1922 to 108 at the peak in June 1929, then declined 41 per cent to 64 in January 1932. Merchandise less than carload lots, which are more representative of retail trade, showed an increase of 14 per cent from December 1922 to 104 at the peak in October 1929 and slumped 22 per cent to 81 in January 1932. These are quantitative indexes and therefore reflect accurately changes in tonnage transported by rail. The slump in car loadings has been greatly aggravated by the competition of auto-trucks, especially on merchandise shipments. Average monthly tonnage passing through the Panama Canal increased 32 per cent from 1,975 thousand tons in 1925 to 2,621 thousand tons in 1929. The monthly average declined 67 per cent from 1929 to 864 thousand tons in 1931. The tonnage for January 1932 was 652 thousand tons or 77 per cent less than in January 1929 (2,859 thousand tons).

Industrial production indexes are published each month in

[4] The sale of house furnishings *increased* about 18 per cent for substantially the same period.

the Federal Reserve Bulletin. These indexes were originally constructed for the Board by Dr. Woodlief Thomas.[5] These are indexes of physical quantities. The base is the period 1923–1925 equals 100 and all indexes are adjusted to eliminate seasonal variations.

The *combined* index increased with only a slight interruption in 1924, from the low of 65 in April, 1921, to 125 at the peak in June, 1929, a gain of 91 per cent. The decline in 2¾ years to 67 in March, 1932, or 46 per cent, was much more rapid than the rise during 8 years. During the same periods manufacturing production rose from 63 to 129 or 105 per cent and fell 50 per cent to 64. Mineral production rose from 71 to 118 in October, 1929, or 66 per cent and fell 29 per cent to 84 in March, 1932.

BUILDING AND CONSTRUCTION

Building and construction is one of the most important types of production. Indexes of value of building contracts awarded are published in the Federal Reserve Bulletins. These indexes show extraordinary fluctuations in the construction industries. All classes of building rose from the low of 43 in February, 1921 to the high of 139 in June, 1928, an advance of 223 per cent. This index for March, 1932, is 26, which is 81 per cent below the peak and nearly 40 per cent below the low of 1921. Residential building has fluctuated even more widely during this period, shooting up from the low of 24 in 1921 to the high of 142 in February, 1928, and down to 15 in March, 1932. The rise was 492 per cent and the drop 90 per cent, bringing this type of building nearly 38 per cent below the low of 1921.

Construction has in certain past depressions been the key industry to keep business alive during the lean years and to lift it out of the slump. In this depression it has been a chief cause to aggravate and prolong the depression.

[5] The methods of construction are fully described in Federal Reserve Bulletins for February and March, 1927.

Employment and Payrolls

Employment and payroll indexes [6] as indicators of production activity and of the total wage bill are valuable if used with due caution. The figures cannot include small establishments or newly established plants and industries; hence they are likely to be misleading during periods of rapid change in industrial production, organization and technique.

The Federal Reserve Board makes use of the employment figures collected by the United States Bureau of Labor Statistics, correcting them with the more complete figures of the Census and adjusting them for seasonal variations. The base is the same as that of the other indexes published by the Board, 1923–1925 equals 100.

The index of total factory employment rose 32 per cent from the low of 80.4 in July 1921 to the high of 106.4 in June 1923. It reached a secondary high of 102.8 in July 1929, 28 per cent above the 1921 low. Since then it has slumped to 66.4 in March 1932, nearly 36 per cent below the 1929 high and 17 per cent below the low of 1921.

The factory payroll index was 72.2 in July 1921, the lowest recorded during that depression except for January 1922. It rose 56 per cent to the peak of 112 in September 1929 and dropped 54 per cent to 52.3 in March 1932, or 22 per cent below the low of 1921.

The declines in production, employment and payrolls have been especially drastic in iron and steel, machinery, textiles, lumber and lumber products and especially automobiles.

Iron and steel production rose more than five-fold from 30 in July 1921 to 155 in June 1929. It then fell 78 per cent to 34 for March 1932. Employment in iron and steel rose 86 per cent from 54.5 in July 1921 to 101.4 in August 1929 and fell 40 per cent to 60.9 for March 1932. The payrolls in iron and steel rose nearly three-fold from 37.4 in July 1921 to

[6] Revised indexes of employment are shown in Federal Reserve Bulletin for November 1930 and of payrolls in the Bulletin for November 1929.

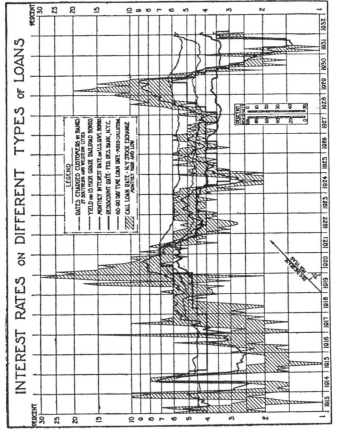

INTEREST RATES ON DIFFERENT TYPES OF LOANS

Note: Data on R.R. Bond Yields not available Aug.–Oct., 1914.

CHART 12

268

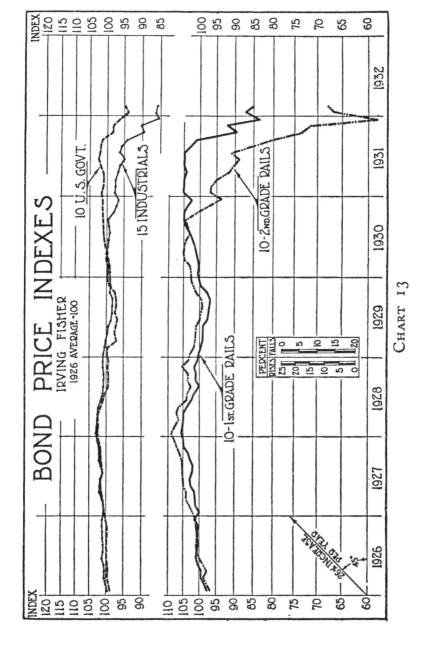

CHART 13

TABLE 20

INDEXES OF PRODUCTION, EMPLOYMENT AND PAYROLL
WITH SEASONAL ADJUSTMENT
1923–1925 averages = 100

	Iron and Steel			Textiles			Paper and Printing			Leather and Products		
	Production	Employment	Payrolls	Production	Employment	Payrolls	Production	Employment	Payrolls	Production	Employment	Payrolls
Low in 1921	30	54.5	37.4	64	71.4	66.1	60	83.9	76.4	70	73.4	72.0
High in 1929	155	101.4	111.6	121	120.8	108.8	128	106.3	114.9	117	96.0	117.8
November 1931	46	65.3	41.2	89	73.6	59.3	97	89.7	90.6	77	70.1	47.0
December 1931	38	65.4	41.0	85	72.2	58.1	97	89.2	91.0	82	75.3	50.3
January 1932	43	64.0	36.3	89	71.1	55.5	101	88.3	85.5	84	75.4	53.3
February 1932	41	62.4	37.2	86	72.4	59.8	98	87.2	83.5	89	78.1	61.4
March 1932	34	60.9	35.4	82	71.0	59.3	99	86.2	82.4	92	80.2	62.3

	Automobiles			Food and Food Products			All Manufacturing		
	Production	Employment	Payrolls	Production	Employment	Payrolls	Production	Employment	Payrolls
Low in 1921	25	31.9	25.2	77	92.4	89.8	63	80.4	76.1
High in 1929	166	131.4	152.0	103	100.1	108.8	129	102.8	111.7
November 1931	36	56.1	42.3	90	85.9	83.0	71	69.3	56.2
December 1931	66	68.8	48.0	89	86.3	82.7	73	69.4	55.8
January 1932	45	67.1	47.7	94	85.3	78.6	71	68.1	52.4
February 1932	35	64.7	52.0	90	83.7	76.3	68	67.8	53.5
March 1932	28	60.9	51.3	84	83.1	74.4	64	66.4	52.3

Sources: *Federal Reserve Bulletins* for March 1927, November 1929, November 1930, and subsequent issues.

111.6 in May 1929, then sunk 68 per cent to 35.4 in March 1932. The low and high points did not fall in the same months in 1921 and 1929 for each industrial group.

Automobile production rose 6⅔ times from 26 in 1921 to 166 in 1929 and dropped 83 per cent to 28 in March 1932.

It will be noted that the index volume of production in all the groups shown was higher in 1932 than at the low in 1921. Employment indexes are somewhat lower than in 1921 in foods and all manufacturing combined. Payroll indexes are smaller in all groups shown, except paper and printing and automobiles.

See Chart 5 in Chapter VIII, p. 99, and Table 20.

INTEREST RATES (FACTOR 9)

The variations in the interest rates on the principal types of loans are given in Chart 12 for comparison. The rates on call loans have always varied the most. The high call loan rates in 1929 indicate the feverish speculative demand during the boom.

Changes in the prices of bonds reflect in part changes in the long term rate of interest and in part changes in the riskiness of the bond as an investment. Hence there is a marked contrast in the movement of the price indexes of Government bonds and first grade and second grade corporations' bonds, as will be noted on Chart 13.

[To find the "real" interest for a given period, take the percentage by which the dollar has increased and add to it the annual interest, raised by said percentage. For 1929 to 1932 the dollar increased by 53 per cent and to the third week of June 1932, by 62 per cent.]

AN OUTLINE OF COMPLETE STABILIZA-
TION PROGRAM

*which, if adopted, would provide stabilization expedi-
ents sufficient to meet all circumstances which could reasonably be expected to arise.*

COMMISSION ON STABILIZATION

1. Create a commission on stabilization.
   Members: Governor of Federal Reserve Board, ex officio
   Comptroller of the Currency, ex officio
   One representative of the Governors of the Federal Reserve banks, to be chosen by them.
   Four other (appointed) members with terms of 3, 6, 9, 12 years; all replacements to be for 12 years.
   The Commission to elect its own chairman.

2. The Secretary of the Treasury to be authorized and directed to execute and deliver to said commission short term U. S. Government 3% bonds.

3. The Commission to offer to every national and state bank and trust company, in proportion to its deposits, its quota of said bonds, and in return be credited with deposits. These deposits to be time [1] deposits bearing the same rate of interest as the

---

[1] Demand deposits could also be used. They would have the advantage of quicker results but the disadvantage of being less acceptable to the banks in time of depression. They would make taxation unnecessary to the extent of the demand deposits. This is precisely what was done during

212

said bonds; thus no expense will be incurred by either party.

4. Said time deposits to be withdrawn only after the expiration of one year or by mutual agreement between the Commission and the individual bank.

5. The bonds are to be the property of the bank and may be resold or hypothecated with the Federal Reserve Banks.

6. The Commission to agree to accept at par at any time said bonds in payment for any of said deposits.

The effect of the bonds as liquid assets for the banks would be to improve their position so as to enable them to increase their loans and investments, thus creating new purchasing power for the public, and raising the price level. The effect on the individual bank would be almost the same as pouring into a bank's vaults the equivalent of its quota of bonds in gold. Only 3% is required as reserve against the time deposits.

This strengthening of the banks' position can be accomplished by telegraph within a day or two, even before the physical delivery or even the printing of the bonds.

7. After the price level has been restored to the legal normal, the commission to stabilize the price level by repeating or reversing the above operations, increasing or decreasing the amount of said bonds and deposits, as may be necessary, to maintain the stated level.

8. Such stabilization to be with the cooperation of the Federal Reserve System, and if possible, of foreign governments and central banks.

COOPERATION OF FEDERAL RESERVE SYSTEM

9. The main policies of the Federal Reserve System to include:

(1) Open market operations—that is, buying and selling eligible bills and securities.

(2) Buying and selling gold or gold certificates in ex-

the World War. The Government paid for war materials out of these deposits and raised the price level thereby (to the country's injury at that time).

change for Federal Reserve notes or other funds (the price of gold being, unless hereafter changed as hereinafter provided, $20.67 per ounce of pure gold, i. e., $1 per 23.22 grains of pure gold).

(3) Adjustment of rediscount rates.

(4) Rationing of credit.

(5) Adjustment of gold reserve ratios of Federal Reserve Banks as hereinafter prescribed.

(6) Advice to member banks and non-member banks, with the object of securing their cooperation in stabilization policy, including, especially, adjustment of discount rates to customers, open market operations and rediscounts with Federal Reserve banks.

(7) Relations, consultation, cooperation, and lawful transactions with non-American banks, including the Bank for International Settlements at Basle known as the World Bank.

(8) Statistical studies.

(9) Publicity.

(10) If the free gold of the system is deemed, at any time, to be too near exhaustion, the system is authorized to utilize its holdings of Government bonds as backing for Federal Reserve notes. This would perpetuate the like provision in the Glass-Steagall bill now limited to one year.

(11) If the securities held by the Federal Reserve System, and available for sale, seem at any time, to be too near exhaustion, the System is authorized to issue and sell, in the open market (and at any later time, rebuy) new interest-bearing debentures in such volume and of such date of maturity and rate of interest as may be deemed by it most suitable.

(12) All net profit or loss from buying and selling said debentures or paying interest thereon shall accrue to the United States Government and shall annually be paid into, or reimbursed from, the Treasury of the United States.

(13) If the gold reserve ratio is deemed to be too near to the prescribed minimum, the System is authorized and di-

rected to lower the legal minimum reserve requirement for Federal Reserve Banks in accordance with and under the conditions and restrictions already prescribed in Section II, subsection c of the Federal Reserve Act;

If, on the other hand, the legal minimum gold reserve ratio is deemed to be too high, the System is authorized and directed to raise the legal minimum ratio for Federal Reserve Banks.

10. If the gold reserve is deemed by the commission to be too near to the prescribed minimum, the commission is authorized, if the other methods already authorized appear inadequate, to raise the official price of gold.

If, on the other hand, the gold reserve ratio is deemed to be too high, the commission is authorized, if the other methods already authorized appear inadequate, to lower the official price of gold.

11. Should, at any time, the price of gold thus be changed, either up or down, the commission is authorized to introduce temporarily a differential between its selling and buying prices sufficient to prevent speculators (for instance, on rumor of a proposed change in price) from taking advantage of the commission, the Federal Reserve System or the United States Government either by buying gold from them at one price and later selling it back to them at a higher price, or by selling gold to them at one price and later buying it back from them at a lower price.

12. At all times the United States Treasury, mints, Government assay offices, and any other agencies authorized to buy or sell gold to employ the same identical prices as those employed by the Federal Reserve System.

The reason why there should be a special safeguard against speculation injurious to the Government is because the Government, unlike an ordinary buyer and seller, now stands ready to buy and sell at the same price instead of making a profit in the selling price over the buying price.

After the price of gold has been sufficiently changed to safeguard the reserve ratio so that the new price may, presumably, again be left unchanged for a considerable period, the differential may be removed so that the buying price and selling price may again coincide.

13. All profits and losses from buying and selling gold to accrue to United States Treasury.

COMMENTS

It will be observed that there is no mandate put upon the commission ever to change the price of gold. Such a change is merely authorized if and when found necessary to prevent inflation or deflation. As long as the retention of the present basis of $20.67 an ounce continues to be compatible with the maintenance of a stable price level, that basis will remain.

But if and when the retention of a constant price of gold and the maintenance of a fairly constant level of prices are found to be incompatible, a change can and should be made. The authorities can be trusted not to make it any sooner than need be. But it is only fair to them that, when given the responsibility to stabilize the price level and to keep the legal gold reserve ratio, they should not be eventually hamstrung in their attempts by the fixity of the price of gold. Inasmuch as the only proper purpose of maintaining a uniform price of gold is to prevent inflation and deflation, no one can properly object to changing the gold price if that purpose can better be served thereby.

Any change, made with such a purpose, is not an abandonment of the gold standard but simply a revaluation of gold to correspond to any great change in its purchasing power. The present price of $20.67 an ounce might conceivably be maintained indefinitely without producing material inflation or deflation, and it is altogether probable that no change would be required in many years.

It is further to be noted that any change which might become necessary after it is once made in a thoroughgoing manner so that the reserve ratio is again moderate—neither absurdly high nor low—this new price will probably stand unchanged for many years.

Under these circumstances there seems no occasion for alarm, on the part of those who regard the figures $20.67 as sacred, over the remote prospect of its being some day changed, especially as any change is authorized only in furtherance of maintaining the gold standard and its chief purpose—stability.

Thus, while all the virtues of the gold standard are retained, its periodical evils are avoided. Instead of those periodical evils of inflation and deflation there will be occasional readjustments in the price of gold. But these changes in the gold price basis will be made solely in order to avoid changes in the commodity price base. In this respect, they will differ from such revaluations as those of France and Italy in recent years. These nations regained the gold standard after war-time inflation, through devaluing the gold franc and lira.

The above provisions make possible the perpetuation of the gold standard under all possible circumstances. They also permit the retention of the present price of gold, $20.67 per ounce, and the corresponding weight of the dollar except when, if ever, a change of price should be necessary to supplement the other efforts to prevent deflation or inflation of the price level. The chief justification of the gold standard has been that it afforded, to some extent, a safeguard against inflation such as has so often occurred when a country has gone off the gold standard and has adopted irredeemable paper money.

But this safeguard against inflation has only been partial. For instance, we experienced a great gold inflation between 1896 and 1920.

Moreover, the gold standard has afforded no safeguard whatever against deflation. England in effect, preferred going off the gold standard rather than suffer further deflation.

Under the present plan there would never be any need of America following the English example by abandoning the gold standard. She would have a gold standard safeguarded against deflation and inflation alike, a gold standard almost fully assimilated to a virtual goods standard—in short, a genuine standard of purchasing power, fair to debtors and creditors alike. It may never be necessary to change the price of gold; but when, if ever, a change should become necessary, it would always be a benefit and never an injury.

If the price of gold is ever raised it will only be because otherwise we should suffer deflation. That is, the price of gold would be raised only when gold became so scarce that its price clearly ought to be raised.

Contrariwise, if the price of gold is ever lowered it will only be because otherwise we would suffer inflation. In other words, the price of gold would be lowered only when gold becomes so superabundant that its price clearly ought to be lowered.

Should, at any time, the price of gold be raised, this operates automatically to raise and thereby improve the reserve ratio in two ways, namely:

(1) It stimulates the sale by gold owners of their gold to the Federal Reserve System and discourages the purchase of gold from it.

(2) It increases the dollar value of the gold in the vaults of the Federal Reserve banks.

If, for instance, the price of gold is increased by 1 per cent, a hundred million ounces of gold in the vaults now worth $20.67 an ounce or 2,067 million dollars is thereupon worth, instead, 1 per cent more, rising, namely, to $20.8767 per ounce or to 2,087.67 million dollars, an increase of 20.67 million dollars which can be entered on the books of the Federal Reserve banks as a profit.

Contrariwise, if at any time the price of gold should be reduced, this operates automatically to reduce the reserve ratio in two ways, namely:

(1) It discourages the sale by gold owners of their gold to the Federal Reserve System and encourages the purchase of gold from it.

(2) It decreases the dollar value of vault gold.

This, of course, registers a loss on the books of the Federal Reserve banks.

There is practically no limit under this plan, to the power of the commission system, either to counteract deflation or to counteract inflation. Its buying power is practically unlimited and, when exercised, it will raise the prices of securities and other goods, not only of those it buys but of the great mass of others. This is true not only because of the sympathetic movement of securities but because the buying power does not cease with its exercise by the system. Those who receive this buying power pass it on by buying other securities and goods of all sorts, raising their price in turn and so on indefinitely. This new buying power is not at the expense of some other buying power as in the case of an individual spending money already in circulation before he gets it. The Federal Reserve notes or other forms of credit are newly created, a net addition to the circulating medium. Until withdrawn this new circulating medium adds permanently to the annual buying power of the country.

To see how resistless is the power of the Federal Reserve System to sustain the price level, under this plan suppose that, as was threatened recently, there should be a nationwide run on banks and continued hoarding, causing an increasing vacuum in our circulating medium; this vacuum, however great, could be filled as fast as created, by pouring out Federal Reserve notes in purchasing securities, or by paying in deposit balances. Yet the gold reserve need never be too low if the price of gold be raised sufficiently. Furthermore, if action were prompt enough there would be no hoarding, as hoarding is the result of deflation. If action were not prompt enough, hoarding might take place; but it could probably be more than neutralized by vigorous action, although the fear that grips the hoarder is apt to be unreasonable and capricious.

For the same reasons the outflow of gold to foreign countries can not prevent safeguarding the price level against deflation so long as there is the power to raise the price of gold.

The only limit to be encountered would be reached when the Federal Reserve System had exhausted the entire legally available security market so as to have gathered within its own walls all Government bonds, and other securities on its eligible list.

To take an example of the reverse sort, suppose there should be a threat of inflation, due, say, to speculative activity resulting in increasing loans and swelling the volume of deposits subject to check. The Federal Reserve could then, if need be, sell newly created debentures without limit, receiving back their own Federal Reserve notes (or deposit balances on their books to the credit of member banks or the United States Government). This shrinkage of outstanding Federal Reserve credit would cause member banks in turn to curtail the credit extended by them to their customers. Otherwise their reserve ratios would be reduced below the legal requirement. This shrinkage would have no limit since there is no limit to the possible issue of debentures.

The importation of gold from abroad can not upset the control of the Federal Reserve over inflation so long as the latter can decrease the price of gold.

Of course, every change in the price of gold changes the rates of foreign exchange. But the slight additional inconvenience caused by this to foreign commerce will be as easily and regularly allowed for as any other, and the inconvenience is small as compared with the advantages obtained in the fact that domestic commerce has a stable level of prices; for foreign commerce is of very small volume, say one-tenth the volume of domestic commerce.

Moreover, at present, several of our chief foreign customers are now off the gold standard, so that there is scarcely any inconvenience added to that we already have. Ultimately, it is altogether likely that all important commercial nations will adopt uniform stabilization laws and policies.

There is only one obstacle to fully safeguarding the price level against both inflation and deflation. It can not stop the danger of Government inflation. The Government can, in its sovereign power, break any or all rules laid down, break away from the gold standard, and inflate the currency to suit itself.

In times of great distress, such as war, this usually happens. There is no way by law to prevent inflation by the Government; for the Government is the law-maker. But as long as the rules here laid down are observed, the commission and Federal Reserve system have full control of the circulating medium, including deposit currency, and can stop either inflation or deflation to any conceivable extent.

SOME TECHNICAL DETAILS

14. If at any time the price of gold is changed as herein provided—

(a) The coinage of gold by the Bureau of the Mint shall cease except as provided under (d) below, although its equivalent, the unlimited purchase of gold at the official price, shall continue.

(b) The redemption, by the United States Treasury, of United States notes, Treasury notes, and all other paper money, now redeemable in gold except gold certificates, shall be accomplished by selling gold bullion therefor, at the official price.

(c) The United States Treasury shall continue to redeem gold certificates, being warehouse receipts, in gold bullion or gold coin at the option of the holder, at the present rate of $20.67 an ounce of pure gold, or 23.22 grains per dollar.

(d) The mint is authorized and directed to coin at the present rate of 23.22 grains of pure gold per dollar such of the gold bullion belonging to the Government as may be required to satisfy any demand for gold coin by holders of gold certificates.

(e) Any (full weight) gold coin in circulation shall be redeemable by the United States Treasury at its face value in gold bullion and shall continue to be full legal tender.

(f) Gold bullion shall be full legal tender at the official price at which the Federal Reserve System sells it, provided this bullion is in the form of standard gold bars nine-tenths fine, officially stamped as to such fineness and as to weight by the United States Government under rules and regulations prescribed by the Secretary of the Treasury.

COMMENTS

The holders of gold certificates or gold coin can thus have no cause for complaint. For they can, at any time, become holders of gold coin; and the holders of gold coin can, if their coined dollars of 23.22 grains each are bigger than the new current gold bullion dollar, melt them into bullion and get more dollars than they originally had; while, on the other hand, if their coined dollars of 23.22 grains are smaller than the new current bullion dollars these coins can be used like token coins, at their face value, or redeemed in the new and bigger bullion dollars.

15. In preparation for the contingency that the price of gold may sometime be changed, the Federal Reserve System is authorized to accumulate systematically gold certificates in exchange for Federal Reserve notes, and the Treasury is authorized, as occasion offers, to retire and destroy systematically such certificataes when not further needed, to the end that, long before the possible contingency arrives of a change in the price of gold, the gold certificates in circulation shall be almost wholly replaced by Federal Reserve notes.

16. If, in the opinion of the commission, there is danger of deflation, Federal Reserve notes returned to Federal Reserve banks may be reissued and put back in circulation either via member banks or otherwise.

17. Six months after the passage of this act all bonds, notes or other contractual obligations then outstanding containing the well-known "gold clause"—"payable in gold coin of the present standard of weight and fineness," or other words to that effect, shall be subject to a tax of——per cent unless both parties shall have within said six months agreed to substitute in said contract the stabilized dollar in place of the gold dollar of the present weight and fineness.

FEDERAL RESERVE

18. If there is danger of deflation, the system is authorized, on due notice in addition to or in conjunction with other

measures already authorized in such a contingency, to lower the minimum reserve requirements of member banks, the reduction to be by a uniform percentage.

If, on the other hand, there is danger of inflation, the system is authorized, on due notice, in addition to, or in conjunction with, other measures already authorized in such a contingency to raise the minimum reserve requirements of member banks, the increase to be by a uniform percentage.

19. Better than the last is the plan proposed by Dr. Riefler of the staff of the Federal Reserve Board and recommended by the Board, whereby bank reserves shall be adjusted according to velocity of deposits, being 5 per cent plus half the daily turnover (with a maximum limit of 15 per cent).

This would operate to control member bank credit very promptly and effectively.

20. The act of March 3, 1865, imposing a tax on state bank notes is to be amended by adding:

"The Federal reserve system is authorized and directed to make a service charge of ——— per cent on all checks cleared for nonmember banks."

An alternative is to tax State banks' deposits, just as their notes were taxed in 1865 and for the same reason: to help bring about a unified national medium of exchange.

21. To the above may well be added the "Stamped money plan" described below in Appendix VII.

Many of the foregoing provisions would be unnecessary if the others were adopted. They are inserted, however, to show the abundance of means available for stabilization under almost all conceivable circumstances, although even the means enumerated do not include all possible ones. Of the various means, we may note that:

(1) Those already more or less consciously used for stabilization purposes, that is to combat inflation and deflation, are changing the rediscount rate and the open market operations.

(2) The speediest in their action on the price level are probably the stamped money plan of paragraph 21 and Appendix VII, the bond deposit plan, described in paragraphs 3–9

supra, and the automatic adjustment of reserves to velocity of deposit turnover of paragraph 19.

(3) The freest from hampering limitations is the plan of changing the price of gold.

APPENDIX VII

OTHER PLANS FOR REFLATION AND STABILIZATION

MAKING GENERAL USE OF ACCEPTANCES

Mr. Andrew W. Robertson, Chairman of the Westinghouse Electric and Manufacturing Company, suggests that, wherever possible, we should all pay our bills by 90 day acceptances—drafts on us by tradesmen. These would to some extent operate like an addition to the medium of exchange and, if widely adopted, would tend appreciably to raise the price level.

SUBSIDIES TO PRODUCERS

A plan for subsidizing producers has been suggested by Col. Malcolm C. Rorty. Enterprises that have been holding back from desirable undertakings could be rewarded by a government subsidy for borrowing from the banks the necessary funds for such undertakings—the enterprisers bidding against one another for the favor.

SUBSIDIES TO RETAILERS

A retailers' subsidy scheme has been suggested by H. B. Brougham and E. F. Harvey. According to this plan, the Government would add a percentage to the daily deposits coming into the banks from the tills of the retailers, thus enabling the retailers to give discounts to their customers. Temporarily, the discounts would reduce retail prices, but eventually the general price level would rise on the increased expenditures—that is, on the increased circulation.

LOANS TO RETAILERS' CUSTOMERS

A scheme is in actual operation (June 1932), known as "The Great Falls, Montana, Plan." It is propounded by Byron DeForest, manager of the Great Falls Credit Exchange. As far as it has gone, it is simply a plan for trusting the humble but embarrassed purchasers. Nearly all steady workmen eventually pay up. Unsecured loans to them are usually as safe as most other loans—provided health remains and the job is restored. The plan enables these storekeepers to raise money by endorsing their customers' notes. The proposal has been thus expressed by Mr. Deforest:

"We propose a 'Finance Corporation' set up by Congress putting at the disposal of the various credit bureaus throughout the United States billions of dollars to be loaned to worthy men and women, said loans to be repaid in easy payments, over as long a period as is necessary, at any rate of interest not to exceed six per cent per annum, and with no security other than the endorsement of the creditor. Such a plan would, at once, release billions of dollars into trade channels."

THE STAMPED MONEY PLAN

Nearly ten billion dollars of deposit currency have disappeared since 1929, and the residue has only 40 per cent of the 1929 velocity. The greater part of this depletion is due to the timidity of business borrowers. They would borrow if they were sure of buyers. If a plan could be devised whereby the buying could start first, the business borrowing would follow.

To stimulate buying, an ingenious scheme of which the following is an adaptation has been suggested, though I cannot find by whom.[1] Let the government print billions of special dollar bills, the reverse side to be divided into 12 spaces, each

---

[1] Since the above was written, I have learned that essentially this plan was proposed by Silvio Gesell of Argentina in 1890. It was, in effect, actually used locally in Germany in 1931. See an article, "Wara," by Hans R. L. Cohrssen in *The New Republic*, August 10, 1932.

the size of a one-cent postage stamp and each space dated; the dates to represent the first day of 12 consecutive months. Let one hundred of these dollars be given to each citizen (or every registered voter, or every person designated in such other way as may be deemed best suited to be fair and not subject to fraud and duplication). This "gift" would be to all of us from all of us (and so no gift at all), the object being merely to increase circulation and raise the price level. Each dollar bill would be legal tender provided it had the required one-cent stamps on it up to that month in which it is tendered. No one could refuse it at par because it would be legal tender; and no holder would be likely to keep it more than one month, lest it cost him another stamp; much less would he hoard it. In many cases it would circulate several times in the same month, at the saving of a cent to each user until the stamp date arrives at the beginning of the next month. Presumably such a dollar would circulate on the average more than 12 times a year. The plan would operate as a stamp tax on hoarding—increasing the velocity as well as the quantity of money.

After all the 12 stamp spaces have been filled, the dollar could be redeemed either by another of the same kind or by an ordinary dollar, at the option of the Government. If the stamped dollar, renewed, runs for nine years (108 months), the funds for this redemption will have already been provided to the government by the public in the 108 cents paid for the affixed stamps, —with 8 cents in excess.

If $100 have been given to each of 40 million people, this excess will amount in all to $8 × 40 million or $320,000,000 revenue for the government.

This unique plan would put immediate purchasing power into the hands of every consumer, including the unemployed. In fact, if desired, it could be confined to the unemployed and the original gift raised to, say, $500 per person, which, for, say, 8 million unemployed, would make the same total issue. It would then help solve two problems at once, immediate unemployment relief and reflation.

These new dollar bills would constitute an addition to the circulating medium. Moreover, they would circulate faster than money ordinarily circulates.[2]

Finally, as soon as the effect in raising the price level was felt appreciably, if not in anticipation of this effect, hoarding of other money would cease and all money, including deposit currency, would quicken its pace. In short, the new money would simply prime the pump or start the machinery going, both by providing new purchasing power and by putting a penalty on any delay in using it.

There would be a slight recession in other circulation medium. The money paid by the public in purchase of the stamps would divert this amount from other uses. But this money diverted is only equal to one per cent of the new money each month. Even if all this money paid in by the public for stamps were kept idle by the government until the 108 months were up, there would always be outstanding (except in the last eight months) more of the (new) dollar bills than of the (old) money paid into the government and held for their redemption. The excess would average for the nine years about two billions, or half of the total issue. But presumably the government would not keep idle all of the money paid in for stamps.[3]

One advantage of this plan is that it puts no added strain on gold reserves. Nor would it involve any raid on the Treasury, nor be special legislation, like the bonus bill (unless specially used as unemployment relief and, in that case, only the sort of special legislation which has long been sanctioned in emergencies). While it might be called a dole if used especially

---

[2] See "The Purchasing Power of Money" by Irving Fisher (Chapter XII), Macmillan, 1931.

[3] There would, of course, be other readjustments. For instance, as soon as hoarded money came out of hiding there might be temporarily in circulation a disproportionate amount of pocket currency.

This would result in the deposit in banks of some of the superfluous or redundant pocket currency—largely Federal Reserve notes. The depositor would receive a deposit credit, thus increasing deposit currency. The Federal Reserve notes would be sent to the Federal Reserve Bank and cancelled, and the 40 per cent gold behind them would be released for reserve against bank deposits.

for unemployment relief, it would at least be a costless dole. In fact, it would actually enrich the rest of us through attacking the dollar disease just as the cancellation of inter-governmental debts would probably enrich, not impoverish, the taxpayers of the United States. These paradoxes will surprise no one who realizes the overwhelming importance of correcting the broken-down price structure.

Nor should there be fear that such a gift to the unemployed would encourage unemployment, for there would be no chance of repeating such a distribution until, or unless, another depression came upon us. Certainly no unemployed person will voluntarily stay unemployed in order to enjoy another $500 years hence.

Meantime, involuntary unemployment would disappear with recovery.

But if, in spite of this argument, gifts to the unemployed or gifts to anybody are objected to, the reader is reminded that the stamped money could be put into circulation, though more slowly, in several other ways.

This strange-appearing plan will not seem so strange if we think of it as a loan to the public from the government, to be repaid in monthly installments of one per cent. It is as if Mr. Everyman were to borrow, on good security, of the Reconstruction Finance Corporation, agreeing to repay in monthly installments, repayment to be made in postage stamps (whether by one person or by 108 persons makes no difference).

There is no one who has any cause for complaint in these transactions. The Government has ample security; that is, repayment is certain. The borrower (the original recipient) gets what seems to him individually a gift, and he seems to pass on to others most of the burden of repayment—although, of course, he himself will be called upon to supply stamps when, in his turn, he receives such dollars. All the stamp-affixers get more benefit than injury because of the up-turn in business which the plan will so speedily bring. Each stamp-affixer will merely feel that he is paying a small "stamp-tax," or sales tax, just as now he pays a stamp-tax on checks. (And in 1898 the individual drawing the check had the trouble of affixing the stamps personally.)

There would, of course, be administrative details to be arranged. It might save some bickering if the person offering one of these dollars in payment for less than a dollar's worth of goods should be required to pay the other party the one cent for the next stamp due (so that the other party would not have to bear more than his one per cent).

The plan could conceivably be put into operation as a private expedient—by individuals, corporations, banks, clearing houses, or municipalities, instead of by the Federal Government, if the latter raised no objection—just as clearing house certificates have been so used; even the help of a legal tender law might not be necessary. It was, in fact, in such a voluntary way that substantially the same plan was used locally in Germany.[4] But properly, of course, the plan should be under the control of the Government to secure any prescribed reflation.

Besides serving as a temporary expedient to break the depression, stop hoarding, and start reflation, the plan could also be adapted to serve as a permanent instrument of stabilization by varying the interval between stamps, or the quantity in circulation, or both. Of course the Government could issue such bills in payment of its own expenses or purchase of bonds. (In fact, the original issue itself could be made in this way instead of as a gift.)

With this power the volume of the bills could, from time to time, be regulated up or down as required. This regulation should, of course, be restricted by law to the sole purpose of stabilization according to an index number.

THE GOLD TRUCE PLAN

Dr. Hermann Scheibler, head of the European branch of

---

[4] This so-called "Wära" money was also backed by a 100% reserve of German marks, so that its substitution for those marks in circulation made no net addition to the total circulating medium, its only superiority being its more rapid circulation. A facsimile of the back of one of these "Wära" notes which had actually circulated and had had stamps affixed is given in Chart 14.

291

my Index Number Institute, has proposed a plan. A resolution of the International Labor Organization, April 29, 1932, states: "To this end the Conference requests the League of Nations to place before its competent bodies as early as possible the proposal for a gold truce." It has been discussed by the Economic Council of the League of Nations.

The essential point of the plan, in Dr. Scheibler's words, is:

"The high contracting powers guarantee each other the possession of their present gold holdings.

"In order to make this guarantee effective the contracting parties report monthly or quarterly on the movements of their gold holdings to an international clearing office. Those countries, which during the period preceding the settling-day received more gold from abroad than they paid out, would hand over this surplus gold to the international clearing office as a long-term loan at a certain rate of interest with provisions for specified sinking fund payments —both being fixed in advance by the gold truce convention. The clearing office would, in turn, forward these amounts of surplus gold to those parties which had a gold deficit for the period under consideration. In short, on each settling-day the status quo as to effective gold holdings would be reestablished between the contracting parties."

This plan would largely remove the fear of gold withdrawals which now paralyze banking and commerce in countries short of gold.

MISCELLANEOUS

Among other "reflationary" expedients that might be used in a depression are:

As during the World War, an embargo could be put on gold. This would greatly enlarge the amount of currency that can maintain parity with gold and so help avoid losing gold parity and going off the gold standard completely.

National banks could be authorized to issue bank notes based on government bonds.[5]

Clearing House certificates could be used as emergency currency, as before the Federal Reserve Act was passed.

ON SILVER AND GOLD

The gold standard is chiefly useful because of the fact that it has a traditional prestige, and of the fact that gold is the most convenient medium for international settlement. The notion that gold has, in itself, stability in value is unwarranted; and in 1932 (the present writing) when so many nations are off the gold standard and some of them seeking something more stable to take its place, it is quite possible that the gold standard may be generally abandoned or modified. One such modification ("the compensated dollar") has been mentioned above.

Another modification would consist in a partial rehabilitation of silver, so as to enable silver to serve with gold in broadening the base of our credit structure.

The demonetization of silver in India by England's action in 1926 caused a fall in the price of silver in terms of gold as well as a fall in silver's purchasing power over commodities. This is well shown by the rise in the commodity price level in China, the only important silver standard country now remaining. This rise of prices in silver standard countries has helped their business and exports, just as the fall of prices in gold standard countries has hurt *their* business and exports.

A rehabilitation of silver would help overcome this handicap to the gold countries as compared with the silver countries. It might be worth the while of the United States for this purpose to bring about a rise in the price of silver in terms of gold. But the principal advantage probably would be the one just named—to broaden the base of our currency. There are several ways in which this might be done. Silver might again lawfully serve for bank reserves. This is the purpose of broadening

[5] Since this was originally written, the Glass-Borah bill has been passed for this purpose.

the base of our credit structure. Apparently there is (1932) not enough gold to maintain the predepression price level with safety. Or if there is enough it may in a few years cease to be enough. This would mean that either we must be resigned to a lower price level and all its embarrassments to debtors, or else, if we do return to the old levels, we must run the risk of again suffering a collapse in the price level.

In any case, to make silver again available for bank reserves would make for a safer and longer continued maintenance of a proper price level. There are various ways of restoring silver. One is bimetallism. But this is not very satisfactory because it is itself so precarious.[6] Sooner or later bimetallism is sure to turn into monometallism of one kind or the other.

Another method is "symmetallism," or linked bars of gold and silver. But this, even if politically feasible, would require going off the gold standard immediately. This, while theoretically desirable, would be fraught with practical complications, including "gold clause" contracts (although, as already indicated, these could be taxed out of existence).

The best plan it seems to me, is one proposed by James H. Rand, Jr. He suggests that we (preferably with other countries) buy silver as we did under the Sherman Act, at market prices and, with the silver so purchased, issue, or stand ready to issue, new gold-silver coins, using in each dollar 40 cents of gold (a "forty per cent gold reserve" as Mr. Rand calls it) and an amount of silver equal to the silver in our present silver dollar. These new dollars would, like our silver dollars, be full legal tender. Certificates (more or less like silver certificates) would be issued, representing these gold-silver coins (or the bullion equivalent).

Subject to a maximum limit, the governmental purchase of silver would be continued until the gold-silver dollar became "intrinsically" worth a dollar, i. e., until the silver bullion in it came to be worth 60 cents. This, with the 40 cents gold, would make up a full value dollar. The silver purchases would then

[6] See "The Mechanics of Bimetallism," by Irving Fisher, (British) *Economic Journal,* 1894.

cease. If and when the silver came to be worth more than 60 cents, say 61 cents, so that the "intrinsic" worth of the gold-silver dollar would be 101 cents, the government would then sell silver bullion instead of buying it, until the gold-silver dollar was no longer intrinsically worth more than one dollar. If and when it again became intrinsically worth less than a dollar, the purchases would recommence. In this way, the gold-silver dollar would be kept at, or very near, par.

Such gold-silver dollars could serve as reserve and yet gold would remain the standard.

There would be limits beyond which the silver purchases and sales could or should not go. No more silver could or should be sold than was possessed by the government and no more should be bought than could be bought without surrendering the gold standard.

SHALL WE KEEP THE GOLD STANDARD?

In case the gold standard is to be entirely abandoned and all nations resort to a managed currency, the place of gold for redeeming other money can be taken by managed fiat paper money, just as, already in the Federal Reserve System, "lawful money," such as our silver dollars and silver certificates (which are "fiat" money in the sense of being legal tender for much more than their "intrinsic" worth), operates as reserve against the deposits of member banks. The new fiat base would preferably be international paper money made legal tender in all countries by treaty.[7]

But going off the gold standard is not an easy matter, especially in the United States.

In Britain it was done as follows: on Sunday, September 20, 1931, the Cabinet met and decided to suspend the provisions of the Bank Acts of 1825 and of 1844 which obligate the Bank of England to buy all gold that is offered at the rate of £3 17s 9d per troy ounce of standard gold (11/12 fine) and to sell to all

[7] This money could be created as a part of a plan for international debt settlement as proposed by James H. Rand, Jr.

purchasers standard gold at the rate of £3 17s 10½d per troy ounce. Notice of this decision was sent to the officers of the Bank of England. Accordingly, when the Bank opened on the morning of Monday, September 21, the officers refused to buy or sell gold. This refusal by the bank officers was illegal until Parliament passed an act later in the day, formally suspending the gold purchase and sale provisions.

In the United States, we have no traditions for such summary legislation. While our Senate was debating the question, our gold would be withdrawn by foreigners and speculators and every bank would be forced to suspend specie payments. No other and more orderly way of going off the gold standard seems practicable for the United States. The legislation would have to come after the harm had been done.

In 1932 there was once an attempt to secure legislation authorizing the Federal Reserve Board to alter the buying and selling prices of gold. One thought in the legislation was that it could be used, in an emergency, to put us off the gold standard summarily by raising to a prohibitive figure the price at which gold would be sold by the government (i. e., used in redemption). In other words, the Board would lower the weight of the gold dollar enormously. The chief virtue of this proposal was that its implications might not be understood until the action was taken! But the very fact that it was not understood prevented its adoption.

One of the chief difficulties for America in getting off the gold standard is the existence of a great mass of gold clause contracts, by which payment is stipulated in gold coin "of the present weight and fineness." It is true that the greenback decision certified the right of Congress to make United States notes legal tender for the payment of debts contracted prior to the legislation. The legal tender act, it is true, related only to contracts to pay money generally and not to contracts to pay a specific kind of money such as "gold coin of the present weight and fineness." But Justice Bradley (12 Wall. 457, 566, 567) said: "I do not understand the majority of the Court to decide that an Act so drawn as to embrace in terms contracts payable in specie would not be constitutional. Such a decision would completely nullify the power claimed for the Government."

But it is probable, I am told on good legal authority, that Congress does not have the power, constitutionally, to abrogate the gold clause contracts.

Apparently the most promising way to handle these gold clause contracts would be to tax prohibitively their fulfillment. The power to tax seems to be almost unlimited.

However, the complications and disturbances which would be incident to going off the gold standard seem, in America, to be so great that for this reason alone it would be advisable, if possible, to retain the gold standard.

There remains one possibility which may be worth mentioning. Since gold today does not really contribute appreciably to the value of other money, but, on the contrary, derives its value almost wholly from other money, it might prove feasible (1) to add to the "lawful money" (now available for reserve against the member bank deposits) enough other "lawful" fiat money to make gold superfluous; (2) to make this other money available for reserve against Federal Reserve notes also; and (3) having thus no further need of gold as a redemption base, demonetarize it to the extent of no longer *requiring* redemption in it, but requiring only that gold money be required to be redeemable in other money, and not the other money in gold. Gold would then still keep parity with other money, could still serve in settlements of international balances, and would still keep its place in gold clause contracts, as Sir Arthur Salter has recently suggested.

Ideally a fiat paper money base would be far superior to any metallic standard; but, as Sir Arthur says, we must wait until we can have confidence that the issuing government will not abuse the privilege. Perhaps if the issue were under the auspices not of one nation only but of a number, there would be security in numbers. No country would be likely to permit the other countries in the agreement to abuse the privilege.

Gold is far from being a satisfactory standard, despite its traditional reputation for being "the best standard which has been tried," and despite the recent efforts of conservative followers of tradition to bolster it up—including the majority report of the League of Nations "Gold Delegation" in June 1932. The majority almost invariably follows tradition right or wrong.

It is interesting to find in conservative England a few economists, business men and bankers who favor a continuance of managed currency. Sir Basil Blackett, a director of the Bank of England, was quoted in the newspapers of October 22, 1931, as saying,

"We are bound to ask whether there is an alternative international standard, such as bimetallism, symmetallism or a non-metallic standard which would work better than gold. Even if there is such an alternative, however, the question will still be asked whether conditions are ripe for its adoption.

"If by sacrificing the stability of exchange Britain can be made the master of its own economic destiny, not to be dragged at the wheels of the chariot of the Federal Reserve System of the United States or the Bank of France, and give real stability to the internal price level, the alternative of a managed sterling currency system is at least worth examining."

The gold standard is too much subject to the accidents of gold discoveries and too easily manipulated, consciously or unconsciously. It sometimes seems, as it were, suddenly to pull a string and precipitate a depression because of accidental coincidental influences depleting some great bank's reserves, as in the case in 1931 of the Bank of England.

A fiat base could be instantly reinforced. It would require far less skill than the open market operations now require to pump the fiat money reserve in or out so as to maintain a really stable price level. Depressions could scarcely occur in any degree worthy of the name. And, in case a depression did occur, instead of "balancing the budget" governments would pay bills with fiat money, thus killing two birds with one stone—solving the problem of public finance and solving the problem of deflation.

Fiat money has a bad name and deservedly. But its shortcomings are purely political, not economic, and economists ought not to be afraid to say so. The old ideas that money must derive its value from something else has been exploded both by theory and experience. Sweden during the war made its paper money more valuable than the gold which was supposed to give it value! In the Ukraine, paper money circulated after the invading German general who issued it and his government had passed off the scene! In neither of these two cases nor in others which might be mentioned could the value of the money be explained by any hope of redemption. Our own silver certificates are redeemable only in silver dollars which are worth "intrinsically" twenty-five cents and which are not redeemable in gold. Before the gold standard act of 1900 there was not even any express policy of parity—only legal tender and quantity limitation. Moreover, if we were now to change this status and to make silver certificates and silver dollars not legal tender but redeemable in gold, requiring, say, a 40 per cent reserve as for Federal Reserve notes, the result would be to weaken not strengthen our monetary system, to put an added strain on our gold reserve, to run the risk of sudden raids and manipulations which might at any time pull the string which would bring deflation with a jerk.

Yet, curiously enough, all our haphazard silver and greenback money now has the sanction of tradition. If it all had not been handed down to us but were today to be proposed as something new, it would be laughed to scorn—as it should be.

If we could only have inherited a logical systematic fiat system dedicated to stability in value, it also would have had the sanction of tradition. But, if this were now proposed as something new, it would probably be laughed to scorn—though it should not be.

Possibly, however, the time has come when such suggestions as those of Sir Basil Blackett can be seriously considered. At any rate our list of good expedients would not be complete without the inclusion of a fiat substitute for gold reserves and as ideal in *economic*, if not in political, theory.

SUMMARY

Whenever there has been any intense interest in the stabilization problem it has always been after some great suffering from inflation or deflation. But after great and rapid deflation, as in 1932, some inflation is required; and after great and rapid inflation, as in 1920, some deflation. Either correction is properly to be called "reflation."

Thus reflation is, in practice, always the first and most urgent problem preliminary to stabilization as a permanent policy.

Practically all the means available for reflation are also available for stabilization and conversely. We have seen that the chief of these means available for the Federal Reserve System are two, both of which are for credit control only: adjustments of rediscount rates, and open market operations.

But any central bank will always be confronted with so many other problems that it can never be the ideal medium for effecting reflation and stabilization, though its influence must always be reckoned with and should always be a cooperative influence. What is really needed is a special agency of the government such as a Stabilization Commission.

We have found as the most important means available to such a stabilization agency:

For Gold Control

The compensated dollar plan
The plan of gold-mine control,
The sterilized or surplus gold plan;

For Credit and Paper Money Control under a Gold Standard

The stamped money plan,
The bond deposit plan.
If the gold standard be abolished the principal method is:

Adjusting legal tender paper money, to be used as a basis for credit instead of gold.

Preferably this paper money should be under international auspices. In that case each nation could have its own system of regulation of the credit structure based on said international paper money just as it may now, based on gold.

Either under the gold standard or a substitute it would be possible for each nation to have its own independent system of regulation. If they all employed the same index number, say, that of wholesale prices in London, they could keep their foreign exchanges substantially fixed, and maintain substantially fixed ratios between their several money units and also between their price levels.

An alternative would be to have one world system of stabilization.

MR. HOOVER'S RELIEF PROGRAM

President Hoover in his annual message on December 8, 1931, submitted to Congress and the country a comprehensive program for emergency relief and several measures which should help to mitigate the fearful booms and crises in business.

The program attempted by the Administration and Congress included: (1) planning public works in advance to give employment in times of depression; (2) an Economic Council to plan production and prevent or care for unemployment; (3) intergovernmental debt revision to restore solvency to Germany and the world; (4) the National Credit Corporation formed of bankers to unfreeze frozen bank assets and relieve distressed depositors; (5) the Railroad Pool for helping weaker railroads to meet interest payments on their bonds; (6) the Home Mortgage Corporation to make real estate borrowing easier and cheaper, thus stimulating building, especially residential building; (7) the Reconstruction Finance Corporation to make loans to distressed farmers, banks and any other distressed businesses so as to thaw out congealed assets and cause money and credit streams again to flow; (8) the Glass-Steagall Act amending the Federal Reserve Act to expand bank credit by making it possible for member banks to obtain loans from Reserve banks on their own promissory notes and to issue Federal Reserve notes secured by United States bonds, thus setting free gold reserves; (9) a vigorous (so it was then hoped) anti-deflation policy on the part of Federal Reserve Banks through lowering rediscount rates and buying United States securities in the open market, thus building up the gold reserves of member banks and encouraging them to inaugurate a more liberal loan policy; (10) further amendments to the Federal Reserve Act unifying and strengthening the banking system by bringing all or almost all banks into the Federal Reserve System; (11) the anti-hoarding campaign; (12) Committees of bankers and industrialists formed for the purpose of setting the unemployed bank reserves to work.

Some relief measures have not fulfilled the hopes entertained when they were conceived. The disappointment has been especially acute with the Public Works program, the Farm Board's Revolving Fund, and the Debt Moratorium.

The Reconstruction Finance Corporation may be described as the peace time prototype of the War Finance Corporation which served so well during the World War. It is referred to as the $2 billion Finance Corporation, but its capital stock was originally limited to $500 million, all of which was "subscribed by the United States of America, payment for which shall be subject to call in whole or in part by the Board of Directors of the Corporation." Later the capital was increased by 2 billion. The Corporation may loan this capital and issue $1.5 billions of its notes and other obligations with maturities of not more than five years. Fifty million dollars were made immediately available to the Secretary of Agriculture for emergency farm relief with the possibility of extending the amount to $200 million. The Corporation was "empowered to make loans, upon such terms and conditions not inconsistent with this act as it may determine, to any bank, savings bank, trust company, building and loan association, insurance company, mortgage bank, Federal intermediate credit bank, agricultural credit corporation, live stock credit corporation, organized under the laws of any state or of the United States, including loans secured by the assets of any bank that is closed, or in process of liquidation." Not more than $200 million is to be used for the relief of closed banks. The Corporation "may also, upon the approval of the Interstate Commerce Commission, make loans to aid in the temporary financing of railroads and railways engaged in interstate commerce," or under construction or in receivership.

APPENDIX VIII

SELECTED BIBLIOGRAPHY

For fuller bibliographies see:

Books about Business Cycles, Illinois University College of Commerce and Business Administration, Bureau of Business Research, Bulletin no. 22, Urbana, Ill., 1928.

Schmid, Anton, "Bibliographie der Konjunktur- und Krisenforschung," *Archiv der Fortschritte betriebswirtschaftlicher Forschung und Lehre,* Vol. IV, 1927, pp. 183–99.

Abbati, A. H., *The Final Buyer,* P. S. King & Son, Ltd., London, 1928.

Adams, Arthur B., *Economics of Business Cycles,* McGraw-Hill Book Co., Inc., New York, 1925.

Adams, Arthur B., *The Trend of Business, 1922–1932,* Harper & Bros., New York, 1932.

Aftalion, Albert, *Les Crises Periodique de Surproduction,* Paris, 1913.

Ahern, J., *Economic Progress and Economic Crises,* London, 1928.

Altman, George T., *An Investigation into the Causes of the Trade Cycle by Way of Mathematical Theory,* George T. Altman, 35 East Wacker Drive, Chicago, Ill., 1932.

Anderson, Montgomery, "An Agricultural Theory of Business Cycles," *The American Economic Review,* Vol. XXI, No. 3, September 1931, pp. 427–46.

244

Beckhart, B. H., *The Discount Policy of the Federal Reserve System*, Henry Holt & Co., New York, 1924.

Beckhart, B. H., *The New York Money Market*, Columbia University Press, New York, 1932.

Berridge, William A., *Cycles of Unemployment in the United States 1903–1922*, Houghton Mifflin Co., Boston & New York, 1929.

Beveridge, Sir William H., *Unemployment, a Problem of Industry*, 2d ed., London, 1910.

Beveridge, Sir William H., "Weather and Harvest Cycles," *Economic Journal*, Vol. XXXI, December, 1921, pp. 449–51.

Beveridge, Sir William H., "Wheat Prices and Rainfall in Western Europe," *Journal of the Royal Statistical Society*, Vol. LXXXV, May, 1922, pp. 412–59.

Bonn, M. J., *The Crisis of Capitalism in America*, John Day Co., New York, 1932.

Bouniatian, Mentor, *Les Crises Économiques*, 2nd ed., M. Giard, Paris, 1930.

Cannan, Edwin, *Modern Currency and the Regulation of Its Value*, P. S. King & Son, Ltd., London, 1931.

Cassel, Gustav, *Theory of Social Economy*, Harcourt, Brace & Co., New York, 1932.

Clark, J. M., *The Economics of Overhead Cost*, University of Chicago Press, Chicago, 1923.

Commons, John R., "Farm Prices and the Value of Gold," *North American Review*, January and February, 1928.

Crum, W. L., "Cycles of Rates on Commercial Paper," *Review of Economic Statistics*, Preliminary Vol. V., January, 1923, pp. 17–29.

Donham, Wallace Brett, *Business Adrift*, McGraw-Hill Book Co., New York, 1931.

Douglas, Paul H. and Director, Aaron, *The Problem of Unemployment*, Macmillan Co., New York, 1931.

Edie, Lionel D., *The Banks and Prosperity*, Harper & Bros., New York, 1931.

Edie, Lionel D., *Money, Bank Credit and Prices*, Harper & Bros., New York, 1928.

Foster, William T. and Catchings, Waddill, *Profits*, Houghton Mifflin Co., Boston and New York, 1925.

Frank, Lawrence K., "A Theory of Business Cycles," *Quarterly Journal of Economics*, August, 1923, pp. 625–42.

Frisch, Ragnar, "A Method of Decomposing an Empirical Series into its Cyclical and Progressive Components," *American Statistical Journal, Supplement*, March 1931, pp. 73–78.

Graham, Frank D., *The Abolition of Unemployment*, Williams and Wilkins, Baltimore, 1932.

Hall, Lincoln W., *Banking Cycles*, University of Pennsylvania Press, Philadelphia, 1927.

Hansen, Alvin Harvey, "The Business Cycle in its Relation to Agriculture," *Farm Economics*, Jan., 1932, pp. 59–67.

Hansen, Alvin Harvey, *Business Cycle Theory*, Ginn & Co., New York, 1927.

Hansen, Alvin Harvey, *Economic Stabilization in an Unbalanced World*, Harcourt, Brace & Co., New York, 1932.

Hardy, C. O., *Credit Policies of the Federal Reserve System*, Brookings Institution, Washington, 1932 (In Press).

Hastings, Hudson B., *Costs and Profits, Their Relation to Business Cycles*, Houghton Mifflin Co., Boston and New York, 1923.

Hawtrey, R. G., *Currency and Credit*, Longmans, Green & Co., New York, 1928.

Hawtrey, R. G., *Trade and Credit*, Longmans, Green & Co., London, 1928.

Hayek, F. A., *Prices and Production*, George Routledge & Sons, London, 1931.

Hexter, Maurice Beck, *Social Consequences of Business Cycles*, Houghton Mifflin Co., Boston and New York, 1925, pp. 206.

Hobson, J. A., *Economics of Unemployment*, G. Allen & Unwin, Ltd., London, 1922.

Hobson, J. A., *The Industrial System*, Longmans, Green & Co., New York, 1909.

Hull, George H., *Industrial Depressions*, Frederick A. Stokes Co., New York, 1911.

Huntington, Ellsworth, *World-Power and Evolution*, New Haven, 1919, Chs. II–IV, pp. 29, 42.

Jerome, Harry, *Migration and Business Cycles*, National Bureau of Economic Research, New York, 1926.

Jevons, Herbert Stanley, "The Causes of Unemployment: III, Trade Fluctuations and Solar Activity," *Contemporary Review*, Vol. XCVI, August, 1909, pp. 165 ff. Reprinted with added preface and summary, as *The Sun's Heat and Trade Activity*, London, 1910.

Jevons, W. Stanley, *Investigations in Currency and Finance*, Edited by H. S. Foxwell, London, 1884.

Jones, Edward D., *Economic Crises*, Macmillan Co., New York, 1900.

Juglar, Clement, *Des Crises Commerciales*, Librairie Guillaumin et C., Paris, 1889.

Kempster, J. W., *Banking Credit and the Crisis*, London General Press, London, 1932.

Keynes, John Maynard, *Essays in Persuasion*, Harcourt, Brace & Co., New York, 1932.

Keynes, John Maynard, *A Treatise on Money*, 2 vols., Harcourt, Brace & Co., New York, 1930.

King, Willford I., "Credit in the Business Cycle," *Burroughs Clearing House*, November, 1930.

King, Willford I., *Employment Hours and Earnings in Prosperity and Depression, United States, 1920–1922*, National Bureau of Economic Research, New York, 1923.

King, Willford I., "The Immediate Cause of the Business Cycle," *American Statistical Association Supplement*, March, 1932, pp. 218–230.

Kondratieff, N. D., "Die langen Wellen der Konjunktur," *Archiv für Sozialwissenschaft und Sozialpolitik*, Bd. 56, Heft 3.

Kondratieff, N. D., "Die Preisdynamik der industriellen und landwirtschaftlichen Waren," *Archiv für Sozialwissenschaft und Sozialpolitik*, Bd. 60, Heft 1.

Kuznets, Simon S., *Cyclical Fluctuations*, Adelphi Co., New York, 1926.

Kuznets, Simon S., "Random Events and Cyclical Oscillations," *Journal of the American Statistical Association*, September, 1929, pp. 258–275.

Kuznets, Simon S., *Secular Movements in Production and Prices*, Houghton Mifflin Co., Boston and New York, 1930.

Lescure, Jean, *Des Crises Générales et Périodiques de Surproduction*, 3rd Ed., L. Tenin, *Bibliothèque d'Economie Politique et Sociologie, III*, Paris, 1923.

Lescure, Jean, "Crises," *Encyclopaedia of the Social Sciences*, Vol. 4, Macmillan Co., New York, 1931, pp. 595–599.

Lightner, Otto C., *The History of Business Depressions*, The Northeastern Press, New York, 1922.

Martin, P. W., *The Problem of Maintaining Purchasing Power*, P. S. King & Son, Ltd., London, 1931.

Mitchell, Wesley C., "Business Cycles," *Encyclopaedia of the Social Sciences*, Vol. III, Macmillan Co., New York, 1930, pp. 93–106.

Mitchell, Wesley C., *Business Cycles*, University of California, 1913.

Mitchell, Wesley C., *Business Cycles, The Problem and Its Setting*, National Bureau of Economic Research, New York, 1927.

Mises, Ludwig, *Geldwertstahlisierung und Konjunkturpolitik*, Verlag von Gustav Fischer, Jena, 1928.

Moon, Parker Thomas, Editor, Collection on: "Depression and Revival," *Proceedings of the American Academy of Political Science*, Vol. XIV, No. 3, June, 1931.

Moon, Parker Thomas, Editor, Collection on: "Can Prices, Production and Employment be Effectively Regulated?"

Proceedings of the Academy of Political Science, Vol. XIV, No. 4, New York, January, 1932.

Moore, Henry L., *Economic Cycles: Their Law and Cause,* Macmillan Co., New York, 1914.

Moore, Henry L., *Generating Economic Cycles,* Macmillan Co., New York, 1923.

Persons, Warren M., *Forecasting Business Cycles,* John Wiley & Sons, Inc., New York, 1931.

Persons, Warren M., "Theories of Business Fluctuations," *Quarterly Journal of Economics,* Vol. XLI, November, 1926, pp. 94–128.

Persons, Warren M., Foster, W. T., and Hittinger, A. J., *The Problem of Business Forecasting,* Houghton Mifflin Co., Boston & New York, 1924.

Pigou, A. C., *Industrial Fluctuations,* Macmillan Co., New York, 1929.

Pownall, G. H., "Periodicity of Crises," *Palgrave's Dictionary of Political Economy,* Vol. I, A-E, Macmillan & Co., Ltd., London, 1925, pp. 466–67.

Reed, H. L., *Federal Reserve Policy, 1921–30,* McGraw-Hill Co., 1930.

Ricci, Umberto, "Les Crises Économiques et la Dépression Présente," *L'Égypte Contemporaine,* Vol. XXII, pp. 249–307.

Riefler, W. W., *Money Rates and Money Markets in the United States,* Harper & Bros., New York, 1930.

Robertson, D. H., *Banking Policy and the Price Level,* P. S. King & Son, Ltd., London, 1926.

Rogers, James Harvey, *America Weighs Her Gold,* Yale University Press, New Haven, 1931.

Roos, C. F., "A Mathematical Theory of Price and Production Fluctuations and Economic Crises," *Journal of Political Economy,* Vol. XXXVIII, No. 5, October, 1930, pp. 501–522.

Salter, Sir Arthur, *Recovery, the Second Effort,* The Century Co., New York, 1932.

Schumpeter, J., *Theorie der Wirtschaftlichen Entwicklung*, Duncker u. Humblot, München, 1926.

Snyder, Carl, *Business Cycles and Business Measurements*, Macmillan Co., 1927.

Sombart, Werner, *Der moderne Kapitalismus*, 3 vols., Vols. I–II, 3rd Ed. Duncker u. Humblot, Munich und Leipsig, 1919; Vol. III, 1927.

Soule, George, *A Planned Society*, Macmillan Co., New York, 1931.

Spiethoff, Arthur, "Krisen," *Handwörterbuch der Staatswissenschaften*, Vol. VI, 4th Ed., Jena 1925, p. 8–91.

Sprague, O. M. W., *History of Crises under the National Banking System*, Supt. of Documents, Washington, 1910.

Sprague, O. M. W., "Major and Minor Trade Fluctuations," *Journal of the Royal Statistical Society*, Vol. XCIV, Part IV, 1931, pp. 540–549.

Strong, Benjamin, *Interpretations of Federal Reserve Policy*, Harper & Bros., New York, 1930.

Thorp, Willard Long and Mitchell, Wesley C., *Business Annals*, National Bureau of Economic Research, Inc., New York, 1926.

Timoshenko, V., The Role of Agricultural Fluctuations in the Business Cycle, *Mich. Bus. Studies* 2, June, 1930.

Tugan-Baranovski, Michel, *Les Crises Industrialles en Angleterre*, Paris, 1913.

Wagemann, Ernst, *Economic Rhythm*, McGraw-Hill Book Co., New York, 1930.

Walker, Karl, *Das Problem unserer Zeit und seine Meisterung*, Rudolf Zitzmann Verlag, Lauf a. Pegnitz.

Warren, G. F. and Pearson, F. A., "Commodity Prices," *Farm Economics*, New York State College of Agriculture, February, 1932, pp. 1659–1705.

Warren, G. F., and Pearson, F. A., "The Future of the General Price Level," *Farm Economics*, New York State College of Agriculture, Jan., 1932, pp. 23–46.

Warren, G. F., and Pearson, F. A., "Prices," *Farm Economics*,

New York State College of Agriculture, Jan., 1932, pp. 1742–51.

Wicksell, Knut, *Vorlesungen über Nationalökonomie; Geld und Kredit*, Verlag von Gustav Fischer, Jena, 1928.

Young, A. A., *Analysis of Banking Statistics for the United States*, Harvard Press, 1928.

The World's Economic Crisis and the Way of Escape, by Sir Arthur Salter, Sir Josiah Stamp, J. Maynard Keynes, Sir Basil Blackett, Henry Clay, Sir W. H. Beveridge, The Century Co., New York, pp. 185.

Interim Report of the Gold Delegation of the Financial Committee of the League of Nations, Series of League of Nations Publications II. Economic and Financial, 1930, II. 26.

Second Interim Report of the Gold Delegation of the Financial Committee of the League of Nations, Series of League of Nations Publications, II. Economic and Financial, 1931, II. A2.

Final Report of the Gold Delegation of the Financial Committee of the League of Nations, Geneva, June 1932.

Report: Committee on Finance and Industry, H. M. Stationery Office, London, 1931.

Report: *The Course and Phases of the World Economic Depression*, Secretariat of the League of Nations, Geneva, 1931.

Report of the Committee of the President's Conference on Unemployment, *Business Cycles and Unemployment*, Mcgraw-Hill Book Co., New York, 1923.

Hearings before the Committee on Banking and Currency of the House of Representatives, on Goldsborough Bill, H.R. 11788, 1923, H.R. 494, 1925.

Hearings before the Committee on Banking and Currency of the House of Representatives, on Strong Bill, H.R. 7895, 1927, H.R. 11806, 1928. (See especially testimony of J. R. Bellerby, W. R. Burgess, John R. Commons, Gustav Cassel, E. A. Goldenweiser, Adolph C. Miller, Edmund Platt, Walter W. Stewart, R. A. Lehfeldt, O. M. W. Sprague, Henry A. Shearer, Benjamin Strong, Owen D. Young, Roy A. Young.)

Hearings before the Sub-Committee on Banking and Currency of the House of Representatives, on Goldsborough Bill (similar to Strong Bill of 1927 and 1928), H.R. 10517, 1932. (See especially testimony of Willford I. King, Irving Fisher, Robert L. Owen.)

Hearings before the Joint Commission of Agricultural Inquiry, Senate, 1921. (See especially testimony of Governor Strong.)

Journals Containing Special Articles on the Subject

Econometrica (beginning January 1933; will give special attention to Booms and Depressions).
Review of Economic Statistics
Journal of the American Statistical Society
Journal of the Royal Statistical Society
American Economic Review
Journal of Political Economy
Quarterly Journal of Economics
Journal of the Royal Economic Society
Vierteljahrshefte zur Konjunkturforschung (Berlin)

INDEX

A

B

C

Editorial Postscript
with Selected Documents

Booms and Depressions received scant attention from reviewers in the standard academic journals of the day and that which it did receive was largely hostile. Writing in the *American Economic Review*, Raymond T. Bowman characterized it as "of little use to the lay reader and of even smaller value to the technical investigator of business cycle phenomena."[a] Harold Barger devoted one paragraph to the work in the *Economic Journal* in which he observed that "what little theory it contains is in no way novel" and "that this book cannot but be something of a disappointment."[b] *Economica*'s reviewer, Ralph Arakie, found fault with the author's preoccupation with a monetary theory of the cycle and was particularly harsh about Fisher's treatment of price behavior between the years of 1923 and 1929 (see pp. 74–75 of the text). Despite the fact that the commodity price level did not rise – and, thus, the expected "warning" about impending instability "failed to put in an appearance" – Fisher had described this as an "inflationary period." The reviewer wondered whether Fisher had grasped the "significance" of this problem "for he is as ardent a stabilizer as ever."[c]

Fisher's essential contribution at that time was conveyed far more effectively to most members of the economics profession in article form than in book form. He had been a prime mover in the formation of the Econometric Society, serving as its first president in 1933. "The Debt-Deflation Theory of Great Depressions" – which appeared in the first volume of the Society's journal – summarized the basic argument set out in *Booms and Depressions*. Events during the year which elapsed between the publication of the book and the article added plausibility to Fisher's thesis. When *Booms and Depressions* had gone to press in the late summer of 1932, Fisher believed that a momentum for recovery had, at last, been solidly established. (For details on his reading of the flow of events at that time, see Volume XIV.) In the version of the "debt-deflation" theory

---

[a] Raymond T. Bowman, *American Economic Review*, March 1933, 127–28.
[b] Harold Barger, *Economic Journal*, December 1933, 681.
[c] Ralph Arakie, *Economica*, November 1933, 484–87.

which appeared in the autumn of 1933, he could properly draw attention to the experience of late 1932 and early 1933 – which culminated in the total paralysis of the U.S. financial system in March 1933 – as tending to confirm the rightness of his analysis.

In the atmosphere of 1933, the distinctive attributes of Fisher's doctrine were unmistakable. From his perspective, deflation was self-evidently harmful and needed to be countered by deliberate measures to "reflate." This position was squarely at odds with one holding that downward adjustments in prices could perform a constructive function. At the time, a respectable number of influential economists supported the latter view. A version of this doctrine – most prominently associated with the work of Professor A.C. Pigou of Cambridge University – maintained that a disequilibrium evidenced by falling prices would be temporary and self-correcting. Lower prices meant that the purchasing power of financial assets would be increased; those enjoying this improvement in their "real balances" would soon be induced to consume more and to save less; the resulting increment in spending would then stabilize the economy at a new equilibrium. In the United States, there was also considerable support for the conclusion that falling prices were not unhealthy for another reason. This line of argument took the following general form: the depression itself was a by-product of the fact that market imperfections had permitted prices and wages to be artificially high. Unemployment and excess capacity had thereby been generated because workers and producers had priced themselves out of the market. Downward flexibility in prices and wages – i.e., deflation – could thus be perceived as a good thing. By contrast, Fisher insisted that deflation had nothing but disastrous consequences.

Fisher was certainly eager to promote the spread of his message among economists. When submitting a truncated version of the argument to Ragnar Frisch, the editor of *Econometrica*, he wrote as follows:

"As you will see, the paper is an attempt to summarize under about 49 categorical statements what is in my *Booms and Depressions*, and my other few writings along these lines, and in more general terms what has been done by others. I wrote to Wesley C. Mitchell asking for his opinion as to whether I had been anticipated, and he wrote back that I had not and that my theory was both new and important. He said that the nearest writer was Veblen, but I find that he is not very near. . . .

If Mitchell is right, I suppose that from a practical point of view at least, my *Booms and Depressions* is my chief contribution to economic science, and as such, I would like to get whatever credit belongs to me and to have the conclusions not only accepted but recognized as mine among the rising generation of economists who are now being marshalled into the Econometric Society. . . .

I am particular in regard to this claim to originality not only because of the practical importance of this matter but also because the conclusions are getting to be so widely accepted and taken as a matter of course that the origin is likely to be overlooked – and all the more because *Booms and Depressions* was written not altogether or even primarily for the student of economic science but in order to accomplish something practical in the way of bringing about recovery from this terrible depression. With that object, the book was written in as popular language as was consistent with accuracy, so that technical students may not realize that it is a new contribution at all. In fact, one careless reviewer referred to it as a 'rehash' of my previous writings, overlooking entirely the parts that were new. I also purposely refrained in the preface from stressing any claims for originality lest it might give the cautious reader the impression that 'economists never agree' and that here is just another theory to be thrown into the cauldron, to be destroyed by the criticism of others.

Between you and me, I think the book has been one of the two books (the other being *Prices* by Warren and Pearson) which have had the greatest influence in bringing about the decisive measures taken by President Roosevelt. The book was in galley when I visited him at Albany a year ago, and at his request I sent him a copy which he afterward wrote me that he had read. Warren has been close to the President, and the last time I saw Warren he told me that one thing the President would never forget is that the debts, though great in 1929 and seemingly reduced, now are really greater relatively to the national wealth today.

Of course, to the President belongs the lion's share of credit for the bold steps taken to get out of the depression, and among those who have influenced him are others, notably Warren, who has probably had more influence than I, but I am sure that I have had *some* influence. I am, humanly speaking, sure that with Congress I have had more influence than any other living economist, partly through *Booms and Depressions*, partly through *The Money Illusion*, partly through personal appearances before Committees of Congress in which the principles of *Booms and Depressions* have been expounded, and partly through many personal contacts. . . ."[a]

When accepting the manuscript of "The Debt-Deflation Theory of Great Depressions" for publication in *Econometrica*, Frisch congratulated Fisher on his achievement and added: "In my opinion it emphasizes one very important aspect of the business cycle problem and I think you are right when you say that this point has not properly been discussed before, so that you really have a claim of priority in this matter. Of course, as you say, many other business cycle theorists have mentioned

---

[a] Fisher to Ragnar Frisch, June 22, 1933, Frisch Papers.

the effect of debts without however drawing all the important consequences which your analysis has now brought into the limelight."[a]

Fisher welcomed this news and responded to Frisch at length.

"... I would suggest that either yourself or someone whom we can enlist should write up the whole available literature in which either debts or deflation, or (more important) both, have been cited in relation to booms and depressions. I have no doubt that many others will be found besides those I have so far found or been told about; and I should expect that more attention has been given in *this* depression than in former depressions, owing partly to the fact that it is the greatest of all depressions (and the bigger the depression, the more these factors stand out); partly to the existence of international debts which are particularly prominent; and partly to the prominence, before the crash, of margin-trading and installment-buying in America.

I shall be surprised, however, if any of the points which I regard as new in my article will be found in the literature – in particular that liquidation may defeat itself.

It seems to me that the primary reason why this central cause and its numerous effects have been overlooked is the 'money illusion.' Most economists are almost as much subject to this as the public, and especially those who are not money economists but who want to 'look through money' to something more 'real,' not realizing that they are looking through a distorting medium and taking for granted that money really measures value, with the result that the 'real' thing is not as they see it. ...

In future studies, both the fact that the monetary unit may swell faster than the number of units of debt shrinks and the fact that the real income shrinks can be elaborated. Both are mentioned in *Booms and Depressions*. Debt embarrassment may be aggravated by either or both. ...

Perhaps I am unduly emphasizing the importance of further studies on debt and deflation. But, if I *am* right, I have a personal interest because, in that case, (1) this paper and *Booms and Depressions* include my chief practical contribution to economic science, and (2) the sooner economic telescopes are pointed in these new directions the sooner we can expect to avoid great depressions in the future.

I am planning to send the article to all students in this field – writers, editors, business leaders, and so forth. Incidentally, I hope that it may help the Econometric Society."[b]

---

[a] Frisch to Fisher, August 19, 1933, Frisch Papers.
[b] Fisher to Frisch, September 4, 1933, Frisch Papers.

Econometrica, Vol. I (October 1933).

THE DEBT-DEFLATION THEORY
OF GREAT DEPRESSIONS

By Irving Fisher

INTRODUCTORY

In *Booms and Depressions*, I have developed, theoretically and statistically, what may be called a debt-deflation theory of great depressions. In the preface, I stated that the results "seem largely new," I spoke thus cautiously because of my unfamiliarity with the vast literature on the subject. Since the book was published its special conclusions have been widely accepted and, so far as I know, no one has yet found them anticipated by previous writers, though several, including myself, have zealously sought to find such anticipations. Two of the best-read authorities in this field assure me that those conclusions are, in the words of one of them, "both new and important."

Partly to specify what some of these special conclusions are which are believed to be new and partly to fit them into the conclusions of other students in this field, I am offering this paper as embodying, in brief, my present "creed" on the whole subject of so-called "cycle theory." My "creed" consists of 49 "articles" some of which are old and some new. I say "creed" because, for brevity, it is purposely expressed dogmatically and without proof. But it is not a creed in the sense that my faith in it does not rest on evidence and that I am not ready to modify it on presentation of new evidence. On the contrary, it is quite tentative. It may serve as a challenge to others and as raw material to help them work out a better product.

Meanwhile the following is a list of my 49 tentative conclusions.

"CYCLE THEORY" IN GENERAL

1. The economic system contains innumerable variables—quantities of "goods" (physical wealth, property rights, and services), the prices of these goods, and their values (the quantities multiplied by the prices). Changes in any or all of this vast array of variables may be due to many causes. Only in imagination can all of these variables remain constant and be kept in equilibrium by the balanced forces of human desires, as manifested through "supply and demand."

2. Economic theory includes a study both of (a) such imaginary, ideal equilibrium—which may be stable or unstable—and (b) disequilibrium. The former is economic statics; the latter, economic dynamics. So-called cycle theory is merely one part of the study of economic dis-equilibrium.

3. The study of dis-equilibrium may proceed in either of two ways.

We may take as our unit for study an actual historical case of great dis-equilibrium, such as, say, the panic of 1873; or we may take as our unit for study any constituent tendency, such as, say, deflation, and discover its general laws, relations to, and combinations with, other tendencies. The former study revolves around events, or *facts;* the latter, around *tendencies.* The former is primarily economic history; the latter is primarily economic science. Both sorts of studies are proper and important. Each helps the other. The panic of 1873 can only be understood in the light of the various tendencies involved—deflation and other; and deflation can only be understood in the light of the various historical manifestations- -1873 and other.

4. The old and apparently still persistent notion of "the" business cycle, as a single, simple, self-generating cycle (analogous to that of a pendulum swinging under influence of the single force of gravity) and as actually realized historically in regularly recurring crises, is a myth. Instead of one force there are many forces. Specifically, instead of one cycle, there are many co-existing cycles, constantly aggravating or neutralizing each other, as well as co-existing with many non-cyclical forces. In other words, while a cycle, conceived as a *fact,* or historical event, is non-existent, there are always innumerable cycles, long and short, big and little, conceived as *tendencies* (as well as numerous non-cyclical tendencies), any historical event being the resultant of all the tendencies then at work. Any one cycle, however perfect and like a sine curve it may tend to be, is sure to be interfered with by other tendencies.

5. The innumerable tendencies making mostly for economic dis-equilibrium may roughly be classified under three groups: (a) growth or trend tendencies, which are steady; (b) haphazard disturbances, which are unsteady; (c) cyclical tendencies, which are unsteady but steadily repeated.

6. There are two sorts of cyclical tendencies. One is "forced" or imposed on the economic mechanism from outside. Such is the yearly rhythm; also the daily rhythm. Both the yearly and the daily rhythm are imposed on us by astronomical forces from outside the economic organization; and there may be others such as from sun spots or transits of Venus. Other examples of "forced" cycles are the monthly and weekly rhythms imposed on us by custom and religion.

The second sort of cyclical tendency is the "free" cycle, not forced from outside, but self-generating, operating analogously to a pendulum or wave motion.

7. It is the "free" type of cycle which is apparently uppermost in the minds of most people when they talk of "the" business cycle. The yearly cycle, though it more nearly approaches a perfect cycle than

any other, is seldom thought of as a cycle at all but referred to as "seasonal variation."

8. There may be equilibrium which, though stable, is so delicately poised that, after departure from it beyond certain limits, instability ensues, just as, at first, a stick may bend under strain, ready all the time to bend back, until a certain point is reached, when it breaks. This simile probably applies when a debtor gets "broke,"or when the breaking of many debtors constitutes a "crash," after which there is no coming back to the original equilibrium. To take another simile, such a disaster is somewhat like the "capsizing" of a ship which, under ordinary conditions, is always near stable equilibrium but which, after being tipped beyond a certain angle, has no longer this tendency to return to equilibrium, but, instead, a tendency to depart further from it.

9. We may tentatively assume that, ordinarily and within wide limits, all, or almost all, economic variables tend, in a general way, toward a stable equilibrium. In our classroom expositions of supply and demand curves, we very properly assume that if the price, say, of sugar is above the point at which supply and demand are equal, it tends to fall; and if below, to rise.

10. Under such assumptions, and taking account of "economic friction," which is always present, it follows that, unless some outside force intervenes, any "free" oscillations about equilibrium must tend progressively to grow smaller and smaller, just as a rocking chair set in motion tends to stop. That is, while "forced" cycles, such as seasonal, tend to continue unabated in amplitude, ordinary "free" cycles tend to cease, giving way to equilibrium.

11. But the exact equilibrium thus sought is seldom reached and never long maintained. New disturbances are, humanly speaking, sure to occur, so that, in actual fact, any variable is almost always above or below the ideal equilibrium.

For example, coffee in Brazil may be over-produced, that is, may be more than it would have been if the producers had known in advance that it could not have been sold at a profit. Or there may be a shortage in the cotton crop. Or factory, or commercial inventories may be under or over the equilibrium point.

Theoretically there may be—in fact, at most times there must be—over- or under-production, over- or under-consumption, over- or underspending, over- or under-saving, over- or under-investment, and over or under everything else. It is as absurd to assume that, for any long period of time, the variables in the economic organization, or any part of them, will "stay put," in perfect equilibrium, as to assume that the Atlantic Ocean can ever be without a wave.

12. The important variables which may, and ordinarily do, stand

above or below equilibrium are: (a) capital items, such as homes, factories, ships, productive capacity generally, inventories, gold, money, credits, and debts; (b) income items, such as real income, volume of trade, shares traded; (c) price items, such as prices of securities, commodities, interest.

13. There may even be a *general* over-production and in either of two senses: (a) there may be, in general, at a particular point of time, over-large inventories or stocks on hand, or (b) there may be, in general, during a particular period of time, an over-rapid flow of production. The classical notion that over-production can only be relative as between different products is erroneous. Aside from the abundance or scarcity of particular products, relative to each other, production as a whole is relative to human desires and aversions, and can as a whole overshoot or undershoot the equilibrium mark.

In fact, except for brief moments, there must always be some degree of general over-production or general under-production and in both senses—stock and flow.

14. But, in practice, general over-production, as popularly imagined, has never, so far as I can discover, been a chief cause of great dis-equilibrium. The reason, or a reason, for the common notion of over-production is mistaking too little money for too much goods.

15. While any deviation from equilibrium of any economic variable theoretically may, and doubtless in practice does, set up some sort of oscillations, the important question is: Which of them have been sufficiently great disturbers to afford any substantial explanation of the great booms and depressions of history?

16. I am not sufficiently familiar with the long detailed history of these disturbances, nor with the colossal literature concerning their alleged explanations, to have reached any definitive conclusions as to the relative importance of all the influences at work. I am eager to learn from others.

17. According to my present opinion, which is purely tentative, there is some grain of truth in most of the alleged explanations commonly offered, but this grain is often small. Any of them may suffice to explain *small* disturbances, but all of them put together have probably been inadequate to explain *big* disturbances.

18. In particular, as explanations of the so-called business cycle, or cycles, when these are really serious, I doubt the adequacy of over-production, under-consumption, over-capacity, price-dislocation, maladjustment between agricultural and industrial prices, over-confidence, over-investment, over-saving, over-spending, and the discrepancy between saving and investment.

19. I venture the opinion, subject to correction on submission of

future evidence, that, in the great booms and depressions, each of the above-named factors has played a subordinate rôle as compared with two dominant factors, namely *over-indebtedness* to start with and *deflation* following soon after; also that where any of the other factors do become conspicuous, they are often merely effects or symptoms of these two. In short, the big bad actors are debt disturbances and price-level disturbances.

While quite ready to change my opinion, I have, at present, a strong conviction that these two economic maladies, the debt disease and the price-level disease (or dollar disease), are, in the great booms and depressions, more important causes than all others put together.

20. Some of the other and usually minor factors often derive some importance when combined with one or both of the two dominant factors.

Thus over-investment and over-speculation are often important; but they would have far less serious results were they not conducted with borrowed money. That is, over-indebtedness may lend importance to over-investment or to over-speculation.

The same is true as to over-confidence. I fancy that over-confidence seldom does any great harm except when, as, and if, it beguiles its victims into debt.

Another example is the mal-adjustment between agricultural and industrial prices, which can be shown to be a result of a change in the general price level.

21. Disturbances in these two factors—debt and the purchasing power of the monetary unit—will set up serious disturbances in all, or nearly all, other economic variables. On the other hand, if debt and deflation are absent, other disturbances are powerless to bring on crises comparable in severity to those of 1837, 1873, or 1929-33.

THE ROLES OF DEBT AND DEFLATION

22. No exhaustive list can be given of the secondary variables affected by the two primary ones, debt and deflation; but they include especially seven, making in all at least nine variables, as follows: debts, circulating media, their velocity of circulation, price levels, net worths, profits, trade, business confidence, interest rates.

23. *The chief interrelations between the nine chief factors may be derived deductively*, assuming, to start with, that general economic equilibrium is disturbed by only the one factor of over-indebtedness, and, in particular, assuming that there is no other influence, whether accidental or designed, tending to affect the price level.

24. Assuming, accordingly, that, at some point of time, a state of over-indebtedness exists, this will tend to lead to liquidation, through

the alarm either of debtors or creditors or both. Then we may deduce the following chain of consequences in nine links: (1) *Debt liquidation* leads to *distress selling* and to (2) *Contraction of deposit currency*, as bank loans are paid off, and to a slowing down of velocity of circulation. This contraction of deposits and of their velocity, precipitated by distress selling, causes (3) *A fall in the level of prices*, in other words, a swelling of the dollar. Assuming, as above stated, that this fall of prices is not interfered with by reflation or otherwise, there must be (4) *A still greater fall in the net worths of business*, precipitating bankruptcies and (5) *A like fall in profits*, which in a "capitalistic," that is, a private-profit society, leads the concerns which are running at a loss to make (6) *A reduction in output, in trade and in employment* of labor. These losses, bankruptcies, and unemployment, lead to (7) *Pessimism and loss of confidence*, which in turn lead to (8) *Hoarding and slowing down still more the velocity of circulation*.

The above eight changes cause (9) *Complicated disturbances in the rates of interest*, in particular, a fall in the nominal, or money, rates and a rise in the real, or commodity, rates of interest.

Evidently debt and deflation go far toward explaining a great mass of phenomena in a very simple logical way.

25. The above chain of causes, consisting of nine links, includes only a few of the interrelations between the nine factors. There are other demonstrable interrelations, both rational and empirical, and doubtless still others which cannot, yet, at least, be formulated at all.[1] There must also be many indirect relations involving variables not included among the nine groups.

26. One of the most important of such interrelations (and probably too little stressed in my *Booms and Depressions*) is the direct effect of lessened money, deposits, and their velocity, in curtailing trade, as evidenced by the fact that trade has been revived locally by emergency money without any raising of the price level.

27. In actual chronology, the order of the nine events is somewhat different from the above "logical" order, and there are reactions and repeated effects. As stated in Appendix I of *Booms and Depressions:*

The following table of our nine factors, occurring and recurring (together with distress selling), gives a fairly typical, though still inadequate, picture of the

---

[1] Many of these interrelations have been shown statistically, and by many writers. Some, which I have so shown and which fit in with the debt-deflation theory, are: that price-change, after a distributed lag, causes, or is followed by, corresponding fluctuations in the volume of trade , employment, bankruptcies, and rate of interest. The results as to price-change and unemployment are contained in Charts II and III, pp. 352–3. See references at the end of this article; also footnote 2, page 345, regarding the charts.

cross-currents of a depression in the approximate order in which it is believed they usually occur. (The first occurrence of each factor and its sub-divisions is indicated by italics. The figures in parenthesis show the sequence in the original exposition.)

I. (7) Mild *Gloom* and Shock to *Confidence*
   (8) Slightly *Reduced Velocity* of Circulation
   (1) Debt *Liquidation*

II. (9) *Money Interest* on Safe Loans Falls
   (9) But Money Interest on Unsafe Loans Rises

III. (2) *Distress Selling*
   (7) More Gloom
   (3) *Fall in Security Prices*
   (1) More Liquidation
   (3) *Fall in Commodity Prices*

IV. (9) *Real Interest Rises;* REAL DEBTS INCREASE
   (7) More Pessimism and Distrust
   (1) More Liquidation
   (2) More Distress Selling
   (8) More Reduction in Velocity

V. (2) More Distress Selling
   (2) *Contraction of Deposit Currency*
   (3) Further Dollar Enlargement

VI. (4) *Reduction in Net Worth*
   (4) Increase in *Bankruptcies*
   (7) More Pessimism and Distrust
   (8) More Slowing in Velocity
   (1) More Liquidation

VII. (5) *Decrease in Profits*
   (5) *Increase in Losses*
   (7) Increase in Pessimism
   (8) Slower Velocity
   (1) More Liquidation
   (6) *Reduction in Volume of Stock Trading*

VIII. (6) *Decrease in Construction*
   (6) *Reduction in Output*
   (6) *Reduction in Trade*
   (6) *Unemployment*
   (7) More Pessimism

IX. (8) *Hoarding*

X. (8) *Runs on Banks*
   (8) *Banks Curtailing Loans* for Self-Protection
   (8) *Banks Selling Investments*
   (8) *Bank Failures*
   (7) Distrust Grows
   (8) More Hoarding
   (1) More Liquidation
   (2) More Distress Selling
   (3) Further Dollar Enlargement

As has been stated, this order (or any order, for that matter) can be only approximate and subject to variations at different times and places. It represents my present guess as to how, if not too much interfered with, the nine factors selected for explicit study in this book are likely in most cases to fall in line.

But, as has also been stated, the idea of a single-line succession is itself inadequate, for while Factor (1) acts on (2), for instance, it also acts *directly* on (7), so that we really need a picture of subdividing streams or, better, an interacting network in which each factor may be pictured as influencing and being influenced by many or all of the others.

Paragraph 24 above gives a logical, and paragraph 27 a chronological, order of the chief variables put out of joint in a depression when once started by over-indebtedness.

28. But it should be noted that, except for the first and last in the "logical" list, namely debt and interest on debts, *all the fluctuations listed come about through a fall of prices.*

29. When over-indebtedness stands alone, that is, does *not* lead to a fall of prices, in other words, when its tendency to do so is counteracted by inflationary forces (whether by accident or design), the resulting "cycle" will be far milder and far more regular.

30. Likewise, when a deflation occurs from other than debt causes and without any great volume of debt, the resulting evils are much less. It is the combination of both--the debt disease coming first, then precipitating the dollar disease—which works the greatest havoc.

31. The two diseases act and react on each other. Pathologists are now discovering that a pair of diseases are sometimes worse than either or than the mere sum of both, so to speak. And we all know that a minor disease may lead to a major one. Just as a bad cold leads to pneumonia, so over-indebtedness leads to deflation.

32. And, vice versa, deflation caused by the debt reacts on the debt. Each dollar of debt still unpaid becomes a bigger dollar, and if the over-indebtedness with which we started was great enough, the liquidation of debts cannot keep up with the fall of prices which it causes. In that case, the liquidation defeats itself. While it diminishes the number of dollars owed, it may not do so as fast as it increases the value of each dollar owed. Then, *the very effort of individuals to lessen their burden of debts increases it, because of the mass effect of the stampede to liquidate in swelling each dollar owed.* Then we have the great paradox which, I submit, is the chief secret of most, if not all, great depressions: *The more the debtors pay, the more they owe.* The more the economic boat tips, the more it tends to tip. It is not tending to right itself, but is capsizing.

33. But if the over-indebtedness is not sufficiently great to make liquidation thus defeat itself, the situation is different and simpler. It is then more analogous to stable equilibrium; the more the boat

rocks the more it will tend to right itself. In that case, we have a truer example of a cycle.

34. In the "capsizing" type in particular, the worst of it is that real incomes are so rapidly and progressively reduced. Idle men and idle machines spell lessened production and lessened real income, the central factor in all economic science. Incidentally this under-production occurs at the very time that there is the illusion of over-production.

35. In this rapid survey, I have not discussed what constitutes over-indebtedness. Suffice it here to note that (a) over-indebtedness is always relative to other items, including national wealth and income and the gold supply, which last is specially important, as evidenced by the recent researches of Warren and Pearson; and (b) it is not a mere one-dimensional magnitude to be measured simply by the number of dollars owed. It must also take account of the distribution in time of the sums coming due. Debts due at once are more embarrassing than debts due years hence; and those payable at the option of the creditor, than those payable at the convenience of the debtor. Thus debt embarrassment is great for call loans and for early maturities.

For practical purposes, we may roughly measure the total national debt embarrassment by taking the total sum currently due, say within the current year, including rent, taxes, interest, installments, sinking fund requirements, maturities and any other definite or rigid commitments for payment on principal.

ILLUSTRATED BY THE DEPRESSION OF 1929-33[2]

36. The depression out of which we are now (I trust) emerging is an example of a debt-deflation depression of the most serious sort. The

[2] Note the charts, pp. 352-7:

Chart I shows: (1) the price level (P) and (2) its percentage rate of rise or fall (P'). When the last named is lagged with the lag distributed according to a probability curve so that the various P''s overlap and cumulate we get $\bar{P}'$, as in Charts II and III. This $\bar{P}'$ is virtually a lagged average of the P''s.

Charts II and *III* show: $\bar{P}'$ contrasted with employment (E). $\bar{P}'$ may be considered as what employment would be if controlled *entirely* by price-change.

Chart IV shows the Swedish official (retail) weekly index number contrasted with the American weekly wholesale and monthly retail indexes.

Chart V shows the estimated internal debt in the United States contrasted with the estimated total money value of wealth. The unshaded extensions of the bars upward show what the 1933 figures would be if enlarged 75 per cent to translate them into 1929 dollars (according to the index number of wholesale commodity prices).

Chart VI shows estimated "fixed" annual charges (actually collected) contrasted with estimated national income. The unshaded extensions of the bars upward show what the 1932 figures would be if enlarged 56 per cent to translate them into 1929 dollars.

Charts VII and *VIII* show the chief available statistics before and after March 4, 1933, grouped in the order indicated in Article 27 above.

debts of 1929 were the greatest knowл, both nominally and really, up to that time.

They were great enough not only to "rock the boat" but to start it capsizing. By March, 1933, liquidation had reduced the debts about 20 per cent, but had increased the dollar about 75 per cent, so that the *real* debt, that is the debt as measured in terms of commodities, was increased about 40 per cent $[(100\% - 20\%) \times (100\% + 75\%) = 140\%]$. Note Chart. V.

37. Unless some counteracting cause comes along to prevent the fall in the price level, such a depression as that of 1929-33 (namely when the more the debtors pay the more they owe) tends to continue, going deeper, in a vicious spiral, for many years. There is then no tendency of the boat to stop tipping until it has capsized. Ultimately, of course, but only after almost universal bankruptcy, the indebtedness must cease to grow greater and begin to grow less. Then comes recovery and a tendency for a new boom-depression sequence. This is the so-called "natural" way out of a depression, via needless and cruel bankruptcy, unemployment, and starvation.

38. On the other hand, if the foregoing analysis is correct, it is always economically possible to stop or prevent such a depression simply by reflating the price level up to the average level at which outstanding debts were contracted by existing debtors and assumed by existing creditors, and then maintaining that level unchanged.

That the price level is controllable is not only claimed by monetary theorists but has recently been evidenced by two great events: (1) Sweden has now for nearly two years maintained a stable price level, practically always within 2 per cent of the chosen par and usually within 1 per cent. Note Chart IV. (2) The fact that immediate reversal of deflation is easily achieved by the use, or even the prospect of use, of appropriate instrumentalities has just been demonstrated by President Roosevelt. Note Charts VII and VIII.

39. Those who imagine that Roosevelt's avowed reflation is not the cause of our recovery but that we had "reached the bottom anyway" are very much mistaken. At any rate, they have given no evidence, so far as I have seen, that we had reached the bottom. And if they are right, my analysis must be woefully wrong. According to all the evidence, under that analysis, debt and deflation, which had wrought havoc up to March 4, 1933, were then stronger than ever and, if let alone, would have wreaked greater wreckage than ever, after March 4. Had no "artificial respiration" been applied, we would soon have seen general bankruptcies of the mortgage guarantee companies, savings banks, life insurance companies, railways, municipalities, and states. By that time the Federal Government would probably have be-

come unable to pay its bills without resort to the printing press, which would itself have been a very belated and unfortunate case of artificial respiration. If even then our rulers should still have insisted on "leaving recovery to nature" and should still have refused to inflate in any way, should vainly have tried to balance the budget and discharge more government employees, to raise taxes, to float, or try to float, more loans, they would soon have ceased to be our rulers. For we would have insolvency of our national government itself, and probably some form of political revolution without waiting for the next legal election. The mid-west farmers had already begun to defy the law.

40. If all this is true, it would be as silly and immoral to "let nature take her course" as for a physician to neglect a case of pneumonia. It would also be a libel on economic science, which has its therapeutics as truly as medical science.

41. If reflation can now so easily and quickly reverse the deadly down-swing of deflation after nearly four years, when it was gathering increased momentum, it would have been still easier, and at any time, to have stopped it earlier. In fact, under President Hoover, recovery was apparently well started by the Federal Reserve open-market purchases, which revived prices and business from May to September 1932. The efforts were not kept up and recovery was stopped by various circumstances, including the political "campaign of fear."

It would have been still easier to have prevented the depression almost altogether. In fact, in my opinion, this would have been done had Governor Strong of the Federal Reserve Bank of New York lived, or had his policies been embraced by other banks and the Federal Reserve Board and pursued consistently after his death.[3] In that case, there would have been nothing worse than the first crash. We would have had the debt disease, but not the dollar disease—the bad cold but not the pneumonia.

42. If the debt-deflation theory of great depressions is essentially correct, the question of controlling the price level assumes a new importance; and those in the drivers' seats—the Federal Reserve Board and the Secretary of the Treasury, or, let us hope, a special stabilization commission—will in future be held to a new accountability.

43. Price level control, or dollar control, would not be a panacea. Even with an ideally stable dollar, we would still be exposed to the

---

[3] Eventually, however, in order to have avoided depression, the gold standard would have had to be abandoned or modified (by devaluation); for, with the gold standard as of 1929, the price levels at that time could not have been maintained indefinitely in the face of: (1) the "scramble for gold" due to the continued extension of the gold standard to include nation after nation; (2) the increasing volume of trade; and (3) the prospective insufficiency of the world gold supply.

debt disease, to the technological-unemployment disease, to over-production, price-dislocation, over-confidence, and many other minor diseases. To find the proper therapy for these diseases will keep economists busy long after we have exterminated the dollar disease.

DEBT STARTERS

44. The over-indebtedness hitherto presupposed must have had its starters. It may be started by many causes, of which the most common appears to be *new opportunities to invest at a big prospective profit*, as compared with ordinary profits and interest, such as through new inventions, new industries, development of new resources, opening of new lands or new markets. Easy money is the great cause of over-borrowing. When an investor thinks he can make over 100 per cent per annum by borrowing at 6 per cent, he will be tempted to borrow, and to invest or speculate with borrowed money. This was a prime cause leading to the over-indebtedness of 1929. Inventions and technological improvements created wonderful investment opportunities, and so caused big debts. Other causes were the left-over war debts, domestic and foreign, public and private, the reconstruction loans to foreigners, and the low interest policy adopted to help England get back on the gold standard in 1925.

Each case of over-indebtedness has its own starter or set of starters. The chief starters of the over-indebtedness leading up to the crisis of 1837 were connected with lucrative investment opportunities from developing the West and Southwest in real estate, cotton, canal building (led by the Erie Canal), steamboats, and turnpikes, opening up each side of the Appalachian Mountains to the other. For the over-indebtedness leading up to the crisis of 1873, the chief starters were the exploitation of railways and of western farms following the Homestead Act. The over-indebtedness leading up to the panic of 1893 was chiefly relative to the gold base which had become too small, because of the injection of too much silver. But the panic of 1893 seems to have had less of the debt ingredient than in most cases, though deflation played a leading rôle.

The starter may, of course, be wholly or in part the pendulum-like back-swing or reaction in recovery from a preceding depression as commonly assumed by cycle theorists. This, of itself, would tend to leave the next depression smaller than the last.

45. When the starter consists of new opportunities to make unusually profitable investments, the bubble of debt tends to be blown bigger and faster than when the starter is great misfortune causing merely non-productive debts. The only notable exception is a great war and even then chiefly because it leads *after it is over* to productive debts for reconstruction purposes.

46. This is quite different from the common naïve opinions of how war results in depression. If the present interpretation is correct, the World War need never have led to a great depression. It is very true that much or most of the inflations could not have been helped because of the exigencies of governmental finance, but the subsequent undue deflations could probably have been avoided entirely.

47. The public psychology of going into debt for gain passes through several more or less distinct phases: (a) the lure of big prospective dividends or gains in *income* in the remote future; (b) the hope of selling at a profit, and realizing a *capital* gain in the immediate future; (c) the vogue of reckless promotions, taking advantage of the habituation of the public to great expectations; (d) the development of downright fraud, imposing on a public which had grown credulous and gullible.

When it is too late the dupes discover scandals like the Hatry, Krueger, and Insull scandals. At least one book has been written to prove that crises are due to frauds of clever promoters. But probably these frauds could never have become so great without the original starters of real opportunities to invest lucratively. There is probably always a very real basis for the "new era" psychology before it runs away with its victims. This was certainly the case before 1929.

48. In summary, we find that: (1) economic changes include steady trends and unsteady occasional disturbances which act as starters for cyclical oscillations of innumerable kinds; (2) among the many occasional disturbances, are new opportunities to invest, especially because of new inventions; (3) these, with other causes, sometimes conspire to lead to a great volume of over-indebtedness; (4) this, in turn, leads to attempts to liquidate; (5) these, in turn, lead (*unless counteracted by reflation*) to falling prices or a swelling dollar; (6) the dollar may swell faster than the number of dollars owed shrinks; (7) in that case, liquidation does not really liquidate but actually aggravates the debts, and the depression grows worse instead of better, as indicated by all nine factors; (8) the ways out are either *via laissez faire* (bankruptcy) or scientific medication (reflation), and reflation might just as well have been applied in the first place.

49. The general correctness of the above "debt-deflation theory of great depressions" is, I believe, evidenced by experience in the present and previous great depressions. Future studies by others will doubtless check up on this opinion. One way is to compare different countries simultaneously. If the "debt-deflation theory" is correct, the infectiousness of depressions internationally is chiefly due to a common gold (or other) monetary standard and there should be found little tendency for a depression to pass from a deflating to an inflating, or stabilizing, country.

SOME NEW FEATURES

As stated at the outset, several features of the above analysis are, as far as I know, new. Some of these are too unimportant or self-evident to stress. The one (No. 32 above; also 36) which I do venture to stress most is the theory that when over-indebtedness is so great as to depress prices faster than liquidation, the mass effort to get out of debt sinks us more deeply into debt.[4] I would also like to emphasize the whole logical articulation of the nine factors, of which debt and deflation are the two chief (Nos. 23, 24, and 28, above). I would call attention to *new investment opportunities* as the important "starter" of over-indebtedness (Nos. 44, 45). Finally, I would emphasize the important corollary, of the debt-deflation theory, that great depressions are curable and preventable through reflation and stabilization (Nos. 38–42).

Yale University

[4] This interaction between liquidation and deflation did not occur to me until 1931, although, with others, I had since 1909 been stressing the fact that deflation tended toward depression and inflation toward a boom

This debt-deflation theory was first stated in my lectures at Yale in 1931, and first stated publicly before the American Association for the Advancement of Science, on January 1, 1932. It is fully set forth in my *Booms and Depressions*, 1932, and some special features of my general views on cycle theory in "Business Cycles as Facts or Tendencies" in *Economische Opstellen Aangeboden aan Prof. C. A. Verrijn Stuart*, Haarlem, 1931. Certain sorts of disequilibrium are discussed in other writings. The rôle of the lag between real and nominal interest is discussed in *The Purchasing Power of Money*, Macmillan, New York, 1911; and more fully in *The Theory of Interest*, Macmillan, New York, 1930, as well as the effects of inequality of foresight. Some statistical verification will be found in "Our Unstable Dollar and the So-called Business Cycle," *Journal of the American Statistical Association*, June, 1925, pp. 179–202, and "The Relation of Employment to the Price Level" (address given before a section of the American Association for the Advancement of Science, Atlantic City, N. J., December 28, 1932, and later published in *Stabilization of Employment*, edited by Charles F. Roos, The Principia Press, Inc., Bloomingdale, Ind., 1933, pp. 152–159). See Charts I, II, III. Some statistical verification will be found in *The Stock Market Crash and After*, Macmillan, New York, 1930.

A selected bibliography of the writings of others is given in Appendix III of *Booms and Depressions*, Adelphi Company, New York, 1932. This bibliography omitted Veblen's *Theory of Business Enterprise*, Charles Scribner's Sons, New York, 1904, Chapter VII of which, Professor Wesley C. Mitchell points out, probably comes nearest to the debt-deflation theory. Hawtrey's writings seem the next nearest. Professor Alvin H. Hansen informs me that Professor Paxson, of the American History Department of the University of Wisconsin, in a course on the History of the West some twenty years ago, stressed the debt factor and its relation to deflation. But, so far as I know, no one hitherto has pointed out how debt liquidation defeats itself via deflation nor several other features of the present "creed." If any clear-cut anticipation exists, it can never have been prominently set forth, for even the word "debt" is missing in the indexes of the treatises on the subject.

CHARTS

The following eight charts are all on the "ratio scale" excepting Charts II, III, V, VI, and curve P' of Chart I. The particular ratio scale used is indicated in each case.

It will be noted that in Charts VII and VIII all curves have a common ratio scale, as indicated by the inset at the right in both charts, except "Brokers' Loans" in Chart VII and "Failures Numbers," "Failures Liabilities," and "Shares Traded" in Chart VIII, which four curves have another, "reduced" i.e., smaller, common scale, as indicated by the inset at the left of Chart VIII.

It will be further noted that "Money in Circulation," "Failures Numbers," and "Failures Liabilities" are inverted.

The full details of how $\overline{P'}$ in Charts II and III is derived from P' in Chart I and also how P' in Chart I is derived from P are given in "Our Unstable Dollar and the So-Called Business Cycle," *Journal of the American Statistical Association*, June, 1925.

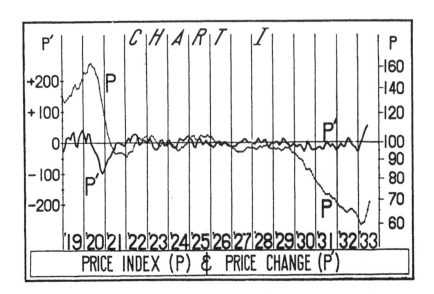

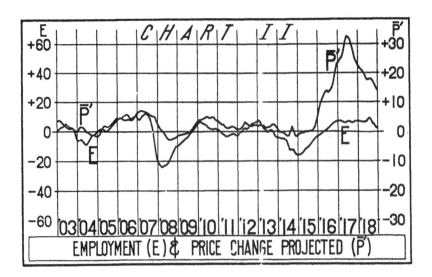

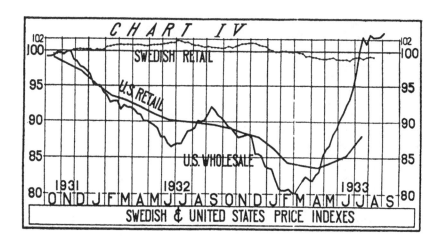

CHART IV

SWEDISH & UNITED STATES PRICE INDEXES

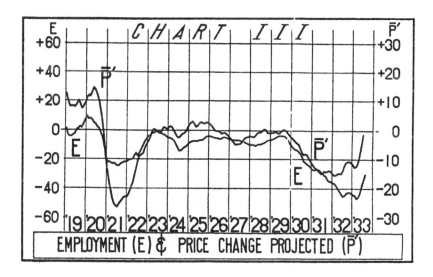

CHART III

EMPLOYMENT (E) & PRICE CHANGE PROJECTED (P̄')

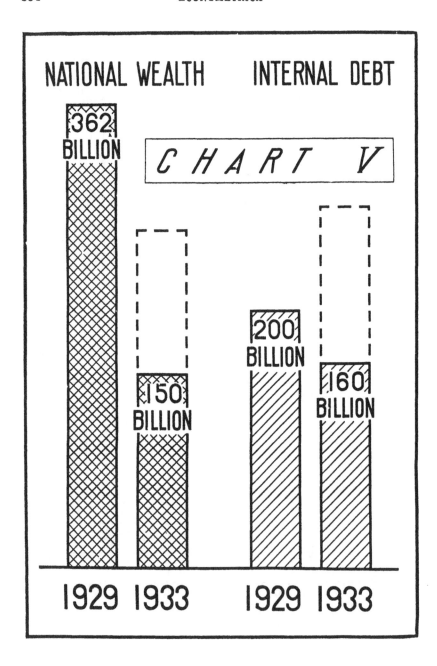

NATIONAL WEALTH   INTERNAL DEBT

362 BILLION

CHART V

200 BILLION

150 BILLION

160 BILLION

1929 1933   1929 1933

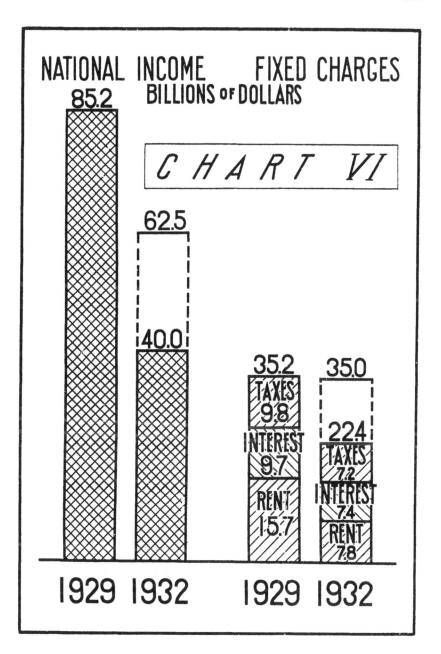

NATIONAL INCOME   FIXED CHARGES
BILLIONS of DOLLARS

85.2

CHART VI

62.5

40.0

35.2
TAXES
9.8
INTEREST
9.7
RENT
15.7

35.0

22.4
TAXES
7.2
INTEREST
7.4
RENT
7.8

1929 1932   1929 1932

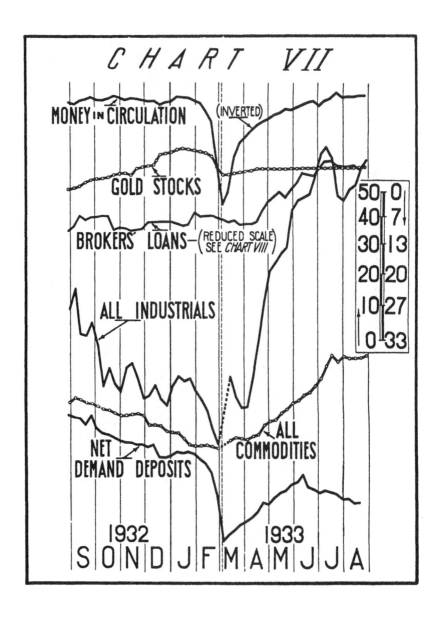

CHART VII

MONEY IN CIRCULATION   (INVERTED)

GOLD STOCKS

BROKERS' LOANS — (REDUCED SCALE)
                  SEE *CHART VIII*

ALL INDUSTRIALS

NET
DEMAND DEPOSITS   ALL COMMODITIES

50 0
40 7
30 13
20 20
10 27
0 33

1932   1933
S O N D J F M A M J J A

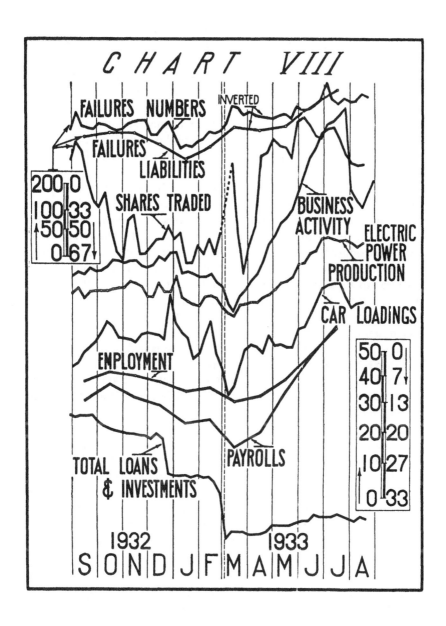

CHART VIII

As part of his campaign for "reflation," Fisher pushed for the introduction of a special currency issue – to be known as "stamp scrip" – which would require that a 2 cent stamp be attached weekly to each dollar of scrip to maintain its exchange value at par. Fisher saw this stratagem as a device for stimulating the velocity of monetary circulation. After all, any one who held scrip had an incentive to spend it, rather than to hold it with its value eroding by 2 percent per week. The idea itself dated from the 1890s and the thinking of Silvio Gesell, a German economist then conducting business in Argentina. Fisher learned about the scheme in mid-1932 and quickly incorporated it into his kit of policy recommendations. In *Booms and Depressions*, it was inserted as a last-minute afterthought.

Fisher attempted – but without success – to sell this plan to the Mayor of New Haven, Connecticut. (See his detailed recommendation in Volume XIV.) In early 1933, his advocacy managed to persuade Senator Bankhead (Democrat of Alabama) and Congressman Pettengill (Democrat of Indiana) to introduce legislation that would put the Federal government in the stamp scrip business. No Congressional action was forthcoming, despite his pleas to President Roosevelt to endorse it as a matter of legislative priority. Fisher, however, kept the idea alive. For example, in May 1933 – when Congress was considering how to finance service charges on debt issued to finance the New Deal's spending programs – he had the formula readily at hand. The debt service charges, he explained, should be paid for in stamp scrip which would be self-liquidating. Thus, when government "issues $220,000,000 of this money (the amount of the anticipated increment in debt service charges) [it] is not going to have to levy any tax to retire it." By requiring a 2 cent stamp each week to validate each dollar of scrip, the government would raise $1.04 in the course of a year which would permit redemption of the scrip and generate 4 cents per dollar's worth of scrip in net revenue.[a] Fisher was no fan of public works spending as re-employment device: he consistently maintained that the focus should be on creating jobs in the private sector and that that objective could best be reached through monetary stimuli. But if public works expenditures were to be the order of the day, they could be made more palatable when they had a monetary ingredient. Despite his best efforts, the stamp scrip scheme for debt-service financing was rejected.

---

[a] Fisher, Hearings before the Committee on Ways and Means, House of Representatives, 73:1, May 19, 1933, 172. When the House of Representatives did not warm to this proposal, Fisher put another version before the Senate Committee on Finance. In this instance, he suggested that the Federal government authorize state governments to issue stamp scrip to fund the latters' contribution to public works projects (in which the sharing was expected to be 70 percent Federal, 30 percent state). (Fisher, Hearings before the Committee on Finance, U.S. Senate, 73:1, May 31, 1933, 337–40.)

He nonetheless continued his propaganda efforts in a tract entitled *Stamp Scrip* (in which he was assisted by Hans R.L. Cohrssen and his brother, Herbert W. Fisher) which appeared in October 1933.

Fisher published two other tracts in 1933: *Inflation?* and *After Reflation, What?* (In both instances, his brother assisted in the preparation.) Their substantive contents amounted to a reiteration of the ideas Fisher had already set out in *Booms and Depressions*, in his *Econometrica* article, and in his correspondence with public officials (see Volume XIV). The state of his thinking on these matters is contained in a paper he presented to the American Academy of Political and Social Science entitled "Monetary Policy of the United States" on November 22, 1933.

– Fisher, "Reflation and Stabilization," *Annals of the American Academy of Political and Social Science*, January 1934.

Reflation and Stabilization[1]

By Irving Fisher

PRESIDENT ROOSEVELT stated on July 3:

The United States of America seeks the kind of dollar which a generation hence will have the same purchasing power and debt paying power as the dollar we hope to attain in the near future.

That is the subject of debate today among all who are interested in the so-called money question.

PRESIDENT GUIDED BY AUTHORITATIVE OPINION

I think I am right in saying that practically all the monetary economists who have made a long and thorough study of this subject agreed with J. Maynard Keynes when he said the day after this utterance of the President, "The President is magnificently right." And yet, perhaps the majority of the people of the United States are not convinced of that fact. It is dangerous to leave a technical subject to majority vote. I should consider the advice and opinion of J. Maynard Keynes superior to that of the layman, even if duplicated one hundred million times.

The President has at his elbow two of the ablest monetary economists in the world. One is Professor Warren of Cornell, whose book on *Prices* I think will convince 99 per cent of the people who read it that he is "magnificently right" in concluding that we cannot permanently maintain the price level that we had in 1926 with the gold that we had at that time, and that if we do not increase the metallic base by de-

valuating the dollar (since there is no other immediate way of doing it) so as to multiply the number of gold dollars at the base of our credit structure, we shall have this same catastrophe repeated; because the depression, beginning with the stock market crash, was very largely due to the insufficiency of the metallic base. Professor James Harvey Rogers, of Yale, who is another of the President's advisers, has written a book called *America Weighs Her Gold*. I think the layman, unversed in monetary economics, before he assumes to have a voting opinion on this subject, and before he assumes to rush through resolutions in chambers of commerce, owes it to the President to read at least one of these books, or those of other authors on the subject.

There are only a score of such men in the world today—a half dozen in this country, a half dozen in England, and the rest scattered through the world— who are entitled to an authoritative opinion which these two advisers of the President have. The average economist is not entitled to such authority, for he is not a monetary economist. This branch of economics is just as special within the field of economics as patent law is in the field of law, and it would be no more absurd for the ordinary lawyer to pronounce upon a patent case (and he will not do so) than for the ordinary economist to count on equal voting strength with the monetary economist.

An even smaller percentage of the bankers have made a study of this subject. Among those who have, I would mention Reginald McKenna, the president of the largest bank in the world or it was until the Chase claimed to be

[1] Paper read at a meeting of the American Academy of Political and Social Science on "Monetary Policy of the United States," November 22, 1933.

the largest. He was Chancellor of the British Exchequer. In 1922, when I was in London, he invited me to come to see him. He said, "I feel lonely among the bankers"; and added, jokingly, "You know, Professor Fisher, you and I are the only two people in the world that understand this subject!"

Professor Sprague is a sincere and able authority on the technique of banking; but he does not have the authority of Professors Warren and Rogers on the price level.

DEFENSE OF PRESIDENT'S MONETARY POLICY

When speaking tonight of the President's problem, I am not including all of the policies. I am not speaking from the political angle. I am not of his party. I did not vote for him. I do not agree with him on many subjects. But on this monetary policy I believe he is "magnificently right."

I am confining myself entirely to the monetary policy as contained in the words which I quoted. If you analyze those words, you will see that this monetary policy is twofold. It consists of reflation, or raising the price level, and of stabilization, or fixing the price level. In regard to reflation, the President said on May 7:

The Administration has the definite objective of raising commodity prices to such an extent that those who have borrowed money will, on the average, be able to repay that money in the kind of a dollar which they borrowed. We do not seek to let them get such a cheap dollar that they will be able to pay back a great deal less than they borrowed; in other words, we seek to correct a wrong and not to create another wrong in the opposite direction.

There has been a great deal of misunderstanding and misrepresentation not only of the President but also of those who have supported him. I, for

one, resent being called an inflationist, and I think the healthy complex that we have in this country against inflation as a social wrong is the outgrowth of the writings of us economists who have tried so long to get people to appreciate the evils of inflation. I could cite at least a half dozen of my books in which I have preached against inflation.

But I am equally opposed to deflation, and I have a keen realization, as most people do not, that deflation is practically 75 per cent of the explanation of the present depression. It is a debt-deflation depression, and debt and deflation act upon each other. There was too much debt to start with. That caused distress selling and shrinkage of bank deposits as loans were liquidated. This shrinkage or contraction of the circulating medium, and the distress selling reduced the price level, or magnified the dollar and increased it to 81 per cent of what it had been in purchasing power, which meant that every thousand-dollar debt became the equivalent of $1810, and was that much harder to pay.

The very effort, therefore, to pay debt, which reduced these bank deposits, resulted in increasing debts; and the more the American people tried to get out of debt, the more they really got in, when the debts are measured in real commodities, which is the only proper measure of debt or of any other value. That is the "mystery" of the depression. We seem to have liquidated 20 per cent, but we have really magnified our debts 40 per cent in four years in terms of real things.

I resent for others that they should be called indefinite inflationists. The Senator who is to speak to you today has been unjustly treated, as has his colleague, Senator Smith. I know, because I was present at a recent conference in Washington at which they both subscribed their names to a statement that went to the President of the United States urging reflation only up to the level of 1926 and no farther.

There are at least ten misunderstandings on this very puzzling subject. I wish to enumerate these and speak briefly of each. The opposition to the President is circulating these ten misunderstandings.

UNCONTROLLED INFLATION

First, it is stated that the objective of the inflationists is an indefinite, uncontrolled inflation. It is not. I know of no responsible man in Washington or outside who is advocating any such thing. They merely want reflation enough to offset the deflation, but no inflation beyond that point.

Second, it is stated that even if there be an *intention* to have the reflation controlled, it will become uncontrollable. There is no evidence for that assertion except that Germany, when she could not balance her budget, got into a vicious spiral of inflation which ended in disaster, and some other countries under like conditions met the same fate.

Third, it is said that this uncontrollability is especially true of inflation through government paper money. As a matter of fact, we have had at least two instances in this country when we stopped it without any trouble. We stopped the greenback inflation, which was paper money inflation, in 1865, after several years of very rapid and injurious inflation. We stopped the inflation that began before the World War and lasted until two years after the war, by the deliberate action of the Federal Reserve System after the meeting of its Board on May 20, 1920, on the challenge of Senator McCormick that it should produce some deflation. The Reserve Banks not only had no difficulty whatever in stopping the in-

flation, but produced an unfortunate deflation for a year.

Fourth, it is declared that history shows that all currency inflation becomes uncontrollable. History, as I have indicated, shows the contrary.

MONEY IN RELATION TO COMMODITIES

Fifth, any raising of the price level by monetary means is asserted to be artificial, and so wrong. That grows out of one of the great money illusions that all prices are determined by supply and demand of the things priced. That is not true. The supply and demand of cotton are not the only things that affect the price of cotton. The supply and demand of money are equally important. If you should exchange cotton for silver, and the price of cotton in terms of silver went up, no one would think of ascribing that rise in prices exclusively to causes connected with cotton. You would want to ask what happened to silver; because cotton going up relatively to silver is silver going down relatively to cotton, and the supply and demand of both are equally important. So the supply and demand of money comes into the price of every commodity. In fact, the supply and demand of cotton cannot be expressed in money without reference to the purchasing power of money.

The purchasing power of money lurks in every price, in every bargain, in every act affecting supply or demand. Yet that is usually overlooked. So when we have a fall in the price of almost everything, as we have had in the last few years, people who do not understand that money enters in, can explain it only by saying that it must be that goods have been overproduced. The truth is, however, it is not too much goods but rather too little money that explains that fall of price.

Yet we assume that the dollar is still the dollar, and everything is priced in it so that it is a proper measure. We ascribe to the goods what belongs to the dollar. This money illusion is the fundamental reason that so few people get anywhere on this subject. I spoke of it as a highly technical subject. As a matter of fact, it is easy for any layman to understand it if he will get the idea that the value of a dollar is not a fixed unit of measure, but is something that must itself be measured by the index number of commodities in general. Until a person has that idea he cannot think straight on this subject.

The supply and demand of money affect the general level of prices, whereas supply and demand of goods affect the deviation from this level of the particular price. The supply and demand of wheat do not fix the price of wheat, but they merely fix the level of wheat relative to the general rise or fall of commodity prices. There is just as much difference between the general level and a particular price as there is between the level of a water reservoir and the height of a wave on its surface. And, paradoxically, it is a great deal easier to fix the general level of the water in a reservoir by controlling the inflow or outflow than it is to fix the height of any wave. It is, in the same way, easier to fix the general level of prices than it is to fix any particular price.

STABILIZATION OF PRICE LEVEL

I think very seldom should we try to resort to price fixing. Many people think that in this reflation, Mr. Roosevelt is trying to fix all prices. No such thing! Reflation merely fixes the general level of prices, and supply and demand should be left free, in my opinion, to fix the deviations from that level for any individual price.

In regard to the artificiality of this, the fixing of the general level of prices merely fixes the purchasing power of the dollar. If we raise the general level of prices to that of 1926, it will mean that we have lowered the purchasing power of the dollar from its present expanded value to what it was in 1926. To fix the purchasing power of a dollar in this way is merely to fix the unit of measure for debts and for the business man's operations, exactly as we fix the yardstick, the pound, the kilowatt, or any other unit of measure. In other words, what the President is trying to do, after he has corrected the swollen dollar, is to make it thereafter a constant unit just as is the bushel basket or any other unit in commerce.

Then it is said that even if there is expansion, it should properly be the result of recovery, and not used as a means of recovery. I am sorry to say that I saw that fallacy in the statement of Professor Sprague. As I understand it, and as I think all the monetary economists who have made a thorough study of it would agree, that is inverting the cause and effect in this depression, because of a wrong diagnosis. If we must wait for recovery to raise the price level, then price-level-raising is not a therapeutic measure at all.

Eighth, it is claimed that stabilization of the price level is impossible by any means, monetary or otherwise. That has been not only disbelieved by monetary economists for years, but recently disproved by the experience of Sweden, which has maintained a stable price level for over one hundred weeks in succession, within 2 per cent at the maximum, and usually within 1 per cent. It is no accident that this has been done, and it demonstrates what we have always maintained, that it is possible to make the price level whatever we choose.

Ninth, it is stated that such stabilization is of no value anyway, and is even injurious. The facts show the contrary.

Tenth, it is said that the only proper stabilization is relative to gold, and that therefore we should restore the orthodox gold standard as soon as possible. That merely grows out of the money illusion. Since we are on a gold standard, we take it for granted that gold should be the standard and that we want to get back to gold, and if some other country is on the gold standard we complain because of the upset of exchange between the two. When Germany and Russia had their great inflation, it would have been quite possible to keep a stable exchange between the two countries, but it would not have meant stability for the mark or the ruble; it would merely have meant that they both were being reduced together. So, if we had a stable exchange between ourselves and France and were both kept on the gold standard, it would not necessarily mean that either the franc or the dollar was stable; it would mean in the last few years that they both had been increased together. What we want is to stabilize both the franc and the dollar, both the mark and the ruble, with reference to real things, commodities, purchasing power, that for which money is a measure.

Temperate Use of Inflation

The gold policy is said to be futile. As a matter of fact, the instant the gold policy was undertaken and the gold prices were bid up by the President, the fall in the volume of trade in this country and the fall of prices which had been going on before that were arrested.

It stands to reason that the President has a tremendous power here. If the President should devaluate the dollar 50 per cent, as he is authorized to do, the four billions of dollars of gold in this country would automatically, without any purchase of gold from abroad, become eight billions.

This power is unlimited except as Congress limits it. I do not think it is necessary to give any greater power than the 50 per cent reduction, but we can often understand a principle from an extreme example. Suppose the President could cut the dollar not in two but in ten. Then the four billion dollars would become forty billion dollars. If you cut the dollar into one hundred, it would be not four billion dollars, but four hundred billion dollars. And if every bank were closed and there were no deposit currency and all the paper money were burned up, that four hundred billion dollars would give us a German inflation. So the President could make a price level as high as the sky, and make a wicked inflation, simply by this one device which he is now using, and using temperately.

I think, as James Harvey Rogers said in tonight's newspapers, those who would destroy this temperate policy, if they succeeded, would have to be responsible for the consequences which might not be so temperate.

Irving Fisher, LL.D., is professor of political economy at Yale University. He is active in national economic and public health movements and international peace efforts. He is author and co-author of many books which have been translated into a number of languages. Among his most recent works are "Stabilizing the Dollar" (1919); "The Money Illusion" (1928); "The Stock Market Crash" (1930); "Booms and Depressions" (1932); "Stamp Scrip," "Inflation?" and "After Inflation, What?" (1933).

For Product Safety Concerns and Information please contact our EU representative GPSR@taylorandfrancis.com Taylor & Francis Verlag GmbH, Kaufingerstraße 24, 80331 München, Germany

Printed and bound by CPI Group (UK) Ltd, Croydon, CR0 4YY
08/05/2025
01864356-0001